History and the Idea of Progress

Symposium on Science, Reason, and Modern Democracy

MICHIGAN STATE UNIVERSITY

History and the Idea of Progress

EDITED BY

Arthur M. Melzer,
Jerry Weinberger,
and M. Richard Zinman

Cornell University Press · *Ithaca and London*

First published 1995 by Cornell University Press.
First printing, Cornell Paperbacks, 1995.
Second printing 1996.

Library of Congress Cataloging-in-Publication Data

History and the idea of progress / edited by Arthur M. Melzer, Jerry Weinberger, and M. Richard Zinman.
p. cm.
Essays collected here were delivered as papers of the Symposium on Science, Reason, and Modern Democracy, held in May 1991 at Michigan State University.
Includes bibliographical references and index.
ISBN 0-8014-2986-2.—ISBN 0-8014-8182-1 (pbk.)
1. History—Philosophy. 2. Progress. I. Melzer, Arthur M. II. Weinberger, J. III. Zinman, M. Richard. IV. Symposium on Science, Reason, and Modern Democracy (1991 : Michigan State University)
D16.8.H6247 1995
901—dc20 94-44598

Printed in the United States of America

♾ The paper in this book meets the minimum requirements of the American National Standard for Information Sciences–Permanence of Paper for Printed Library Materials, ANSI Z39.48-1984.

CONTENTS

ACKNOWLEDGMENTS

This volume of essays is the second to be published by the Symposium on Science, Reason, and Modern Democracy and Cornell University Press. Established in 1989 in the Department of Political Science at Michigan State University, the Symposium sponsors teaching, research, and public lectures on the relationship between liberal democracy and the turbulent currents of modern rationalism. The twelve essays collected here were first delivered as papers in the Symposium's second annual program: a lecture series that ran from October 1990 through April 1991 and a three-day conference held in May 1991. This program and, indeed, all of the Symposium's activities during 1990–91 were made possible by grants from the Lynde and Harry Bradley Foundation of Milwaukee, Wisconsin, the Carthage Foundation of Pittsburgh, Pennsylvania, and the Earhart Foundation of Ann Arbor, Michigan. We gratefully acknowledge their continuing support.

The Department of Political Science at Michigan State University has provided a home in which the Symposium can flourish. James Madison College and the Honors College have provided valuable encouragement and assistance. We thank our colleagues in each of these institutions. In particular, we thank Kenneth E. Corey, Dean of the College of Social Science, Brian Silver, Chair of the Department of Political Science, Kenneth Waltzer, former Acting Dean of James Madison College, Donald Lammers, Director of the Honors College, Louis Hunt, the Symposium's first postdoctoral fellow, and David Martin, our undergraduate assistant, for their special contributions during our second year. Karen Albrecht, Rhonda Burns, Joyce Burrell, and Iris Dunn—the administrative staff of the Department of Political Science—smoothed the path for us throughout the year. Ms. Albrecht, the Symposium's Administrative Coordinator, played an especially important role in the preparation of this volume. They have our gratitude for their fine work.

The Symposium's 1990–91 program was enlivened by the participation of the following commentators: Charles Fairbanks, Eugene Genovese, Charles L. Griswold, Louis Hunt, William Kristol, Anthony J. Parel, Patrick Riley, Nicholas van de Walle, Bernard Yack, and Catherine Zuckert. We appreciate their seriousness and thoughtfulness. We also thank Folke Lindahl and Marc Plattner, who chaired panels at the conference.

Finally, it is a pleasure to acknowledge the gentle guidance of Roger Haydon, our editor at Cornell University Press.

A. M. M
J. W.
M. R. Z.

East Lansing, Michigan

Introduction

ARTHUR M. MELZER, JERRY WEINBERGER,
AND M. RICHARD ZINMAN

An old *New Yorker* cartoon depicts a man and his wife in their bedroom as dawn breaks. From their furniture and the clothing they wear, we can see that it is the late Middle Ages. While the woman slowly rouses herself from bed, her husband stands at the window, staring intently. He points to a faint glow issuing from beyond the horizon and says, "Look, dear. It's the Renaissance!"

Today, we all find ourselves in the position of that man. At the dawn of the third millennium, with the end of the Cold War, the sudden collapse of communism, and the apparent decline of socialism, we know that one historical epoch has come to an end. We strain to understand the world that will replace it.

This inarticulate wonder, which developed slowly along with events, was suddenly ignited into a headline-grabbing debate in the summer of 1989 by the publication of a brief, fifteen-page article titled "The End of History?" by Francis Fukuyama. No one agreed with its thesis, and yet everyone felt a driving need to say so in print and at length. Many dismissed it as intellectual sensationalism or an ill-mannered display of Western triumphalism. But, in fact, it raised important, indeed inevitable, questions. The furor has now died down, but the questions remain—as they will for a very long time to come. This book represents an early attempt to clarify and address some of them.

In a situation such as ours, it is best to begin by posing the largest possible question, on the assumption that later it will be easier to lower one's sights than to raise them. Thus, as Fukuyama asked, in light of epochal world events, should we not reconsider the long-discredited Hegelian idea of history as a rational process, having an intelligible order, purpose, and completion? It was largely world events, after all, that discredited Hegel in the first place: World War I, the rise of communism and fascism. So now that it has become imaginable to interpret these events as horrible but relatively short-lived detours from the main trend of modern Western history—even as exceptions that prove the rule—we must ask once again whether there is not, after all, some intelligible, and perhaps completable, process driving that history.

Surely no one is suggesting that henceforth there will be no serious change or conflict. On the contrary, it seems obvious that we are in for a period of particularly great turbulence. But history in the grand sense has been characterized by conflicts over fundamental principles: the rivalry of monarchy, aristocracy, and democracy; the struggles between church and state, or Protestantism and Catholicism; the conflict among fascism, communism, and capitalism. What is extraordinary about the present moment is that, within the West, there no longer exists a rival principle. Liberal democracy stands virtually alone, unopposed on the historical stage. To be sure, this principle has not yet been fully realized in practice, and even if it were, there would remain a hundred technical problems, philosophical reservations and general, noisy discontents. But the basic fact remains: our world now contains no comprehensive ideological alternative to liberal democracy. Searching history, one looks hard, perhaps in vain, for another such mono-ideological period. Moreover, at this moment the unitary Western principle is also spreading to large and ever greater portions of the non-Western world.

It is neither smugness nor myopia, then, that leads serious people to ask whether the Western ideals of equality and freedom are essentially the final principles of human political life or whether, after this brief and deceptive lull, history will resume its movement, bringing the rebirth of theocracy or fascism, or some altogether new ideological alternative. Once this basic question is posed, others follow in its wake.

Those inclining to the first alternative must ask what the historical process is, that it should culminate in liberal democracy. Has this political system triumphed because it provides the complete answer to the human drive for justice and happiness? Or the best practicable answer? Or is it somehow the most powerful without being best? More generally, mustn't one distinguish between the radical doctrines of history found in Hegel or Marx and the more limited theories of progress developed in the Renaissance and Enlightenment? The latter made progress a possibility but not a necessity: they did not remove responsibility from human actors, nor did they promise an end to history. Thus, if liberal democracy does represent some kind of peak or culmination, it is still important to ask, Is it the result of the "historical process" or of an uncertain and endless struggle for "human progress"?

Those, on the contrary, who doubt the finality of the liberal democratic model must try to conceive what will replace it. If history is not over, then where is it going? Most people eager to look beyond liberal democracy do so in the name of freedom and equality. Thus, behind their scorn and skepticism, don't they still assume the finality of these ideals?

Some will object that it is useless to try to see very far into the future, that what we can see are the present flaws of liberal democracy. Indeed, if the collapse of its rival has made liberal democracy seem triumphant and invincible, it has also turned it in on itself in moody introspection. Hasn't the spread of Western capitalism and the globalization of the economy produced lower living standards and economic dislocation in the developed world? Doesn't the competitive individualism of liberal democratic society eventually undermine every form of community, including the family? Mustn't the exaggerated promises of freedom and equality used to legitimate this society eventually generate radical expectations and movements that will either undermine or push beyond it? Doesn't the Enlightenment rationalism that first gave rise to liberal democracy ultimately destroy itself, as various postmodern critics of reason proclaim, leaving liberal democracy without foundations, adrift on a sea of mere custom and commitment? And can liberal democracy, weakened in all these ways, be counted on always to prevail—internally and externally—against the ever-renascent dangers of nationalism, fundamentalism, and other forms of political fanaticism?

Finally, persons on all sides of the debate must take a step back and ask, Just what is at stake in this debate, and why do we engage in it? How did our current preoccupation with progress and history first arise, and what sustains it? Liberal democracy grew from the soil of the Enlightenment idea of progress. Can it survive without it? What role, moral or psychological, do conceptions of history play in the belief structure of modern life? Are they the nonsubjective basis for our moral beliefs and commitments, a secular substitute for providence, an evasion of mortality, a necessary postulate of moral idealism?

Great events raise great questions. Needless to say, the essays contained in this book do not aspire to answer, or to address, all of them. They shed some light where much more is needed.

In the opening section of the book, the argument for the end of history is presented in two separate essays. First, Francis Fukuyama restates his position. One cannot understand the course of modern history, he argues, simply in terms of scientific and economic progress. There is another, more fundamental, motor of history: the Hegelian principle of the struggle for recognition. As history unfolds, human reason eventually grasps that each individual has but one rational interest—to be recognized as an autonomous person. This interest requires mutual recognition on the part of all, and thus points to the values and institutions of liberal democracy. With the triumph of liberal democracy, it can now be said that reason—and so also history—has reached its destination.

But is it legitimate to employ the Hegelian concept of recognition in isolation from the large and implausible metaphysical claims that seem to ground the Hegelian system? Terry Pinkard argues that it is. The end-of-history thesis does not depend on some mysterious, supernatural entity that controls practical affairs from above. In a comparison of the *Logic*, the *Phenomenology of Spirit*, and the *Philosophy of Right*, Pinkard shows that in both thought and politics the movement of history is toward the overcoming of metaphysics: in thought, a concept comes to be seen as "not an entity but a position in a series of inferences," and in politics the citizen comes to be understood as a social construction based on the (liberal democratic) principle of mutual recognition. In both cases, the end of history simply means that there are no contradictions or problems in how we think about being, or in how we live in a community, that compel us to some new ontology or principles of social organization.

We thus have no philosophic reasons to doubt the evidence that seems so powerfully to announce the arrival of history's completion.

The next section of the book contains four essays that investigate the philosophical provenance of the idea of history and its relation to the liberal democratic ideal. Harvey Mansfield claims that Machiavelli invented the idea of progress. To do so, Machiavelli had to overcome the classical conception of history as a cycle as well as the Christian notion that history leads to redemption. He sought to base politics openly on the amoral truth that all men are motivated by the harsh needs for acquisition and security. By doing so, he believed that one could overcome the basic disagreements about justice and the good which produced the endless cycle of regimes and ways of life spoken of by the ancients. His politics were redemptive in that just one way of life—the Machiavellian one—could be established and maintained permanently. But Machiavelli did not think it possible to end, only to manage, the violent and principled clashes between those who think it really matters, in terms of justice and the good, that they and not others should rule. The ancient cycle thus becomes the hidden engine of stability. According to Mansfield, Machiavelli's idea of progress is superior to its bland successors—the scientific ideal of universal comfort and the moral ideal of universal peace. For Machiavelli's progress retains the turbulent arena of politics, with its bold and ambitious actors, as the place where a new kind of virtue can flourish. This new virtue is at once manipulated by political science and yet more akin to real daring than anything imagined by the ancients.

Kant, as Susan Shell argues, regards Machiavelli's idea of redemption as simply monstrous. For Kant, we have a moral duty to hope that moral virtue will be rewarded, and thus to hope that history is the progressive and yet infinite approximation of a universal civil society that administers law or justice. We can therefore look for signs that history establishes the conditions in which the human faculties can flourish and in which morality and happiness will be united. Thus conceived, human history is the self-conception and self-realization of the *idea* of humanity—of an idea become real and yet freed altogether from the shackles of unfathomable nature. At the same time, however, Kant set the tone for our abiding discomfort with universal, progressive history, because in the end he could not accept the fact that progress sacrifices the happiness of earlier generations for the sake of later ones, and thus affronts the moral worth and autonomy of every individual. Faith in progress is ultimately not a moral faith. And so Kant dabbled in, but ultimately rejected, the philosophy of history.

Hegel did not. But Joseph Cropsey questions Fukuyama's and Pinkard's effort to separate Hegel and metaphysics. Knowledge of the end of history does require knowledge of the whole of things, which, it turns out, we simply do not have. At best, he says, we have knowledge of a set of alternatives or problems that confront us without any possibility of resolution. And if we did have knowledge of the whole, it is hard to think that it would point to our liberal democratic regime as the best possible political order. For however good it is, that regime is in principle too permeable by alien and destructive forces—indeed, too unhappy with itself and lacking in moral resources—to qualify as the perfect regime that history has in mind. At best, says Cropsey, the end-of-history thesis is a useful fiction that can goad us to improve and defend our liberal, constitutional society and institutions.

Finally, Werner Dannhauser explores the view of Nietzsche and Spengler that the end of history is really the advent of the "last man." Why is it, he asks, that at the time of liberalism's greatest triumph there is such a pervading sadness, uncertainty, and sense of malaise in the West? Perhaps because our triumph brings us face to face with the ultimate disappointment: the fact that the real goal of progress, the "end of history" in the relevant sense, is the death to which each individual is fated with absolute certainty. In the light of this awful truth, perhaps what we are left with is either religious faith or, if that fails, virtue—with the attempt to live an honorable life and die an honorable death. With this perception we come full circle to the issue first raised by Mansfield. When Machiavelli redefined virtue as clever boldness, was he timidly hiding from the ancient wisdom that nothing really abides and that we must all learn how to die? Was Machiavelli's bold revolution the first step toward the progress of the last man, the man for whom peace and physical comfort hide the most terrible of all realities?

The book's last section contains six contemporary reflections, some of them quite practical, about the meaning of progress and the end of history. Samuel Huntington reminds us that the present end of ideological divisions surely does not promise the cessation of political conflict. Indeed, the old strife between regime forms will be replaced by struggles among civilizations divided from one another by religion, ethnicity, and culture: within outposts of the Christian West, between Catholic and Orthodox; between the Western and the Islamic worlds; between Slav and Turk; between Hindu and Muslim; and in Africa, among animist and Muslim and Christian. Such conflict was suppressed by the West's struggle to sort out its internal disputes. But now that the West is at peace—and this is all that the end of history can really mean—the harsh differences that have divided humanity from time immemorial will spring back to life.

Conor Cruise O'Brien follows up the theme broached by Huntington, noting that the history now ended was the story of a West divided between anglophone and francophone Enlightenments. The former was limited and reformist, the latter utopian and animated by proselytizing zeal. The fallen communist empire was the most extreme wing of the more enthusiastic Enlightenment, which was carried by force to far-flung cultures and peoples in whom it never took genuine root. But for these remote peoples, it was the only model of Western values, and with its force now gone and its example discredited, the promise of the more moderate Enlightenment seems to have little chance against the forces of religion, tradition, and nationalism.

The next essays speculate on the future prospects for political liberalism at the putative end of history. Alan Gilbert questions the stability of liberal principles supposed by universal history. Far from being stable, the moral principle at the root of mutual recognition—the autonomy of the individual—is an ever-fertile source of radical critique which will always upset established liberal hierarchies and inequalities. To think that mutual recognition means elections, representative government, and free markets, as Fukuyama claims, is simply to mistake the real forces and ultimate direction of change in the modern world. Jean Bethke Elshtain tells us that the fractures within contemporary feminism reveal that liberalism is far from being a stable end of history. Rather, in the feminist era liberalism is rent anew by the tensions between utopianism and the recognition of nature's limits, between radically different conceptions of individual rights, and ultimately between opposing conceptions of what constitutes a genuine political and moral community.

Richard Rorty shows how he understands the end of history and its implications for left-wing intellectuals in the West. We learn, says Rorty, that, for the intellectuals, history was always really over, because it never moved at the behest of the intellectuals' big ideas. We now can *say* that history is over, because we finally recognize this truth and can now give up the conceit that we should spin out concepts of a redeemed social order, understood in such terms as "capitalism," "bourgeois culture," and (more recently) "Discourse" and "Language," and all similar grand, totalizing concepts that ring hollow in the present world. At best, says Rorty, we can but cultivate our own gardens in order to relieve some human misery, with no false assurances that we have a conceptual handle on its causes or remedies in every possible world.

Christopher Lasch brings the volume to a close on an even more somber note. He argues that the end of the Cold War has loosened the strings that once held together the many contradictions and tensions contained within liberal culture. Our capitalist and Enlightenment faith says that everything is possible, but the groaning environment tells us otherwise; our individualism corrodes the family, that essential socializing institution in a liberal democracy; our faith in planning and social engineering replaces informal modes of social control with formal, state-centered, and ineffectual ones. As a result, the civic culture collapses as we tout the apparent victory of our constitutional and economic system. If history is over, says Lasch, we cannot be happy with the final act as we see it played out before our eyes.

The essays in this volume show clearly that the end-of-history controversy is no mere speculative or academic matter. Indeed, it captures perfectly the ambivalence of our present fin-de-siècle cultural mood. We have for so long thought about the ways and means of progress that we are now caught short when its fruits seem finally to have arrived. Thus we not only exult in success but also sense that in victory something important has been lost. And either way, we feel a foreboding sense that something is over and that we no longer know what we are now supposed to *do.* Politics never waits for such paralysis, however, and the astounding and disruptive powers bequeathed to us by progress are too great to remain unused, if they do not in fact have a life and energy of their own. The press of everyday affairs will thus require that we take a stand on our present mood—either by learning how to live safely with nothing much to do, or else by getting over the loss we have sustained and then proceeding resolutely with what is yet to be done.

Part I

THE REVIVAL OF THE IDEA OF HISTORY AS A RATIONAL PROCESS

1 On the Possibility of Writing A Universal History

FRANCIS FUKUYAMA

The writing of a universal history, that is, a history that finds a coherent pattern to the evolution of human societies when taking into account the experiences of all peoples in all times, is itself not a universal practice. Plato and Aristotle conceived of history as cyclical, the latter believing that the human cycle of regimes would be embedded within a larger natural cycle of natural catastrophes which would end all civilized life and force history to start over again.[1] The first true universal histories were Christian, for unlike classical political thought, Christianity asserted the universal equality of all people in the sight of God, and therefore a common destiny for humanity as a whole.[2] For Saint Augustine, for example, the end of history would come on the day of judgment, whereupon earthly life would end and give way to the kingdom of heaven.

Among modern political philosophers, however, Immanuel Kant was the first to raise the possibility of writing a universal history in his 1784 essay *An Idea for a Universal History from a Cosmopolitan Point of View.* Kant wrote that he could only propose, but not complete, this task, something attempted seriously for the first time by his successor Georg Wilhelm Friedrich Hegel. Hegel fulfilled the terms of reference of Kant's initial proposal by seeing the unity of the historical process as one of the realization of freedom in the here-and-now, and his famous dialectic is essentially the working-out of what Kant identified as the selfish but progressive antagonism of man's "asocial sociability."

It is safe to say that the idea of a universal history has not fared well in the twentieth century, as a result of the two waves of criticism of the Hegelian synthesis represented by Marx and Nietzsche. Marx was, of course, the most famous and influential writer of a universal history; he borrowed from Hegel both the latter's historicist framework and the idea of the end of history. Marx understood the historical process as being driven by material or economic forces, and he put the end of history not in the liberal society arising out of the French Revolution but in a communist utopia. The efforts of real-world communist societies to use the concept of a progressive history to justify mass terror and police-state tactics deeply discredited the idea of "history" itself well before the breakdown of real-world communist societies in the 1980s. The second, Nietzschean wave, in whose shadow we live today, attacked the concept of a universal history directly by denying that history in the Hegelian sense was an intelligible concept. The historical process was neither progressive nor terminable; the sequence of civilizations in which Hegel saw a rational pattern was simply the meaningless succession of isolated cultures, each speaking their mutually unintelligible "language of good and evil."

Neither of these broad attacks on the possibility of a universal history leading to modern liberal democracy would have been as compelling as they were, however, were it not for the crisis of European politics which paralleled the impasse reached by Western rationalism. The horrific sequence of events in the first half of the century, including two world wars, the rise of Nazism, Stalinism, and the Holocaust, and finally the turning of modern natural science against humankind in the form of military technology and environmental damage, engendered a tremendous pessimism concerning the existence of a coherent and progressive historical process. For the political inventions of modernity—the totalitarian states of Nazi Germany and the Soviet Union—put modern technology and modern political organization in the service of evil, such as to produce tyrannies of a scale and monstrosity scarcely conceivable in premodern times. Thus the tremendous political pessimism of our time arises directly out of the twin crises of Western politics and Western philosophy in the early twentieth century.

It is precisely the failure of all of the major alternatives to liberal democracy in the last three decades of the twentieth century, however, that suggests the need to reconsider once again the possibility of reconstructing a universal history. For fascism burned itself out quickly through military defeat in 1945, and communism collapsed of its internal contradictions by the end of the 1980s. There were alternatives remaining to modern liberal democracy—most notably, Islamic fundamentalism—but there were no competitive ideologies that could threaten liberalism on its own home turf.[3] Moreover, if we broaden our horizons from the last two decades to the last two hundred years, it is clear that the seven-hundred-year growth of the idea of democracy noted by Alexis de Tocqueville in the 1830s has continued unabated since the time he wrote. While there were only three liberal democracies in the modern sense in 1790, there are something over sixty today, comprising about 2.2 billion people, or over 40 percent of the world's population.[4] The progress toward democracy has not been linear: there were twelve fewer in 1940 than in 1914, and many democratic regimes were overthrown in Latin America in the 1960s and 1970s.[5] But the existence of troughs in this long-term evolution does not vitiate the existence of a coherent trend, any more than recessions make long-term economic growth impossible. The widespread legitimacy of liberal ideas in areas that had formerly been written off as outside the mainstream of democratic civilization—in southern Europe, in Latin America, and finally within the former communist bloc—suggests that the possibility of a universal history needs to be revisited. The spread of democratic ideas in the late twentieth century does not by itself prove either that there is a directionality to history or that these gains will be consolidated in the near future. It does suggest, however, that the terrible events of the first half of the century represent not the essential characteristic of modernity but only a tragic bypath, and that the possibility of the existence of a coherent historical process be raised again, without recourse to the authority of earlier formulators of universal histories.

Any contemporary effort to write a universal history must start with the phenomenon of modern natural science, a useful starting point because it is the only important social activity that by common consensus is both cumulative and directional, even if its ultimate impact on human happiness is ambiguous. Certain truths about the manipulability of nature are known to us which were not known to Isaac Newton, simply because we live later. The progressive conquest of nature made possible with the development of the scientific method in the sixteenth and seventeenth centuries has proceeded according to certain definite rules laid down not by humans but by nature and nature's laws. In this respect, Thomas Kuhn's skepticism about the ultimate truth of any scientific horizon or "paradigm" is irrelevant, because the social consequences of science rest not on nature's ultimate intelligibility, but on the human ability to successfully manipulate nature for human purposes.[6]

The unfolding of modern natural science has had a uniform effect on all societies that have experienced it, for two reasons. In the first place, technology confers decisive military advantages on those countries that possess it, and given the continuing possibility of war in the international system of states, no state that values its independence can ignore the need for defensive modernization. There have been numerous examples of defensive modernizations in recent centuries, including the Ottoman reforms of Mahmud II, the reforms of G. J. D. von Scharnhorst and A. N. von Gneisenau in Prussia after the latter's defeat at Jena by Napoleon, the reforms in Meiji Japan following the visit of Commodore Perry, and most recently *perestroika* in the former Soviet Union, which was initially undertaken by the Mikhail Gorbachev leadership in order to remain technologically competitive with the United States.[7] Military competition requires not just the import of advanced technologies but the wholesale modernization of societies to enable them to create, produce, and deploy those technologies. Thus the Turkish and Japanese reforms encompassed the creation of a national bureaucracy, mass education, uniform tax codes, and the like.

Second, modern natural science establishes a uniform horizon of economic production possibilities. Technology makes possible the limitless accumulation of wealth, and thus the satisfaction of an ever-expanding set of human desires. This process guarantees an increasing homogenization of all human societies, regardless of their historical origins or cultural inheritances. All countries undergoing economic modernization must increasingly resemble one another: they must unify nationally on the basis of a centralized state, urbanize, replace such traditional forms of social organization as tribe, sect, and family with economically rational ones based on function and efficiency, and provide for the universal education of their citizens. Such societies have become increasingly linked with one another through global markets and the spread of a universal consumer culture.

Moreover, the logic of modern natural science would seem to dictate a universal evolution in the direction of capitalism. This conclusion would not have been readily accepted a generation or two ago, when many in the West would have pointed to Josef Stalin's Soviet Union as an example of a country that had achieved the highest levels of industrial modernity without either political or economic freedom. The experiences of the Soviet Union, China, and other socialist countries in the last third of the century indicate, however, that while highly centralized economies are able to reach the level of industrialization achieved by the Europe of the 1950s, they are woefully inadequate in creating what have been termed complex "postindustrial" economies in which information and technological innovation play a much larger role.

Just as the logic of economic development may point in the direction of capitalism, it also seems to point in the direction of liberal democracy. In a famous 1959 article, Seymour Martin Lipset pointed out that there is an extremely high correlation between stable democracy and economic development, and with factors that accompany development such as urbanization, education, and the like.[8] In the years since this correlation was first pointed out, little has happened to disprove it. That is, the most highly industrialized nations remain the most democratic, and it is precisely those countries that have undergone a major process of socioeconomic modernization—including Spain, Portugal, Greece, the Afrikaner community in South Africa, the former Soviet Union, China, Brazil, South Korea, and Taiwan—that have experienced democratic reform movements. With the liberal revolution that has swept through the former Soviet bloc, an entire category of countries that were both industrialized and nondemocratic has been eliminated.

But although there is an undeniable empirical correlation between high levels of industrialization and stable democracy, it is not at all clear that this comes about for economic reasons. Talcott Parson's assertion that democracy is a natural outgrowth of development[9] is belied by the existence of any number of countries that have piled up impressive growth records under authoritarian rule, such as Japan and Germany in the second half of the nineteenth century, and Russia in the first decade and a half of the twentieth. Brazil, South Korea, Singapore, and Thailand have all prospered under various forms of military or authoritarian rule.

And indeed, as Joseph Schumpeter argued fifty years ago and Singapore's Lee Kuan Yew argues today, there are good reasons for thinking that democracies do not, as a rule, make economically rational choices. In a democracies, losers in the economic marketplace can use their political power to protect themselves through tariffs, quotas, subsidies to failing industries, and the like. Democracies on the whole also tend to transfer more income through welfare payments and allocate public money according to political rather than to economic criteria. To take an example closer to home, American democracy has not been particularly effective in dealing with the enormous federal deficits accumulated during the 1980s because it has been unable to decide how to allocate the relative pain of spending cuts and tax increases. The sorts of inefficiencies typical of democratic societies could in theory be avoided by an economically enlightened authoritarian government.[10]

Thus, although there is an undeniable connection between development and democracy, the reasons for the choice of democratic government cannot be fundamentally economic. Like all essentially economic theories of history, the one based on modern natural science is able to give an account of the fundamental directionality of history and can explain many significant features of modernity: why residents of industrialized countries tend to live in cities and work for bureaucratic superiors rather than eke out a living as peasant smallholders and obey the authority of priests. But it cannot in the end provide us with more than an indirect reason for the choice of liberal democracy as a form of government.

The failure of an economic account of history leads us back to Hegel rather than Marx, and to Hegel's completely noneconomic account of the historical process.[11] Hegel gives us the opportunity to reinterpret modern liberal democracy in terms rather different from those of our own Anglo-Saxon tradition of liberalism emanating from Hobbes and Locke.[12] This Hegelian understanding is a more noble vision of what liberalism represents, and is in the end a more accurate account of what people around the world mean when they say they want freedom and democracy—from Spain, Portugal, Argentina, and South Korea to Czechoslovakia, China, and the Soviet Union.

For Hegel, history was based not on the unfolding of modern natural science but on what he called the "struggle for recognition." To uncover the meaning of the "struggle for recognition," we need to go back to Hegel's account of the beginning of history, an account quite comparable to the "state of nature" teachings of the early modern theorists of liberalism who preceded Hegel—Hobbes, Locke, and Rousseau. In the *Phenomenology of Mind,* he described a primitive "first man" living at the beginning of history, a prototypical human being who possessed those fundamental human attributes that existed prior to civil society and the historical process.

Hegel's "first man" shares with the animals certain basic natural desires, such as the desire for food, for sleep, for shelter, and above all for the preservation of his own life. But Hegel's "first man" is radically different from the animals in that he desires not only real, tangible objects but nonmaterial ones as well. Above all, he desires the desire of other men, that is, to be recognized by another human consciousness.

Hegel's "first man" differs from the animals in a second way as well. This man wants not only to be recognized by other men, but to be recognized *as a man.* And what constitutes man's identity as man, the most fundamental and uniquely human characteristic, is his ability to risk his own life. Thus the "first man"'s encounter with other men leads to a violent struggle in which each contestant seeks to make the other "recognize" him by risking his own life. Human beings, in other words, are proud of themselves, and their pride leads them not into a peaceful civil society, but to a violent struggle to the death for pure prestige.

In contrast to an Anglo-Saxon philosopher such as Hobbes, who defined freedom as the absence of physical constraint, Hegel understands freedom as the absence of natural determination, that is, as man's ability to overcome or negate his own animal nature as well as the natural environment around him, and even nature's laws. He is, in short, capable of true moral choice, that is, choice between two courses of action not simply on the basis of the greater utility of one over another but because of an inherent metaphysical freedom to make and adhere to his own rules. And man's specific dignity lies not in a superior calculating ability that makes him a cleverer machine than the lower animals, but precisely in this capacity for free moral choice which manifests itself as a desire for recognition. By risking his life, man proves that he can act contrary to his most powerful and basic instinct, the instinct for self-preservation. And that is why it is important that the primeval battle at the beginning of history be over prestige alone, or over an apparent trifle like a medal or a flag that signifies recognition.

This "bloody battle" can have one of three results. It can lead to the death of both combatants, in which case life itself, human and natural, ends. It can lead to the death of one of the contestants, in which case the survivor remains unsatisfied because the other human consciousness cannot recognize him. Or, finally, the battle can terminate in the relationship of lordship and bondage, in which one of the contestants decides to submit to a life of slavery rather than face the risk of violent death.

The psychological concept underlying "recognition" was not invented by Hegel. It is as old as Western political philosophy itself, and refers to a thoroughly familiar part of the human personality. In the history of political philosophy, there has been no consistent word used to refer to the psychological phenomenon of the "desire for recognition": Plato spoke of spiritedness (*thymos*), Machiavelli of man's desire for glory, Hobbes of pride or vainglory, Rousseau of *amour-propre*, Alexander Hamilton of the love of fame, James Madison of ambition, Hegel of recognition, and Nietzsche of man as the "beast with red cheeks." All of these terms refer to that part of man which feels the need to place value on things—himself in the first instance, but on the people, actions, or things around him as well. It is the part of the personality which is the fundamental source of the emotions of pride, anger, and shame.

The first extended analysis of the phenomenon of recognition in the Western philosophical tradition appears, quite appropriately, in Plato's *Republic*. Book IV contains Socrates' famous discussion of the tripartite division of the soul. Socrates begins by distinguishing desire and reason as separate phenomena. Desire impels men to acquire things outside themselves, such as food, drink, and shelter. Reason may at times override desire, as when a hungry man forebears from eating an apple because he knows it is poisoned. But are desire and reason sufficient to explain the whole of human behavior? Socrates tells the story of a certain Leontius, who passes a pile of corpses, bodies of men recently executed, and tries not to look at them. After an internal struggle, he finally gives in to an overpowering desire to view the bodies and then grows angry at himself for having done so.

One could interpret Leontius' internal struggle as nothing more than the struggle between two desires: the desire to look at the corpses competing with a natural disgust at viewing a dead human body. This would be in keeping with Hobbes's mechanistic psychology, which interprets the will as simply "the last appetite in deliberating." But to interpret Leontius' behavior as nothing more than a clash of desires does not explain his anger with himself. For he presumably would not have been angry had he succeeded in restraining himself: on the contrary, he would have felt a different but related emotion, pride. A moment's reflection will indicate that Leontius' anger could come neither from the desiring part nor from the calculating part of the soul, because Leontius was not indifferent to the outcome of his inner struggle. It therefore had to come from a third and altogether different part, which Socrates calls *thymos.*

Thymos emerges in the *Republic* as being somehow related to the value one sets on oneself, what we today might call "self-image" or "self-esteem." Leontius believed that he was someone who could comport himself with a certain dignity and self-restraint, and when he failed to live up to his self-image, he grew angry. *Thymos* is something like an innate human sense of justice: we believe ourselves to have a certain worth, and when other people act as though we are worth less—when they do not *recognize* that worth at its correct value—then anger bursts forth. The intimate relationship between self-evaluation and anger can be seen in the English word synonymous with anger, "indignation." "Dignity" refers to a person's sense of worthiness; "indignation" arises when something happens to offend that sense of worth. Conversely, when other people see that we are not living up to our own self-image, we feel shame; and when we are evaluated justly (i.e., in proportion to our sense of self-worth), we feel pride.

It is instructive to compare the Hegelian account of the beginning of history with the Anglo-Saxon version which is the basis of our own American liberalism. For these two differ precisely in the relative moral evaluation they give to *thymos* or the desire for recognition, on the one hand, and self-preservation of the body, on the other.

The similarities between Hobbes's "state of nature" and Hegel's bloody battle are striking. In the first place, both are characterized by extreme violence: the primary social reality is not love or concord but a war of "every man against every man." And although Hobbes does not use the term "struggle for recognition," the stakes in his original war of all against all are essentially the same as for Hegel. To quote from the *Leviathan:* "For every man looks that his companion should value him at the same rate he sets upon himself; and upon all signs of contempt or undervaluing naturally endeavors, as far as he dares . . . to extort a greater value from his contemners. . . ." According to Hobbes, men may fight over necessities, but more often than not they fight over "trifles" like "a word, a smile, a different opinion." They fight, in other words, over recognition. Hobbes the great materialist ends up describing the nature of the "first man" in terms not much different from those of the idealist Hegel. That is, the passion that first and foremost drives men into the war of all against all is not the quest for security but the satisfaction of the pride and vanity of a few ambitious men.

Where Hobbes and Hegel differ fundamentally, however, and where the Anglo-Saxon tradition of liberalism takes its decisive turn, is in the relative moral weight assigned to the passions of pride or vanity (i.e., "recognition") on the one hand, and to the fear of violent death on the other. Hegel, as we have seen, believes that the willingness to risk one's life in a battle for pure prestige is in some sense what makes human beings human, the foundation of human freedom.

Hobbes, on the other hand, finds nothing whatsoever morally redeeming in the pride of the aristocratic master. Indeed, it is precisely this desire for recognition, this willingness to fight over a "trifle" like a medal or a flag, which is the source of all violence and human misery in the state of nature. For him, the strongest human passion is the fear of violent death, and the strongest moral imperative—the "law of nature"—is the preservation of one's own physical existence. Self-preservation is the fundamental moral fact: all concepts of justice and right for Hobbes are founded in the rational pursuit of self-preservation, while injustice and wrong are those things that lead to violence, war, and death. For Hobbes and Locke, and for their followers who wrote the American Declaration of Independence and the Constitution, the only legitimate government is one that can adequately preserve life and prevent a return to the war of all against all. Liberal society involved the following bargain: in return for the security of their lives and property, men must give up their unjust pride and vanity. The liberal state thus implies the subordination of *thymos,* or the desire for recognition, to a combination of desire and reason—Tocqueville's famous "self-interest rightly understood." Those who seek to show themselves superior to other men, to dominate them on the basis of superior virtue, those noble characters who struggle against their "human all too human" limitations, are to be persuaded of the folly of their pride.

The elevation of self-preservation over the thymotic desire for recognition which is the basis of our liberal tradition has led to a persistent unease with the society thereby produced, and with the prototypical product of that society, the so-called bourgeois. That unease is ultimately traceable to a single moral fact, that the bourgeois is preoccupied primarily with his own material well-being, and is not public-spirited, virtuous, or dedicated to the larger community around him: in short, he is selfish. The typical citizen of a Lockean society is a person composed entirely of desire and reason but lacking in *thymos.*

As noted earlier, Hegel provides us with an alternative account of liberalism which is at once nobler and more accurate. For Hegel, the struggle for recognition does not end with the primordial bloody battle, but continues to drive all of subsequent human history. The bloody battle terminates not in civil society but in a world divided between masters, who risked their lives, and slaves, who accepted a life of servitude because they gave in to their natural fear of death. The relationship of lordship and bondage in subsequent years takes a wide variety of forms in all of the unequal, aristocratic societies that have characterized the greater part of human history.

Lordship and bondage is an unstable relationship, however, because it is ultimately unsatisfying for both the master and the slave. The master desires recognition by another human being, that is, recognition of his worth and human dignity by another human being possessing worth and dignity. But instead he is recognized by the slave, whose humanity is unachieved because he has given in to his natural fear of death. The master's worth is therefore recognized by someone not quite human. This then constitutes the tragedy of the master: he risks his life for the sake of recognition on the part of a slave who is not worthy of recognizing him. The master remains less than satisfied. Moreover, the master remains fundamentally unchanging over time. He does not need to work, because he has a slave to work for him, and he has easy access to all of the things that are necessary to maintain his life. His life therefore becomes a static and unchanging life of leisure and consumption; he can be killed, as Alexandre Kojève points out, but he cannot be educated.

The slave is also unsatisfied. His lack of satisfaction, however, leads not to deadening stasis, as in the case of the master, but to creative and enriching change. By submitting to the master, the slave of course is not recognized as a human being: on the contrary, he is treated as a thing, a tool for the satisfaction of the master's wants. Recognition is entirely one-way. But this total absence of recognition is what leads the slave to desire change—particularly for the slaves, whose humanity is not recognized in any way. With the coming of the French and American Revolutions, the distinction between masters and slaves is abolished: the former slaves are transformed into their own masters through popular sovereignty and the rule of law. History ends with these revolutions because the slave has, in principle, finally found what he was seeking all these years, that is, recognition of his dignity and freedom.

For Hegel, the liberal society that emerges at the end of history is a reciprocal and equal agreement among citizens mutually to recognize one another's human dignity. If Hobbesean or Lockean liberalism can be interpreted as the pursuit of rational self-interest, Hegelian "liberalism" can be seen as the pursuit of *rational recognition;* that is, recognition on a universal basis in which the dignity of each person as a free and autonomous human being is recognized by all. In a Lockean liberal state, rights are a means to the preservation of a private sphere, wherein men seek their true happiness. In the Hegelian state, rights are seen as ends in themselves. What is at stake for us when we choose to live in a liberal democracy is not merely the fact that it allows us the freedom to accumulate property and satisfy the desiring parts of our souls. The more important and ultimately more satisfying thing it provides us with is recognition of our human dignity. The liberal democratic state values us at our own sense of self-worth. Thus both the desiring and thymotic parts of our souls find satisfaction.

The desire for recognition was very much at the root of the anticommunist revolutions in the Eastern bloc in the late 1980s. The fundamental impulse for the reforms undertaken in the Soviet Union and China was indeed economic. It lay in the inability of centralized command economies to meet the requirements of "post-industrial" society. But even if we accept this as the long-term explanation for the breakdown of communism, we cannot understand the totality of the revolutionary phenomenon unless we appreciate the demand for recognition which accompanied the economic crisis. People did not go into the streets of Leipzig, Prague, Timisoara, Beijing, or Moscow demanding that the government give them a postindustrial economy. Their passionate anger was aroused over their perceptions of injustice which had nothing to do with economics: the jailing or murder of a priest, the revelation of corruption on the part of a local official, the martyring of a demonstrator at the hands of a trigger-happy security service, the closing of a newspaper, or the refusal of powerful officials to accept a list of demands. In the accounts of the resistance in St. Petersberg to the hardline coup in August 1991, those who rallied to the side of the "democrats" frequently asserted that they risked their lives because they no longer wanted to be humiliated by the authorities or treated as slaves. They explained that they wanted to walk with their backs straight and, in the words of one participant, "did not want to trade their dignity for a piece of sausage." And they demanded less a market economy than a government that recognized their elementary rights under a rule of law, a government that did not lie to them about the crimes and stupidities it had committed in the past, that would allow them freely to express their thymotic opinions about right and wrong, and that would ultimately treat them not as children but as adults capable of governing themselves.

Recognition has been a driving force not only in the politics of the postcommunist world, but in American political life as well.

We are accustomed to thinking about politics as a clash of interest groups, each trying to get a bigger slice of the economic pie. But in fact, much of the political conflict in this country revolves around questions of dignity and the demand for equal recognition, as indicated by the following three examples:

> The issue of sexual harassment, which was discussed at great length during the Clarence Thomas confirmation hearings, is preeminently an issue concerning the respect shown to women in the workplace. The immense anger felt by many women as a result of Anita Hill's treatment arose directly out of their belief that her dignity had not been recognized, either by Judge Thomas or by the Judiciary Committee.
>
> Today, we build wheelchair ramps to the front doors of public buildings rather than hide them discreetly at the side or back. The issue is not so much one of convenience, since either entrance gets you inside. The question is rather one of dignity, to show that a handicapped person can enter through the front door just as well as anyone else.
>
> Finally, the pain caused by racism or homelessness is of course in large measure economic, but there is an important recognition component as well. In Ralph Ellison's phrase, a black is an "invisible man" to whites, not seen as a full human being. You may help feed a homeless man by giving him money, but you injure his dignity when you fail to look him in the eye as you do so.

Despite continuing preoccupation with economic questions, recognition of equal dignity—not just for economically underprivileged workers, but for blacks, women, the handicapped, homosexuals, and other groups yet unrecognized as being unrecognized—has moved permanently to the forefront of American politics.

Thymos, then, can provide the missing link between liberal economics and liberal politics. Desire and reason are together sufficient to explain the process of industrialization, and a large part of economic life more generally. But they cannot explain the striving for liberal democracy, which ultimately arises out of the thymotic part of the soul. The social changes that accompany advanced industrialization, in particular universal education, appear to liberate a certain demand for recognition which did not exist among poorer and less educated people. As people become wealthier, more cosmopolitan, and better educated, and as society as a whole achieves a greater equality of condition, they demand not simply more wealth but recognition of their status. If human beings did not care about recognition, if they were composed of nothing but reason and desire, they would be perfectly content to live in a South Korea under military dictatorship, or under the enlightened technocratic administration of Francoist Spain, or in a Guomindang-led Taiwan hell-bent on rapid economic growth. And yet citizens of these countries are something more than desire and reason: they have pride and belief in their own dignity, and want that dignity to be recognized, above all by the government of the country they live in. They want to be treated not as children incapable of mastering themselves but as adults aware of their own value and able to control their own lives.

A discussion of whether history is a coherent and directional process inevitably raises the question of history's end. Hegel's great interpreter, Alexander Kojève, said categorically that history had ended with the French Revolution because the quest for recognition had been satisfied. That is, the struggle for recognition propelled human societies through all of the previous "stages of history" and accounted for the master-slave dialectic, the rise of aristocratic societies, religious fanaticism, nationalism, and finally modern liberal democracy. Of these different political forms, only modern liberal democracy could rationally and fully satisfy human thymotic strivings by providing all people with universal and equal recognition. The historical process was completed because people finally found what they had been looking for through all the previous millennia of struggle.

Thus the question of whether history has ended in these Hegelian terms boils down to the question of whether universal recognition is "fully satisfying," as Kojève says. There are two broad critiques of the adequacy of the universal recognition available in modern liberal democracies, one from the left and the other from the right.

The critique from the left argues that liberal democracy ultimately fails because it recognizes equal people unequally. In this respect, capitalism and modern democracy work at cross-purposes, for the capitalist division of labor and the workings of the free market necessarily result in economic inequality and consequently in inequality of recognition. The dignity of a garbage man will never receive the recognition accorded that of a theoretical physicist; and this difference in recognition is not a problem that can be solved by material prosperity.

The critique from the right, by contrast, argues that the defect of liberal democracy is that it recognizes inherently unequal people equally, and thereby dehumanizes them just as fully. It is based on the observation that, contrary to the Declaration of Independence, all men are *not* created equal in certain crucial respects. The right that makes this critique is not represented by anyone on the contemporary American political spectrum, but comes from the philosopher Friedrich Nietzsche.

It is my intuition that this is ultimately the more powerful of the two critiques of universal recognition. For Nietzsche would point out that, even if all men were indeed created equal, no human greatness, no creativity, no aspiration or achievement could come about except as a result of the desire to be recognized as greater than other people. This is true not only of military and political leaders but of composers, poets, philosophers, even of bureaucrats engaged in interagency battles.

For Nietzsche, then, the deepest problem of modernity was that it created a civilization of "last men," human beings who were satisfied merely with equal recognition or who, worse yet, had completely subordinated their *thymos* to a combination of reason and desire. The last man is the human being who is content with himself, and with a life of endless material accumulation, a being without striving, sacrifice, risk, or ideals. Thus the deepest problem of liberal democracy is not that it fails to fulfill the promise of equal recognition, but rather that by its very success in providing "peace and prosperity" it closes off an entire area of human aspiration and leaves those who came after with stunted souls.

The problem of the "last man" is intimately related to the problem of the "first man." That is, it seems unlikely that all men will be content to become such contemptible creatures, preoccupied with endless consumerism and petty self-interest. They are, after all, human beings with pride, and they will rebel at the prospect of a world bereft of ideals and struggle. And if they cannot struggle against injustice and oppression because the world has somehow become "filled up" with successful democracies, then they may well seek to struggle against justice, peace, and prosperity. The fear of becoming a last man has the potential of restarting history once again, and if this ever happens in the future, the consequences will be much more terrible than at the beginning of history, because our modern weapons cannot be uninvented.

A final question is the degree to which Americans, as a society, are in danger of becoming last men. This question is not susceptible to a definitive answer. But I suggest that while as a society we are in some way dedicated to the principle of equal recognition, our lives are in fact filled with a continuing struggle for *unequal* recognition. Most of us do not want to be recognized merely as the equals of our fellows, we want to be better. This desire is apparent in business: capitalist competition is driven not just by greed but by the desire to be recognized as the fastest-growing retailer or the highest-quality automobile manufacturer. It is present in American politics, where the electoral process provides a natural outlet for those who want public acclaim. The very design of our political system, however, seeks to constrain ambitious natures through a complicated series of constitutional checks and balances, so that American democratic politics will always be something less than fully satisfying for the most ambitious natures. Finally, there is the entire realm of sports, whose primary objective is to produce winners and losers, and even the arts, which can also be a realm of thymotic competition.

So the prospect of becoming last men is, in a certain sense, a constant challenge rather than a pervasive reality. In the future, liberal democracies will most likely continue to acquiesce in the human desire to be recognized as greater than one's fellows. And while this desire will in some sense contradict the principle of a free and equal society, the survival of the desire to be recognized as greater than others in ways that nonetheless avoid tyranny will have much to do with the long-term health and durability of liberal democracy.

2 Hegel on History, Self-Determination, and the Absolute

TERRY PINKARD

There is a well-known, received view of Hegel which is still widely influential. Part of this view sees Hegel as the last great (or the final and silly) end of grand theorizing about the place of human affairs in the cosmos and the direction that history is taking. For Hegel, the object of philosophical study is supposed to be the Absolute (always capitalized), and the man for the job is an academic in Prussia: Hegel himself. In the received view, history is the march of God in human affairs, with the march supposedly heading toward nineteenth-century Prussia, where God is to set up base camp, presumably to stay. Moreover, this march is supposed to follow, strictly and with Prussian rigor, a three-step movement of thesis, antithesis, and synthesis. This view is often taken as an expression of nineteenth-century self-congratulatory optimism or even as an egregious example of old-fashioned, pre-*Bundesrepublik* German hubris. Given that Hegel supposedly said so many bombastic things (all of which are of course, fully unbelievable to us more rational souls in this more scientific and enlightened age), why should anybody pay any attention to him, except for the obvious role he played in shaping Marx's views on society and history and for his other historical influences? Some believe that the most that can be said for him is that even though his metaphysics of God's coming to self-awareness through us in history is crazy metaphysics, his thoughts on politics and history justify our rereading the Hegelian texts for those core insights, all of which are detachable from his outrageous metaphysical views.[1]

I shall argue that just about everything in this received picture is wrong. Hegel did not hold this outrageous metaphysics, nor is his political thought completely detachable from his more general intellectual project. Nor did he subscribe to the view, quite often attributed to him, that the world or history was structured in terms of thesis, antithesis, and synthesis (a gross misrepresentation first made by the obscure and well-forgotten Heinrich Moritz Chalybäus).[2] In fact, so I shall argue, Hegel's true radicality and importance as a thinker is only just now coming to be understood. Taken in his own terms, Hegel is not the final expression of a completely outmoded metaphysics but the harbinger of a postmetaphysical mode of thought. I also shall argue that understanding Hegel in this way sheds some new light on his understanding of history and makes it even more challenging than it has usually been taken to be since Hegel's death.

To make this case, however, I must first go into some background about why Hegel would have been driven to the view of history he finally came to hold. As with all things Hegelian, this task requires a bit of a roundabout way to the final goal.

Hegel's *Logic* and the Absolute

Hegel's conception of his program cannot be separated from what he understood the cultural role of philosophy in modernity to be. On Hegel's view, what is most distinctive about modernity is its conception of itself as self-justifying and self-legitimating.[3] Modern culture takes itself to rely only on reason, and reason, unlike faith, can be expected to give an account of itself. We cannot be content, therefore, with what Kant called dogmatism (and what Hegel called positivity), that is, with ending any account of our epistemic or moral lives in terms of something that we are told we simply must accept. Hegel therefore concludes that it is crucial to modern culture that there be an *absolute,* that is, a nonarbitrary, nondogmatic stopping point capable of giving an account of itself. Such claims no doubt strike some as simply another piece of esoteric Teutonic romanticism, and they raise large issues about how such sweeping and grandiose claims could possibly be worked out. In order therefore to get a grasp on these seemingly unwieldy assertions on Hegel's part, it is necessary to see what Hegel meant by taking the cultural project of modernity to be attempting to provide a fully self-grounding cultural life based on the authority of science and philosophy. The best way to begin is with a short overview of what is generally taken to be the most obscure of Hegel's theses—namely, those concerning the absolute—and with that expression of his thought which is considered most esoteric—namely, his *Science of Logic.*

Hegel takes the 'absolute' to be an account of what we can call the *categorical determinateness of appearance,* that is, why the appearing world has the essential structure it does, and whether this appearing world is the world as it really is. Hegel thought that our time has given us a glimpse of what this absolute might be and that, furthermore, it has shown us a *nonmetaphysical* absolute: not an abstract supersensible entity posited to explain the determinateness of the appearing world but the ongoing self-justifying practices of the modern human community.[4] The first part of the story thus begins with the *Science of Logic,* in which the general form of the absolute is developed.

The *Logic* has three parts, "Being," "Essence," and "Concept." Each represents a basic way in which the world may be said to appear to human beings, that is, a basic type of categorial thought. The first part, "Being," portrays the logical structure of a nominalist world, that is, a characterization of the world exclusively in terms of individuals that possess only particular qualitative and quantitative features, and he shows how this type of account of appearance undermines itself. For example, consider trying to explain how it is possible that two individual red spots share a common color. When one tries to explain this shared determinateness of these two red individuals, one inevitably ends up positing some kind of abstract supersensible entity that philosophers often call a universal (for example, 'redness'). One ends up, that is, explaining the determinateness of the appearing world by means of an underlying metaphysical entity. In the language of Hegelian dialectic, if we start with "Being" (nominalism), we therefore quickly find ourselves with the logic of "Essence" (in positing metaphysical substructures that stand behind appearance and explain why appearance is the way it is). Metaphysical thought is characterized by the reflective positing of such supersensible entities beyond (or behind) appearance which are available only to the mind's eye or to reflective thought. We have appearance on the one hand, with its many types of individuals; and we have the essences lying behind appearance which explain its determinateness.

Part of the great novelty of Hegel's *Logic* was to see that although metaphysical thought was most naturally at home in this 'logic of essence,' it nevertheless undermined itself just as nominalism had done. Once one begins looking for a determining ground of appearance outside of appearance, only two routes are open: metaphysical realism and subjective idealism. If we take the first route, metaphysical realism, we posit some metaphysical ground of appearance in things that are beyond appearance, but we then eventually lose the ability to give any characterization of that ground; we cannot know anything about it, and therefore it becomes something about which we can say nothing. We talk about it without saying anything. Kant's doctrine of unknowable things-in-themselves is, for Hegel, a self-conscious statement about what metaphysicians had been up to all along.

What is the other route? If the determining ground of appearance is not in supersensible metaphysical entities, then it must be in the nature of the human mind itself. On this view—subjective idealism—the mind is seen as *imposing* the basic categorial determinateness on the world of appearance. However, this view turns the world in itself into something like an indeterminate great white light that we color in ourselves, and any idea of a determinate world independent of our activities vanishes. Metaphysical realism and subjective idealism are thus the mirror twins of each other, and the history of modern philosophy displays a kind of ongoing oscillation from one to the other. Each is necessarily locked into some kind of odd philosophical tango with its other, and this odd dance continues in our time. For example, the various conceptions of alternative 'conceptual frameworks' popular in Anglo-American philosophy from the 1960s through the 1980s are forms of such subjective idealism. Note the metaphorical language that is used in these modern remnants of subjective idealism: we employ these conceptual frameworks to carve up the world into distinct categorial types. The same holds true for some of the continental attempts at seeing everything in terms of Language or Textuality. Even those theories of pragmatism which stress truth as a function of what works turn the world into a function of *our* needs and interests and thus are also forms of subjective idealism. Even a contemporary pragmatist such as Richard Rorty, who sees himself as avoiding the opposition of idealism versus realism altogether, still sees the determinateness of the world as constituted by a series of what he calls conversations; like the pragmatist he is, Rorty too really offers a variant on the dialectic of subjective idealism.[5] The result of both metaphysical realism and subjective idealism is inevitably skepticism about whether this or that scheme actually reflects 'the' world as it really is.

As Hegel saw, the solution to the dialectic of metaphysical realism and subjective idealism is not more metaphysical realism and subjective idealism. The only way out of the endless oscillation between the two is to construct a different type of characterization in which we do not look *behind* the appearances for any determining essence or substructure whatsoever. This process occurs in what Hegel calls the logic of Concept (I use the capitalization to distinguish it as a type of thinking). In the logic of Concept, we look only to the common appearing world that we share, and we understand it in terms of the various holistic set of beliefs and attitudes that we have come to have. We understand the world not as determined by a conceptual scheme but as manifesting itself to us in a conceptual (or linguistic) form.

The concepts we use to articulate this world are not themselves abstract metaphysical entities that stand behind appearance. A concept is not an entity but a position in a system of inferences. (That is why the "Doctrine of Concept" is the study of inferences, both formal and material.) Outside of these schemes of inference are no metaphysical entities determining their truth. In the logic of Concept, we get a different picture of people *in* a world, people who describe that world in terms of holistically understood conceptual structures, without any metaphysical anchors that would supposedly link their beliefs to the world. Hegel does not deny, of course, that our system of thoughts has a nonmetaphysical causal connection to the world; his claim is that at the level of Concept, there is no metaphysically ultimate basis or metaphysically justifying ground outside the system of thoughts themselves: there is only the internal connectedness of those thoughts which show within their own structure how they link up with the world. In that sense, the system of thoughts is, in Hegel's terms, self-mediating, requiring nothing metaphysical outside of itself to mediate it: it does not require an intuition into any kind of metaphysical essence to underwrite its own authoritativeness, and it is therefore, in Hegel's term, absolute.[6] As it turns out later in his system, these 'pure thoughts' are the expressions of the ongoing linguistic and cultural practices of the human community. As Hegel will argue, once we learn to take the nonmetaphysical stance of the Concept, we will come to see history and society differently. But that takes us to the second part of the story.

History and Self-Identity

Kierkegaard remarks that if Hegel had said of his *Logic* that it is simply a giant game, it would be a great work. Instead, Hegel claims it is the way the world is and thus it is only comical.[7] Hegel himself saw that he needed an account of why we would think that such a project as that sketched in the *Logic* is even possible.[8] His account of this possibility is his 1807 *Phenomenology of Spirit*, published before the *Logic* and the rest of the system.

The *Phenomenology of Spirit* is a treatment of what he calls historical "formations of consciousness" in terms of what they take to be authoritative for themselves, that is, to be required for them.[9] These formations of consciousness are taken as forms of *Geist*, what Hegel calls "spirit." Spirit is Hegel's term for a reflective form of life, that is, a way in which human life has instanced itself in a set of practices and shared standards, which has its own specific history, and which has developed within itself a set of institutions and practices whose function is to reflect on the authoritative conceptions that distinguish that form of life. As forms of life develop practices for reflecting on and evaluating the authoritativeness of their grounds of belief as to whether these practices achieve the aims they set for themselves, they become what Hegel calls spirit: a self-conscious and reflective form of collective social life. The *Phenomenology of Spirit* is the treatment of the ways in which the accounts given by historical forms of life have generated skepticism about themselves purely by virtue of the terms they set for themselves as determining what counts for them as success. By generating such skepticism, these forms of life thereby gradually undermine themselves. Later reflective forms of life, which understand themselves as linked in a historical narrative with those earlier forms, can understand their own requirements—what is authoritative for them—as having been required by virtue of the failure of the past accounts and must see their own accounts as resolving those skeptical objections in their new terms.[10] (Hegel refers to this capacity to generate self-undermining skeptical doubts about what a form of life takes as authoritative for itself as its negativity.) As a form of life develops reflective practices, it finds, for example, that the various grounds that it takes as authoritative for itself can clash with one another in ways that do not seem resolvable: it can find that its practices fail to satisfy certain criteria that have come to count for it as specifying what will be judged to be a successful practice; or it can find that the aims it sets for itself and of which its form of life promises fulfillment themselves come to be necessarily unfulfillable within its set of practices; or it can find that it requires its participants to do things that conflict with other things it also requires them to do, thus provoking tragic social clashes. When a form of life encounters these kinds of skepticisms, the participants in that form of life seek to reassure themselves that what they have come to take as authoritative reasons really are authoritative reasons and that therefore both they and the world really are as they have come to take them to be. Moreover, Hegel holds that these social practices of affirmation and reassurance can take many different shapes other than just philosophical reflection—for example, tragic drama, comedy, religious practice, quests, and so on.

This focus on reflective forms of life is crucial for Hegel. For Hegel, we are social beings not merely in the trivial senses that we learn to speak a particular language, live in a historically situated community, and have our beliefs conditioned by our social environment. We are social in a deeper sense in that who we take ourselves to be is constituted by the form of life in which we have been brought up, and what is distinctive about that form of life consists of the kinds of reasons which it takes as authoritative for itself. As the authoritativeness of those reasons breaks down because of the way in which our attempts at reassurance in the face of skepticism undermine themselves, our sense of who we have come to be therefore also changes and breaks down. The *Phenomenology of Spirit* traces the successive history of those attempts at reflective reassurance and the ways in which they come to undermine themselves. It develops a story of how these reflective forms of life succeed each other by incorporating the past accounts of what was authoritative into a different account that understands what is required for it to be required by virtue of the failures of previous accounts. When a form of life undermines itself by finding that its skeptical doubts about what is authoritative for itself are not satisfactorily resolved by the accounts it frames for itself to reassure itself about those doubts, then either it or a succeeding form of life must alter the account so that it comes to have new aims consistent with what the old account actually accomplished (which, in Hegel's view, is what the Roman form of life did with the preceding Greek form of life); or it must advance a new set of aims that supersede the old aims by including them as components of itself (which, for example, is what the early European culture did with the older Roman form of life). Indeed history itself is possible only by virtue of the way in which spirit, *Geist,* reflects on what is taken as authoritative for itself and the ways in which those later developments can be seen to be the completions of earlier forms, as fulfilling the aims that the older form of life within the terms it set for itself could not accomplish. This is not to say that earlier forms 'aim' at later forms in some fated manner. It says only that they (or something very much like them) could in retrospect be understood to have provided a new understanding both of what is authoritative and why it counts as authoritative which resolves the insufficiencies of the earlier ones (for example, in the way in which Augustine showed how early Christian civilization within its own standpoint could understand itself as resolving the problems of the preceding pagan Roman civilization; or in the way in which early modernity explained to itself how it had resolved the insufficiencies of medieval life).

Part of the task of the *Phenomenology* is to show how its own historical approach to questions of knowledge and action is legitimated. It does this by showing how nonhistorical accounts of what is authoritative for us undermine themselves and require a type of historical explanation to resolve those insufficiencies. In the opening chapters of the work, Hegel examines a collection of post-Enlightenment theories of knowledge which are all couched in terms of a supposedly direct awareness of objects, and he shows how these undermine themselves by failing to achieve the aims that count for them as constituting success in the theory of knowledge. A succeeding attempt at construing knowledge in terms of self-sufficient practical activity also turns out to be insufficient; holding that what can be known is relative to our plans and projects, it finds that the kind of independent, 'fixed self' which is involved in the idea of plans and projects turns out to be not indeed fixed but to be itself caught in various webs of mutual recognition and of contingently determined relations of mastery and servitude. The attempts to rectify that fault by the construction of accounts of an independent fixed self through the practices of stoicism or skepticism similarly undermine themselves.

All the accounts that try to underwrite some conception of ourselves as self-sufficient knowers who are either immediately in touch with the objects of sense (or with the supersensible world through the mediation of the understanding), or who are immediately in touch with our own fixed selves as setting various practical projects therefore turn out to require an appeal to impersonal reason (the "view from nowhere," to use Thomas Nagel's term for such an account).[11] However, the various accounts of our epistemic and practical activities—of who we are—in the terms of an impersonal reason that would transcend any particular social practice themselves turn out to fail on the terms they set for themselves. Hegel argues that these failures in early modern European life require the conclusion that even reason itself must be understood in terms of the ways it has been embodied in determinate forms of historically situated reflective social practice. Hegel runs through the failure of the otherwise-successful methods of modern natural science to provide foundational answers to social and political conflicts and the way in which the project of establishing a self-grounding ideal of freedom seemed to require accounts of our individual and collective lives in terms of some supposedly fixed "inner quality" of ourselves—such as Faustian self-determination, emotionalist religion, or the activities and social practices surrounding the character ideal of the detached yet sincere gentleman and the *honnête homme* of early modern French culture—which themselves also came ultimately to be understood as having undermined themselves.

Indeed, it was what Hegel took to be the failure of the appeal to impersonal reason in early modern European life to realize the project of "self-grounding" satisfactorily which provoked the crisis that motivated the modern European form of life to move away from considering our individual and collective lives as being constituted by some fixed metaphysical quality and instead as being nonmetaphysically constituted by free-standing social practices. But this move itself provoked a new set of crises for European life, since it was not clear to Hegel's contemporaries—as it is still not clear to us—that the modern form of life is not itself self-undermining in exactly the same way that Hegel claims that older forms of life generated a sense of their own insufficiencies. In particular, in Hegel's own day, it was not clear that the best form of life was not already a thing of the past: either in ancient Greece or (in a set of beliefs becoming increasingly popular in his day) in the religiosity of medieval Europe. Moreover, competing for the attention of those who wished neither to restore Greece nor to return to the Middle Ages were the appeals to varying forms of pietist religious revival, to forms of social thought inspired by the Enlightenment, to various doctrines of revolutionary freedom, and to the growing romantic movement having to do with the nonrational exploration of the individual and collective 'self.'

Hegel's response in the *Phenomenology* to these alleged alternatives to modern life was to offer a complex dialectical history of the forms that 'spirit' had assumed in the past and to show both how each had undermined itself and how the insufficiencies of these forms of life had required each succeeding form of life to understand what was mandatory for itself to have been required by the failures of what had preceded it. Hegel's actual arguments concerning this progression are of course, complex and controversial; their complexity precludes their being discussed in depth here, but their general direction can nonetheless be at least outlined. Against the background of the longing for ancient Greece prevalent among many of his contemporaries, Hegel tried to show how the ancient Greek form of life on its own terms had undermined itself and had set the stage for its denouement in Roman life. Greek life had based itself on a form of *Sittlichkeit*, 'ethical life,' in which the individual's immediate identification with his social roles enabled him to be fully free in following out his socially determined nature; but the demands that Greek life had placed on such socialized agents to become free individuals by distinguishing themselves in the pursuit of glory or by gaining recognition from appropriate others placed contradictory demands on the actors in Greek life.[12] Thus in the tragedy *Antigone* we see the dramatization of how Antigone, a Greek woman, can have a free self only in her attachment to family life and to her brother, which in turn leads her to defy Creon's edicts against her performing the appropriate burial rites on her slain brother. The clash between Antigone and Creon thus represented conflicts within Greek life itself, namely, clashes between the principles that governed family life and the principles that governed public life (and thus a struggle between men and women), and a clash between the Greek assumption of a self-restoring ethical life and the way in which the internal contradictoriness of its ethical life prevented such a process from occurring. Through its accounts of itself, Greek life thus came to subvert itself and declined into various pursuits of private independence which were expressed by its later stoical and skeptical philosophies. In realizing the aims of the stoical and skeptical accounts that had completed classical Greek life, Roman civilization had in turn led to a completely legalistic and alienated form of life, which in turn undermined itself and was supplanted by medieval conceptions of faith and chivalry. As this aristocratic ethos culminated in the early modern creation of a 'groundless self' detached from all its ends and prior to all its choices of ends, European life experienced a pivotal crisis in its history. Both the emotionalist religious revival of the seventeenth and eighteenth centuries and the intellectual movement of the eighteenth century called the Enlightenment had each attempted to respond to the problems brought on by that early modern experience of the groundless self by finding a new set of 'grounds' which would supposedly be available to any reflective person; their respective failures to make good on their own promises transformed the early modern experience of groundlessness into the fully modern project of self-grounding, conceptually articulated by Rousseau and then Kant, and practically articulated by the explosion of the French Revolution, which itself led to a variety both of modern subjectivistic accounts of autonomy and morality and of modern romantic practices having to do with the exploration of the self. These themselves are then answered, Hegel argues, by incorporating them within a conception of a fully modern *religious* community. To understand that part of the story, however, we must look at Hegel's arguments about the connection between modernity and self-determination a bit more closely.

Modernity

The *Phenomenology* argues that a form of life is constituted by the norms it takes to be authoritative for itself, and the authoritativeness of these norms has to do with their intelligibility and justifiability to the agents in the form of life for which they are norms. Hegel's controversial theses about his own time have to do with how the intelligibility of those norms comes to depend on how those norms can be reflectively justified to the kind of self-distancing agents of the modern world, and that the central authoritative norm for the modern world is what he calls freedom.

To understand why in general Hegel would make such an argument, it is necessary to sketch out, however briefly, his views on why modernity came to take the shape it did and why he would hold that the principle of modern life must be understood to be that of freedom. His arguments for these views occur in the sections of the *Phenomenology* having to do with the formation and education (the *Bildung*) of the early modern European community and the role the aristocratic ethic played in that formation.

Out of the debris of the collapse of the Roman Empire and the ensuing economic and social chaos, the warrior class that emerged came to understand itself as a collection of aristocrats, as people for whom what counted was the ideal of cultivation (*Bildung*), of forming oneself into a truly noble character for whom something like the ideal of glory or honor was authoritative.[13] The aristocratic ethic became established as a cult of violence and a code of chivalry, in which one gained honor by risking death for glory, with honor always being something that counted only in the eyes of other aristocrats.

The legitimacy of a whole set of institutions and practices, such as the restriction of political power to the nobility, rested on that medieval and early modern aristocratic ethic. The aristocrat was taken to be particularly well suited for political power because he pursued not his own interest but the impersonal interest of honor in the eyes of others; the commoner, particularly the crass merchant and bourgeois, was particularly unsuited for political power because he pursued his own self-interest and thus could not be trusted to put the common good ahead of his own. The truth of the matter, however, was something different. The noble took himself to be acting only out of concern with his honor, and he took the rewards (duchies, sinecures, various offices) of his 'selfless' activities to be part of his honor. In doing so, however, he had constituted himself as a fully detached self, a kind of point in social space, a self that was prior to all its chosen ends, and that was constituted entirely by recognition from others. Hegel argues that this conception of aristocratic honor as existing only in recognition from others logically led to the legitimation of something like absolute monarchy as the point or summit from which all recognition and thus all honor stemmed. Once established, however, absolute monarchy undermined the whole idea of aristocracy.

It is illustrative to see how the normative and the nonnormative explanations of this historical period relate. Louis XIV's childhood experience of the *Fronde* (a revolt against the king in which many nobles participated) helped to motivate him later to construct a separate palace at Versailles and to have the chief nobility reside at that palace. By keeping the nobility under his watch and by dominating the etiquette of court life, he destroyed the independent power of the nobility as a threat to himself and thereby succeeded in firmly establishing himself as the absolute monarch. The honor of the aristocrats at Versailles came to reside in seeking recognition from the Sun King himself, and the old Valois warrior-aristocrats became the Bourbon courtier-aristocrats; words, not swords, became the weapons of battle at the Versailles court. This aristocrat-courtier's whole reason for existence came to be recognition from the Sun King—the Versailles aristocrat-courtier's passionate dream was to be able to hold Louis's coat as he dressed—and his wealth increasingly came from his own shrewd investments, not as a reward for his service as a warrior. (Indeed, the provincial aristocracy that tried to live off its traditional rents found itself increasingly impoverished vis à vis the shrewd urban investors at the Versailles court.) With that development, the Bourbon aristocrat-courtier thus lost the distinction between himself and the bourgeois-commoner he was supposed both to despise and to be 'above.' The aristocrat-courtier thus came to be self-consciously distanced from all his activities, a 'pure self' prior to all ends, for whom all more general ends could therefore be understood only as expressions of vanity, as the disguised preferences of a person or group. With the collapse of the aristocratic ethic, it appeared that there was no natural (that is, discoverable) hierarchy of ends; there were only alienated selves, logical points of social practice, prior to all determinate ends. With this experience of groundlessness, the modern world begins.

The social causes and empirical details of the way in which Louis XIV managed to wrest power from the aristocracy and vest almost all of it in himself are not at issue for Hegel. What is at issue is how this particular historical sequence is to be made intelligible as a normative development. In Hegel's reconstruction, the transition from the Valois warrior-knights to the final Bourbon courtier-aristocrats and the inevitable self-undermining of that aristocratic ethos have a dialectical form: reason-giving based on authoritative grounds; skepticism generated out of those grounds themselves; attempts at reassurance (through, for example, the plays of Pierre Corneille, in which the distinctions between aristocrats and the bourgeoisie are made to seem natural and eternal, and in which the idea of self-identity as exhausted in the perceptions of others is made to seem inevitable and proper); the failure of those attempts; and the resulting experience of groundlessness itself. The contingent series of events culminating in the destruction of the power of the nobility at Versailles may thus be seen as the logical development of the self-undermining nature of the aristocratic ethic and its eventual breakdown *as a norm.*

Seen from a detached viewpoint, the modern experience of groundlessness could have gone in one of three directions. First, it could have sought a new set of grounds, an attempt that was made in one way by the emotionalist religious movements of the seventeenth, eighteenth, and nineteenth centuries and in another way by the European Enlightenment. Both these movements turned out to be self-undermining in similar ways in that each tried to give an account of how the groundless self, detached from all tradition and authority, could nonetheless discover a set of authoritative reasons for belief and action. The emotionalist religious movements held that the emotions immediately disclosed God to the hearts of the faithful and that, by attending to their own inner lives, individuals could discover within themselves something of universal validity; they failed in achieving this end because they set themselves up for the Enlightenment charges that detachment from authority and tradition itself calls into question such immediate, emotional experience as a ground of knowledge. The Enlightenment assumed on its part that a detached, unbiased, and sometimes ironic standpoint toward things—its character ideal of the rational *philosophe* replacing that of the earlier character ideal of the gentlemen—would produce an impersonally true account.[14] It found that this conception itself, however, culminated in a generally utilitarian account of evaluating claims to belief and action in terms of whether they satisfied human desires, and, having done that, the Enlightenment discovered that it had no real answer to Rousseau's charge that it had thereby no criterion for determining which desires were really our own and were therefore worthy of satisfaction. To put it another way, Rousseau showed the Enlightenment that its utilitarian self was just as detached and groundless as the aristocratic self and that it lacked the conceptual resources to reassure itself that this groundlessness was in fact legitimate and justified.

Hegel took the failures of emotionalist religion and so-called unbiased Enlightenment thought to resolve the modern problem of groundlessness to have set the stage for freedom's becoming the basic norm of modernity. In Hegel's eyes this was the crucial Rousseauian insight that led Kant to label Rousseau the "Newton of the moral world."[15] Rousseau saw that a socially determined groundless self could be free only insofar as it had desires determined by a social order which would be identical with what the agent would herself *will*. In this way, an agent's socially determined desires could be seen by her to issue from her own will and thus to be her own desires. This view marks the Rousseauian transformation of the early modern experience of groundlessness into the modern project of self-grounding. The story of how we get from this all-too-abbreviated description of the collapse of the aristocratic ethic to the project of self-grounding (not to mention how it gets taken up in both Kantianism and romanticism) is of course complex and requires more explanation than this space allows. The overall point, though, is that the reason that freedom came to play its determining role in modernity has to do with the fact that the experience of groundlessness in early modern Europe necessitated the move to the project of self-grounding. Freedom was not adopted as the norm because it was a 'good' that somehow won out over other competing 'goods,' but because it emerged as *the* principle necessary to make up for the historical insufficiencies of what had been authoritative for the early modern period.

The norm of freedom is authoritative, so Hegel argues, for all the appearances of modern life. It is authoritative, for example, for thought: nothing can be taken as given, everything must be capable of justification by rational, reflective thought. (Hegel's own *Logic* undertakes to show how reflective thought can be self-certifying.) The end of the *Phenomenology* itself, 'absolute knowing,' is a reflection on the accounts that the modern community must within its own free-standing social practices give of what is authoritative for it. Absolute knowing, the 'account of all the accounts' takes itself quite self-consciously to be moving completely *within* the terms that it sets for itself and to be self-legitimating, not as having its claims 'made true' by any set of transcendent metaphysical entities. Unlike the past accounts that the *Phenomenology* surveys, it does not take its authoritative norms as being anything external to the social practices of the modern community itself. Absolute knowing is the internal reflection on the modern community's taking authoritative norms to come only from within the structure of the practices it uses to legitimate and authenticate itself and to understand the legitimacy of those practices in terms of the ways they make up for the historical insufficiencies of the past. It is *absolute* in that it supposedly can deliver an account of what is authoritative for it, an account capable of reassuring itself against its own self-generated skeptical objections to itself—that is, in other words, self-certifying.

Self-Determination and Social Life

After writing the *Phenomenology,* Hegel went on to write what became known as the 'system,' which appeared in its outline form in the various editions of his *Encyclopedia of the Philosophical Sciences* and parts of which appeared in more detailed form in his two mature books, *The Science of Logic* (written immediately after the *Phenomenology*) and the later *Philosophy of Right.* It is, however, the *Phenomenology*'s culmination in 'absolute knowing' which provided Hegel with the project that informs his system.[16] The *Phenomenology* constructs what Hegel takes to be the fundamentals of the modern project, which has to do with freedom construed as self-determination. This project has its theoretical side in the attempt to construct a self-grounding system of thought (to be realized in Hegel's own system) and its practical side in its attempt to construct an institutional basis for a self-grounding form of life.

Thus a large part of the project of the system consists in a reflection on what it is for us, people for whom the principle of freedom is authoritative, to reflect on who we have come to be. Hegel's *Logic* is a reflection on free, self-grounding thought's systematic elaboration of the different accounts that it can give of its explanatory power.[17] Reflections on the way in which freedom is embodied in social life are carried out by Hegel in that section of the *Encyclopedia* labeled the philosophy of "Objective Spirit," which he expanded into his well-known book the *Philosophy of Right.* In that work, he begins with a conception of groundless agents thinking of themselves as self-determining, that is, as agents who cannot take as authoritative for themselves any set of reasons to accept any basic institution or practice unless those reasons somehow can be seen to be compatible with their understanding of themselves as free and independent. His procedure there, as in all parts of the system, is to show how certain conceptions are embedded in other conceptions, and how accounts using those conceptions require other, richer accounts in order for them to be able to resolve the kinds of contradictions and skeptical objections which they generate when taken alone. In particular, in "Objective Spirit," he wishes to show how the kinds of implicit standards embedded in the social practices surrounding a set of recognizable institutional setups can be explicated and made explicit in such a way that they can be comprehended as a set of sustainable norms of action which are also compatible with being understood as realizations of the modern norm of freedom.

Hegel's conception of freedom is decisively nonmetaphysical. Whether one is free is not for him a question of whether one could do otherwise, or of whether one's metaphysically free will is capable of affecting appearance, or of whether one is coerced. Instead, Hegel explicates freedom in terms of the kinds of reasons an agent uses in thinking and acting and whether he can be said to identify himself with the actions and beliefs those reasons require—in his words, with whether he can be at home (*bei sich*) with himself in acting on beliefs based on those reasons. He derives his conception of freedom from his understanding of what he took freedom to mean within the context of ancient Greek life (or at least within the context of the nineteenth century's highly idealized version of Greek life). The ancient idealized Greek form of *Sittlichkeit*—of a communal understanding that certain basic practices count as valid simply because they are the way things are done—gave the Greeks a social world in which each citizen could be reflectively at home. Unambiguously defined social roles called for very specific actions, such that in acting on the basis of his social roles, the Greek citizen was therefore always clear about what he was doing. Moreover, because he knew and could cite the socially sanctioned reasons for the action, he also knew *why* he was acting. Because he found his self-identity fully constituted by the social roles he played, he also fully identified himself with those actions.

Hegel develops his conception of freedom on the basis of this understanding of Greek life. For Hegel, to be free, one has to know what one is doing, why one is doing it, and one must identify appropriately with what one does.[18] The issue as to whether one is free in one's actions is thus not an issue about what causes one to act; it is an issue of one's identification with one's actions, with whether one is at home in them or is instead alienated from them.

The question of whether one is free in one's actions is thus independent of all issues concerning the causal history of one's choices or behavior.

It is Hegel's thesis in his later system that the modern world has for various contingent reasons produced a set of social institutions that enable the principle of freedom to be fully realized; that is, it has produced a set of institutions whose social roles allow modern agents to be at home with themselves and therefore to fulfill the conditions necessary to count as free agents. These modern institutions themselves are made intelligible to modern agents by their being shown to be the ways in which the conflicts between the dominant accounts that modern agents give of themselves are to be resolved. These dominant accounts have to do with the modern insistence on each person's possession of certain very general rights (on what Hegel calls "Abstract Right") and with the modern practice of the reflective morality of conscience (what Hegel somewhat misleading just calls "Morality"). Given our history, we *must* think of ourselves as agents having certain objectively established rights. We have developed a form of self-understanding in which we think of ourselves as independent rights-bearers, a form which is consistent with others' thinking of themselves as independent rights-bearers and with our equally recognizing one another as such independent rights-bearers. These rights must count for us as objectively established rights (and are sometimes misleadingly called natural rights).

What gives the legitimacy to this form of self-conception is, of course, the basic norm of freedom itself, and that norm also requires (for both systemic and historical reasons) that we also think of ourselves as subjects, as moral agents, as not merely doing the right thing (as acting in accordance with morality) but as doing it on the basis of our recognizing and acknowledging it as the right thing—that is, that each can understand her actions be her own actions. Thus, the objectivity and impersonality we assign to these abstract rights clash with the subjectivity of the claims to autonomy we necessarily make as modern agents. The result is that modern life makes us, in Hegel's nice metaphor, into "amphibious animals" living in "two worlds which contradict one another."[19] Or, as we might put it, modern life generates conflicting intuitions about what is authoritative for ourselves.

Hegel holds that the modern social institutions of family, civil society, and the state serve to mediate and to overcome this contradiction between objective rights and subjective morality and autonomy. They establish a modern form of *Sittlichkeit,* a communal sense of a set of social practices which embody a shared understanding that this is the way things are done with which individuals nonetheless can identify; and they thus allow freedom to be fully realized within the self-reflective, self-distancing practices of the modern world. These institutions serve the logical function within the 'system' of overcoming the conflicts of modern life, and in social life they also serve the purposes of *Bildung* (that is, they serve to educate, and to cultivate character). To put it in looser, non-Hegelian terms: the problem for modern agents is that they are supposed to be self-determining, to write their own scripts, but 'abstract right' and 'morality' give them no determinate guidelines for which scripts to write. The three institutionalized practices of modern *Sittlichkeit*—family, civil society, state—give these agents general scripts that provide them with roles to play, and with which they can identify, because these scripts embody patterns of aims with which agents in the modern world for historical and systemic reasons necessarily identify and which structure both their wills and their emotional lives.

Hegel does not see these institutionalized practices of ethical life as simply supplying different types of goods, each of which must then be balanced off against the others. If that were what he was arguing, then it would be enough simply to distinguish the roles analytically from one another or just give an overall description of the various goods involved in them (as Michael Walzer does in *Spheres of Justice).*[20] Instead, each of the three forms of modern *Sittlichkeit* is supposed to make up for the insufficiencies in the way the others function as realizations of 'freedom as self-determination.' Moreover, so Hegel also argues, these roles are not optional in the sense that if one were to opt out of family life, civil society, or citizenship, one could be said only to be worse off, that is, to have failed to realize some particular good. Hegel's whole point is that without playing these modern roles one cannot be said to be free, and freedom is a nonoptional determination of modern life.

The modern family realizes freedom, so Hegel argues, by virtue of its being structured around companionate marriage with the related goods of privacy, intimacy, and nurturing and with the ideal of rearing the children to attain independence on their own.[21] Unlike families in antiquity, the modern family based on companionate marriage is started by an act of free choice, even though the bonds that supposedly hold such families together are those of affection and shared self-identity. This is not a sociological claim (it is all too evident that many modern families are no such thing) but a claim about how the family and its associated roles are best understood as embodying the modern norm of freedom, independently of whether particular people actually live up to these expectations. This form of self-understanding gives us certain ends of actions that appear as 'natural facts' to modern individuals: the ideal of love in marriage, the way in which children are educated to become independent people, and so on.[22] It also gives a more determinate content to the idea of self-determination. We decide whom to marry, we decide whether to stay in the marriage, and yet we also develop natural ties of affection in such families. In acting as a family member, in having one's self-identity bound up with it, one conceives of oneself as self-directing in a way not possible for members of premodern families. The family thus realizes freedom in that it provides an institutional arrangement within which agents are provided with ends with which they can identify and with a clear set of practices which enables them to know both what they are doing and why they are doing it.

But our self-understanding as members of modern families cannot provide us with a fully rational set of ends, because taken alone its ends would conflict with many of the more particular ends that modern life also seems to require. The intimate emotional ties of the modern family can be smothering as well as nurturing, and the emotional strains put on the family can be high. To carve out one's own self-identity, to be truly self-directing, one needs to step out of family life. Therefore, the practices of modern companionate marriage require there to be a complementary set of practices having to do with a conception of civil society as being composed of markets and the mediating institutions of private associations. Unlike the family, civil society is held together by bonds of both rational and mutual self-interest among individuals, and the mediating organizations of people organized around common interests (for example, professional associations) which give the individual a kind of *recognized* place in the social space of the community and thus endow his or her life with a certain substantiality.

Civil society is a social unity based on the idea of cooperation for mutual benefit (and, to use John Rawls's language, also cooperation on a basis of mutual respect). The problem with civil society is that the cooperation which structures it is contingent on a variety of factors. For example, it is contingent on such things as people's possessing moral motives of general beneficence; or of their putting other families' interests or other associations' interests on the same level as their own families' and associations'; or of there actually being perceptible benefits for both parties in transactions. In the highly competitive world of capitalist markets, those otherwise-nice ideals have a tendency to drop out of the picture. In that rough-and-tumble world, moreover, those with more wealth can acquire more power and can ally against those with less power; those who because of contingent factors accumulate both wealth and power can then begin to dictate to others what they can do with their lives, a result that creates at the heart of these societies a conflict between the claims of freedom and having one's life directed by others. Moreover, given the motives of benefiting oneself which civil society both embodies and encourages, such developments are likely. People who understand themselves as independent will not long accept that kind of position of servitude.

This problem with civil society furnishes part of the rationale for the introduction of the modern, constitutionalist bureaucratic state based on rule of law (which, interestingly, Hegel also thinks should be monarchical).[23] Hegel's conception of the state—what could be better called political community—is meant to supply something like a common point of view, which is lacking in civil society, and this is, as Hegel puts it a requirement of 'spirit' for the realization of freedom.[24] The constitution of such a modern state both commands and defines a universal way of life, namely, the social role of citizenship. As citizens we each play a universalistic role, abstracted from the particularities of race, sex, and class. The idea of the universal way of life of citizenship takes up and refines the practices based on 'abstract right' and 'morality.' The *equality* of legal *persons* as rights-bearers, which leads to the *inequalities* of wealth within civil society, becomes reintroduced as an *equality of citizens*; legal equality, that is, becomes refined into political equality. Moreover, because it is universal, it mirrors in the political arena the universalistic claims of morality and gives institutional support to them. In a constitutional political order, we thus fully become modern *individuals* and achieve the kind of institutionally secured mutual recognition that is necessary for having a coherent self-consciousness.

What would be deficient about an arrangement having all the trappings of modern social life but lacking this form of modern political community would lie in its accounts that it gives itself about what is authoritative for itself and therefore in the way it can understand its social and political practices to make sense. Or, again, in looser terms, it would be deficient in the stories that it tells itself about why this and not that is necessary for itself. The lack of an appropriately modern state to accompany the other institutions of modernity would create a failure therefore of self-consciousness, a lack of a set of practices which could be explicated into a coherent account of ourselves and of what we take as authoritative for ourselves. It would be a form of life which could therefore not be at home with itself, and, so Hegel argues, it would eventually come to lose faith in itself and to despair of what it is doing—it would become a form of what Hegel in the *Phenomenology* calls the "unhappy consciousness"—because it could not reassure itself that its practices make sense and are thereby rational. The modern state (or political community) is thus the condition for a rational and therefore reconciled form of modern life—specifically, a rational shape for a form of life which tries to account for itself in terms of freedom. Or, to put it another way, modern political community as constitutional politics is the necessary condition under which a reflective form of life can come to a full self-consciousness about itself and reconcile itself with itself. (Hegel also has some controversial views on how this modern political community presupposes a certain religious view of the world; those views of life are, unfortunately, too complex to be given much consideration here.)[25]

The Final Stage of History?

This conception of the internal coherence of bourgeois constitutional life led Hegel to one of his most controversial and least understood theses, that having to do with the final stage of history (sometimes called the end of history).[26] It is least understood because more than any other part of Hegel's system, it is supposed to have been dominated by the metaphysical view that God acts in history, a view we late moderns seem to find unacceptable.

To understand Hegel's thesis, we must keep in mind, first, that in the lectures that were posthumously published as the *Philosophy of History,* he was concerned only with world history, not with regional history (not with the histories, for example, of Germany, Peru, or Texas). Second, he was concerned in those lectures only with political history and with the self-understandings essential to cooperative political practice; thus, he focuses there exclusively on the development of the state, not with all forms of social life. Third, Hegel clearly and explicitly argues that the world history of political life is to be taken as a story of spirit—the reflective social practice of the human community—coming to an understanding of political life as embodying institutions organized around the expression and development of freedom, or self-determination. In this famous shorthand of the progress of world history, he says, "The East knew and to the present day knows only that one is free; the Greek and Roman world, that some are free; the Germanic world knows that all are free."[27] That is, the development of the world history is a story of the progressive realization of the social conditions for the full equality of freedom. Finally, Hegel seems to claim that this progression from inequality to full equality of freedom is necessary, part of an inner teleology of history.

We should note that the only seemingly metaphysical claim in all this discussion involves the claim that this progression is teleological and necessary. Hegel is arguing that there is an inner and inherent teleology to the human community's understanding of itself as involved in cooperative social life. However, we have already seen this conception of teleology at work in the *Phenomenology.* It is the kind of teleology inherent in the moves from skepticism to attempts at reassurance, and from the ways in which the insufficiencies of those accounts require a different account that understands itself as required by virtue of the insufficiencies of what preceded it. The general theme of Hegel's narrative of political history—the development of freedom—does not therefore express any metaphysical assumptions about God's directing history; rather it expresses the kind of claim made earlier in the *Phenomenology* that accounts of knowledge are best understood in terms of this kind of historical dialectic in which what a form of life takes as required for itself is legitimated by being understood as being itself required by the failures and insufficiencies of the previous form of life. The teleology of history is the movement from self-undermining conceptions of what is authoritative for human beings to a fully rational form of self-understanding which is capable of resolving its own skepticism about itself. No stage is *fated* to arise after a previous stage; but a new stage is required if the insufficiencies of the previous stage are to be resolved. Modernity turns out to be that stage of history in which the accounts of what is authoritative are capable of satisfactorily answering the kinds of skeptical objections which are generated against them. It is thus not implausible to interpret Hegel as taking this to be the end of that particular story, to have as a result a sustainable self-understanding of who we are and what we are about.

I do not mean here to be defending all of what Hegel says about history. For example, he seems simply to assume that only one community at a time can play the role of the avant garde in constructing the accounts of what can be authoritative for us. Moreover, like all good nineteenth-century European men, he has only the scantiest appreciation for the roles that women and non-Western cultures have played in this development. Surprisingly, he often shows little understanding of the ways in which the enslaved and colonized have changed the self-understandings of those who enslaved and colonized them (which is all the more surprising in that the master/slave dialectic in the *Phenomenology of Spirit* may be taken as a powerful argument that they do).

Hegel's claim about the final stage of history is thus not some metaphysical, quasi-eschatological thesis. It does seem nonetheless to be the rather strikingly bold thesis that, as far as the conceptualization of freedom is concerned, we have reached a point at which there is nothing in principle left to be worked out. Even so, Hegel clearly thought that this thesis about the 'final stage of history' does not rule out three things. First, it does not rule out the idea that world history may now proceed on a different trajectory, even though he denies that we can predict what that trajectory might be.[28] Second, it does not claim that there will be no new and important events. Europe will continue to develop, as will India and Latin America. Whatever occurs at the regional level, however, cannot alter our conception of what the story of the world has been about, namely, the development of our basic understanding of what is essential for the embodiment of freedom in cooperative social life. Third, it does not imply that all important political questions have been answered. How many houses of parliament? How widely should free speech extend? How much power should the civil servants have? None of these questions is taken to be answered at the so-called end of history; if anything, it is only the question of the framework in which the questions arise which has been taken to be answered decisively. Those questions all presupposed that whatever the answer turns out to be, it must be couched very roughly in terms of modern families, markets, and constitutional rule of law.

The real thesis about the so-called end of history is thus a thesis about the rational completeness of the modern constitutional, market-oriented state as providing a rational form of self-understanding. With that, Hegel's story about political and social life ends. Or does it?

The Hegelian Fallout

It is obvious that the Hegelian project has not won widespread contemporary acceptance. In fact, as we all know, Hegel has for the most part simply lapsed into obscurity, a character to be trotted out in surveys of the nineteenth century. Faithful Hegelians would therefore have to ask themselves what internal reasons there could be for such a breakdown of the Hegelian project. One clear historical reason is that the project was not understood by almost any of Hegel's pupils. Hegel was understood by many of them as fundamentally a new metaphysical thinker who had integrated God, nature, and industry and thereby rescued metaphysics from the destructive attacks on it by Kant's critical philosophy. To the later nineteenth century this metaphysical Hegel appeared as a means of reconciling positions like Darwinism and traditional Christianity. Taken in this way, however, Hegel was, on good Hegelian grounds, bound to lapse into obscurity, because if the motivations that had driven traditional metaphysics had lost their authoritativeness for us, a latter-day metaphysical Hegel was hardly going to be able to revive them. Appearing as a premodern figure rather than as the self-conscious theorist of modernity which he is, Hegel would be doomed to obscurity on grounds that should be readily apparent to readers of the *Phenomenology of Spirit*.

This metaphysical misreading is a misunderstanding of the Hegelian project, although an easy one to make. But there are other criticisms that can be leveled even at the rather nonmetaphysical Hegelianism outlined here. First of all, one might hold that finding a self-legitimating point of view within the kind of historically situated theory of knowledge which Hegel propounds is not an achievable task, and that Hegel should stand convicted of Sartre's accusation against him of epistemological optimism. Perhaps this charge can be sustained, but doing so would require us to give a different account of knowledge which would sidestep the need for this kind of self-reflexive, historicist theory—perhaps either a foundationalist account such as the one the logical empiricists of the early twentieth century tried to give, some 'therapeutic' account such as the later Wittgenstein recommended, or some self-correcting fallibilist account of knowledge—but it is certainly not self-evident that such accounts answer the kinds of problems of historicism and relativism on which Hegelian theory explicitly focuses. If anything, they need to be able to articulate and defend a kind of historical narrative in which they situate themselves and in which their form of accounting for things has a privileged place.

Another way of leveling the charge of epistemological optimism against Hegel came from those of his students who held that the complete type of account which Hegel apparently thought was given in modernity could not be achieved in contemporary bourgeois constitutionalism but only in some other form of social life. The young Marx tried something like this line of thought, arguing that Hegel too optimistically postulates a continuity between our identities as members of market society and as universalized political citizens. If that is the case, the story of history as the rise of freedom is perhaps not yet over, and we are still developing a form of cooperative social and political life which is sustainable by agents engaged in fully mutual recognition. Other young Hegelians tried this strategy—for example, Lorenz von Stein, who claimed that we need a theory of social democracy in addition to bourgeois constitutionalism.[29]

Another way of taking the Hegelian project is to see it as not having irretrievably broken down at all. One might accept the project of the *Phenomenology* and reject on the basis of the *Phenomenology*'s own dialectic the 'system's' claims to being complete; the form of modern life which we have reached, so one might argue, can itself only be provisional and is already developing its self-undermining skeptical claims within itself. That is, it could be that internal to the structure of bourgeois constitutionalism are self-understandings that lead to a breakdown of that form of life for the same kinds of reasons that Hegel understood caused earlier forms of life to break down. Perhaps capitalist society with its enforced mobility and its cycles of economic creativity and destruction may not be able to sustain the kind of mutual recognition which gives people a firm sense of self-identity, forcing them instead to seek their self-identity in illusory imaginative ways, such as in status symbols, conformism, hedonistic consumerism, and so on. The so-called postmodern ironic attitude may be just a symptom of this loss of mutual recognition and sustainable self-identity, and what is celebrated as postmodernism may actually be only the internal disintegration described by Hegelianism. This would be a Hegelian development, because it would show that a new account necessarily develops out of the contradictions and incoherences of a former set of accounts of what is authoritative. It might also have the interesting consequence of showing orthodox (that is, *Philosophy of Right*) Hegelianism to fail on its own terms, not on terms imported from outside it.

Thus one might hold that the whole project has never broken down except in its orthodox form. Perhaps in a revised version of the *Phenomenology*'s program, we would have to understand the system as provisional, to take Hegel's own reconstruction as holding at best for the European life in his day, and we would have to assume that what the system takes as authoritative for itself is bound to develop its own negative and to require some other type of account which we ourselves perhaps cannot foresee.[30]

Such a full-fledged reconstruction cannot, alas, be undertaken in this essay. Nevertheless, I hope I have shown that perhaps things are not so bad for Hegelianism as they seem, even if Hegelianism is in temporary eclipse. Hegel's concerns with the 'absolute' and with the structure of our collective and personal self-identities are too important to go away. And even if Hegel does not give us all the answers, I have argued that he points us in the right direction in which to look for them.

Part II

RETROSPECTIVE: ON THE HISTORY OF THE IDEA OF HISTORY

3 Machiavelli and the Idea of Progress

HARVEY C. MANSFIELD

Machiavelli is not often given credit for the revolutionary change he initiated and in time accomplished. He began a project—later picked up and developed by other modern philosophers—for a permanent, irreversible improvement in human affairs—establishing a new political regime. The project is often called modernity, though today modernity is understood no longer as a project but rather as a historical force—one that may have come to an end. To Machiavelli's new political science was added a new natural science, together with a protective blanket known as "epistemology," which science still cannot quite do without. How Machiavelli was responsible for modernity, I shall outline as best I can.

Perhaps one reason that Machiavelli is not often given credit as founder of modernity is that he does not claim it. He does not put himself at the head of a party of progress claiming to speak for all mankind. So far as there exist Machiavellians, they have always been known as enemies of mankind. And if one wishes to take a more generous view of Old Nick, one still finds his humanity to be bounded, envenomed, and contradictory. In the last chapter of *The Prince* he surely calls for progress in Italy, but by an exhortation to seize Italy and free her from the "barbarians"—who must be the civilized monarchies of France and Spain. Even Machiavelli's patriotism is divided between Italy and Florence, whose interests he well knew were not identical. He says that "by experience one sees that only princes and armed republics make very great progress" (*grandissimi progressi, The Prince,* 12), but the statement is made in the context of rejecting the use of mercenary arms and does not seem to promise more freedom for everybody. How can one promote the happiness of all unless mankind are at peace?

Yet at the beginning of the *Discourses on Livy* Machiavelli states that he is driven by a "natural desire," as if it were not merely his choice, to "work, without any respect, for those things I believe will bring common benefit to each." Those things are "new modes and orders," political arrangements in the widest sense of everything pertaining to rule. Here Machiavelli claims to "work" (*operare*), if not speak, on behalf of humanity, and humanity is described as what is common to every individualized "each." The promised benefit does not appear to be a collective project, such as modern science, to which all might variously contribute. Such a project might actualize humanity as a progressive force regardless of its political divisions. But Machiavelli works through those divisions, the princes and armed republics. Each individual, it is true, has a common interest with all other individuals in being well governed, but it is obviously not an interest held *in* common because governments are divided against one another. How will Machiavelli make "each" the beneficiary of political innovation?—innovation that not only maintains political divisions but also enlivens them with new modes and orders of war?

Another, insufficiently noticed, subdivision of humanity besides the strictly political ones can be found in Machiavelli: the sect. The sect, sometimes identified with religion (*Discourses on Livy* II 5), is a more comprehensive phenomenon than the government. It includes language, customs, and morality; it is the whole climate of opinion surrounding and inspiring government. It can be understood as government in a wide sense, as Machiavelli shows by speaking of the "Christian republic" that comprises Christian states (*Discourses* I 12). But of course the Christian republic too is divided, and Machiavelli does not hesitate in his exhortatory mood to call some of its states barbarians, as we have seen. Nonetheless, it is by attending to the phenomenon of sect that we may approach Machiavelli's thought on progress.

Machiavelli faced two main obstacles to the idea of progress, and both are involved with sect. They are the notion of the cycle, arising from classical political philosophy, and Christianity. The notion of the cycle says that all human things change by turning in a circle, of which progress is merely one phase, to be followed by decay. Christianity says that human events began from a perfect beginning, followed by the Fall and the Redemption, and look forward to the Second Coming. Here too progress is only part of the story, and it is not achieved by man unaided. The modern idea of progress had to overcome the classical cycle and Christian redemption in order to establish itself. A careful study of Machiavelli on these two points would help us understand progress better than we can through our contemporary perspective, for it would make us aware of possible alternatives. Then we could see how the idea of progress looks as a choice, before the alternatives have receded from view. Our perspective is posthistorical; it is disillusionment with the idea of progress which takes for granted the establishment of that idea against its rivals. Our objection is to the situation in which history has left (or thrown) us, not to history itself. But Machiavelli had to defeat his two main rivals, and he did not yet speak of history in any but the classical sense of "inquiry."

The cycle and Christianity come together in Machiavelli's discussion of the cycle of sects (*Discourses* II 5; cf. *Florentine Histories* V I). There Machiavelli considers the causes of the oblivion of sects. Sects change; they even have life spans limited to between 1,666 and three thousand years. So the world is older than any sect, including the "Christian sect." Those who survey the changes of sects, the philosophers, have a longer and broader view than those founders who are concerned merely with "the ordering of a new sect." Although the causes of change are three—men, heaven, and nature—Machiavelli suggests the possibility that a single man surviving a near-universal natural or heaven-sent disaster might be able to control the "human generation" that remains. Such a man, blessed as it were with the opportunity Noah had, could remake the past *a suo modo* and so project his new enterprise (*impresa*) into the future. He could actualize the power (*potenza*) of humanity, not merely its possible intellect in the Averroistic sense that Dante had spoken of. The Christian sect, unlike other less universal and less competent religions, has shown men how to unify mankind and capture the world for their own benefit.

That partial and compressed interpretation of a single Machiavellian discourse hurries his argument, but since there is no room for patient interpretation, let it suffice to note the strategy. Machiavelli brings together his two enemies and uses the one against the other. On the one hand, the Christian sect is treated like any other as within a natural cycle according to the classical conception. On the other, the superiority of the Christian sect, which lies not in its truth or divinity but in its political acumen, is used to suggest how men might escape from the cycle and create a universal sect that would lead mankind to progress. To explain Machiavelli's strategy, I shall now discuss the cycle and Christianity in turn.

Machiavelli's consideration of the cycle depends on his borrowing from Polybius (*Discourses* I 2), but it is easier and still faithful to his intent to look to Aristotle for the classical notion of the cycle. Aristotle understands the cycle as one of three kinds of revolution, all of which are endemic to the human situation. Machiavelli means to replace them with one revolution, *the* modern revolution, a revolution that puts an end to revolution, at least in the grandest sense.

For Aristotle, the first meaning of revolution is *stasis,* or uprising, a public disturbance visible to all. The second meaning is a change of regime, a new beginning or a new principle of rule. *Arché* means both rule and beginning. It is simultaneously a beginning in accordance with a principle and ruling in accordance with a beginning. Such a beginning is never *de novo,* as from a state of nature in which there was no previous regime. For Aristotle, man is a political animal by nature. So every new regime consists in the change of an old regime. Every regime moves in a certain direction in accordance with its principle, the principle that is reflected in its form, or structure, of government. For example, democracy moves toward the end reflected in its democratic form; that end is to live democratically. The rulers of the regime have a certain awareness of their direction toward an end, which they declare or claim to be just. Being partisan creatures, they do not have a full awareness of the end, but they have a certain awareness; and with that certain awareness, they take responsibility for the character of the regime. They blame others, their enemies foreign and domestic, and they praise themselves, always insisting on a contrast between the two. Every regime, therefore, has a self-definition that is partisan.

A *stasis*, however, can occur without a change of regime. A coup d'état in a servile banana republic would be an example: a public change that does not alter the nature of the regime. Or, one could have a change of regime over decades or centuries without a stasis—or gradual change that steals over a government without its consent or even recognition, as from new ideas or new technology not initiated by the government, or initiated without a comprehension of the consequences. But the most dramatic event is an uprising together with a change of regime, as in the French Revolution.

A third meaning of revolution is revolution in the literal sense of cycle (*kuklos*). In that meaning we see that regimes have an end that they do not foresee or desire: their death. They may degenerate from internal causes, or may be destroyed by a natural catastrophe external to them, a flood or an earthquake. This third meaning is connected to the partial or partisan nature of the regime. Because every regime is partisan, no regime does full justice to the facts. But the facts, because they are facts, will eventually catch up with the regime. Because every regime is partial, no regime is permanent. No regime can last in perpetuity because none rules in accordance with truth and nature. The statement that man is by nature a political animal does not mean that man knows what he is doing in politics.

So the likely course of such revolutions is a cycle—a return to the beginning so that we can make the same mistakes all over again. Two moral lessons may be drawn from the cyclical view of revolution. First, human beings are limited. We are freed by nature to set a certain direction for ourselves, but that direction, being partisan, is limited in duration. Yet, second, human beings are thereby freed to be moral. As no regime is permanent, the mediocre goal of survival or stability is not imposed on us. Not only an individual life but also our common way of life will come to an end. And even fame has a term when oblivion overtakes history. So a regime can try to be virtuous for the sake of virtue. Why not? Neither individual nor regime is going to last forever.

What is the role of the philosopher, that is, the political philosopher, in this picture? It is to improve his own regime and others if he can. Such a task could possibly lead to revolution or urging a revolution if the philosopher lives in a bad regime or sees bad regimes around him. But he would also point out the limits of action. Good regimes tend to be followed by less good or even bad regimes, bad or less good regimes by good ones. Isocrates once remarked that a reasonable man should wonder whether it is better to be born in good times that will worsen or in bad times that will improve. Aristotle says that the most virtuous are least likely to rebel (*Politics* 1301a38–40). The most virtuous for him would be philosophers. Philosophers are few. Those who are very few will always need allies to make a revolution, and those allies being less virtuous, they will always be dubious and untrustworthy. If philosophers make a revolution in their company, the result may be no better than the regime they rebelled against.

With modern revolutionaries, however, we find on the contrary that the most virtuous are thought most likely to revolt. The culmination of the most dramatic modern revolution was called the reign of virtue by Robespierre (not a philosopher but the disciple of Rousseau). From his new modes and orders, Machiavelli expected a revival of "ancient virtue." Modern revolutions are not shunned but led by philosophers. A modern revolution in thought precedes the great modern revolutions in deed. So said Tocqueville in his book on the ancien régime, the prerevolutionary regime in France. The French Revolution was prepared by the destructive work of philosophers throughout the eighteenth century under the protection and sometimes the encouragement of the ancien régime. Edmund Burke declared that the French Revolution was "the first, complete revolution." It was a revolution in sentiments, manners, and moral opinions which reached "even to the constitution of the human mind." In speaking of a revolution in the constitution of the human mind Burke probably was referring to the unprecedented atheism of the French Revolution. This was the first revolution to be founded on the idea that there is no power in the human mind superior to human reason or human will. But that principle one can find already in the philosophy of Descartes as the principle of doubt, and in Locke as the denial of innate ideas. Machiavelli's slogan "one's own arms" has the same meaning.

Thus the French Revolution brings the modern philosophical revolution into view. It tears away the veil covering the cowardly hesitations of philosophers who did not openly proclaim their atheism. Modern revolutions were inspired by political philosophers seeking a permanent improvement in human affairs. They envisaged a permanent regime that would be the best regime actualized by The Revolution, which would be a combination of *stasis* and change of regime. The change of regime might begin before the *stasis,* as with the intellectual changes in eighteenth-century France. Intellectual change produced social and cultural changes by which, for example, the church became a less reactionary force. And then the *stasis* brought the latent principle into broad daylight by a change of regime.

But even The Revolution, begun by modern philosophers and actualized in modern governments, is not accomplished all at once. Rather than being unchanging like the regime of ancient Egypt, the new regime has a principle of change, a direction that cannot change. Its permanency is not in being changeless but in being irreversible. That is what is meant by progress. In the notion of progress, the cycle or circle that Aristotle spoke of is flattened out to a linear motion that has one direction and does not return to the beginning. The linear progress may indeed proceed by dialectical stages, as with Hegel and Marx, rather than by simple accumulation of improvements. But that complication does not affect the single essential direction of human history.

The consequence of replacing Aristotle's revolutionary cycle with the modern revolution of progress is to overcome the limits to the possible achievements of human politics. First, those limits arising from the supposed fixity of human nature can be surpassed. Men are much more malleable than Aristotle and his friends believed. And second, one can institute an impartial regime not essentially subject to being overthrown, as the regime was in Aristotle's understanding. The problem in Aristotle's regime arose from the fact that he accepted the inevitability of human partiality in politics. His remedy for partiality was the mixed regime. But the remedy was not a cure, and the mixed regime was, for the most part, an aspiration based on arguments requiring an ability to persuade along with people who were persuadable. It was, therefore, very unlikely, if not utopian.

What is the general character of the modern impartial regime? For Aristotle, the typical partisan conflict is between the many and the few, the people and the nobles. To replace that conflict, the general formula for the modern impartial regime is to remove one of the two parties, the people as a political actor. Then let the elite compete before the people for its favor. The idea begins with Machiavelli, who makes a distinction between peoples and princes, a distinction of human natures (or humors, *umori*) which can be found in all regimes, whether popular or oligarchical (*The Prince* 9; *Discourses* I 4–6). Today we say that the people elects the government. The people, thereby, becomes the judge of all government. It does not form a government itself; the people does not rule. Today's liberal democracy is, of course, very different from Machiavelli's kinky preferences for martial republics and Borgia-like principalities. But there is a certain generic resemblance in the impartiality of outlook and new attitude toward the people. Both we and Machiavelli are more favorable to popular judgment than were the ancients, and less favorable to popular rule. The impartial regime is actualized by lowering the moral standard: if the people are not competent to rule, at least they can judge the competence of those who are. Virtue comes to mean something closer to stability, or survival, because that is what the people can understand. Indeed, outstanding virtue is dangerous. Virtue can lead to revolution because it turns people against consensus and compromise. But a certain minimum or mediocre virtue is guaranteed by the impartial regime—or is required by it. Such, especially, is the virtue of respecting others' rights.

The revolution establishing the new regime is, to repeat, The Revolution, because it is irreversible. Machiavelli's role in it is commonly underestimated, not to say overlooked, not only because he does not head a party of humanity but also because he admires the ancients and appeals, as I said, to "ancient virtue." His treatment of the cycle in *Discourses* I 2 is often misinterpreted as favorable, hence hostile to the idea of progress; and his proposal in *Discourses* III 1 for reviving republics, kingdoms, and sects by returning them back "toward the beginnings" (*verso i principii*) is also thought to be reactionary rather than progressive. A quick look at these two chapters will help to overcome such misunderstandings.

Machiavelli begins *Discourses* I 2 by distinguishing two kinds of republics according to their beginnings. One kind receives its laws from "one alone" and "at a stroke," for example Sparta from Lycurgus; the other gets its laws by chance, at many times, and through accidents, as did Rome. At first it seems that the first kind is better, but Machiavelli gradually makes us see that the second kind can become perfect, even if it does not begin so, by the occurrence of accidents. These two kinds of republics suggest the difficulty Machiavelli himself faces in legislating his new modes and orders; he casually mentions here the "accident" that displaced him from office as secretary to the Florentine republic. Machiavelli must legislate with his books alone and at a stroke, yet he must do so with a view to the accidents that will displace him and his influence. He who begins the progressive revolution must take thought for the followers who will both succeed and supersede him.

Machiavelli then confronts Rome's accidental perfection with the classical cycle. He follows the argument in Polybius' text so closely that the differences become obvious to anyone making the comparison (though many commentators do not bother). He seems to have chosen Polybius to represent classical political science because Livy does not discuss the cycle, and Plato and Aristotle do not discuss Rome, Machiavelli's exemplar of accidental perfection. Machiavelli begins by saying "in the beginning of the world": a Christian notion of unique creation obviously contradictory to the notion of a cycle in human affairs, yet un-Christian in denying a perfect beginning. Again we see Machiavelli using the ancients and Christianity against each other. Among many revealing differences of detail between his account and that of Polybius, the main one is that what Polybius attributes to nature Machiavelli attributes to chance. Not being political animals by nature, men are free both to behave like beasts in accordance with their origins and to advance toward a perfect republic not subject to the vicissitudes of a natural cycle.

At the end of the chapter Machiavelli denies the endogenous premise of the cycle of regimes that regimes fail because of their own faults; he simply remarks that any republic revolving in the cycle would fall subject to a better-ordered neighbor. Contrary to the assumption of the ancients, foreign policy is more vital than domestic policy. Rome was the regime whose domestic order—or disorder between the Senate and the people—was determined by its readiness to seek empire through conquest. Like Polybius, Machiavelli mixes together two distinct cycles, the cycle of regimes and the cycle of civilizations. The former presumes, as I said, that regimes fail because of their own faults; the latter, that they are destroyed from without by natural catastrophes. But while Polybius mixes them to show that nature is a force greater than Rome, and human partisanship generally, Machiavelli does so to suggest an expansion of human power. A cure for human partisanship can be found, not the classical palliative that mixes virtues in a mixed regime and holds nature in reserve so that men can start again after they fail, but a new mix of partisan humors loosed from restraint. Machiavelli's new regime, not subject to the "pestiferous" faults of the six classical governments, can save civilization without the necessity for outside intervention. He does not refer again in the *Discourses* to the cycle (he does in *Florentine Histories* V 1, also leaving a way out); it has been replaced by his "perfect republic." Instead of using the cycle to signify the circular inevitability of good and bad in politics and the incapacity of human intention, Machiavelli appropriates the classical cycle to introduce the very contraries of those limitations.

Nor is his call, in *Discourses* III 1, to return toward (not to) the beginning, if one means a sect or republic to live a long time, a move against progress. In his statement, returning toward the beginning is neither conservative nor cyclical. Human institutions must have had some goodness in them, he says, to gain their first reputation; but the goodness becomes corrupt in time. Returning toward the beginning, then, means returning to the condition of being new and exciting, and it is done not by resuming the original constitution but by curing the corruptions that come with growth. The aim is not to curb growth, but to further growth. As compared to *Discourses* II 5, where Machiavelli speaks of "purges" and thus implies that early men were healthy, he now offers as a cure changes (*alterazioni*) for the better which both return toward the beginning and maintain one's acquisitions. "Mixed bodies," he says, do not last if they are not renewed. Perhaps the mixture in mixed bodies is of natural limitation and human improvement. Then Machiavelli's idea of progress is toward the overcoming of natural limitation, but in such a way as never to leave nature, understood as necessity, behind. A state must return toward the beginning that nature provides while making that beginning its own, but without conquering the necessity that makes men operate well.

The Roman republic had "orders" that returned it toward the beginning, such as tribunes and censors and other institutions to oppose ambition, but they had to be "brought to life" by the virtue of "one citizen" who "spiritedly" seeks to execute them against the ambitious. Not a renewal of piety but sensational executions are the device of recall. Such executions revive in men the fear of punishment, the original fear from which government, whether human or divine, protects them. To protect men from fear, governments must periodically (Machiavelli proposes every ten years) remind them of fear, lest they become complacent, corrupt, and lawless. Progress cannot take itself for granted; it cannot continue without a vivid reminder of the contrast with the beginning. Returning toward the beginning applies the spur necessary to progress. Machiavelli even promises that had Rome followed his recipe of sensational executions and virtuous examples, "it follows of necessity" that it would never have become corrupt. This amazing possibility, the first statement of the modern impartial republic, shows how far Machiavelli has departed from the classical cycle.

Sensational executions are not, I said, a renewal of piety—or are they? Machiavelli continues in this same chapter to consider the renewal of the Christian sect, when it had fallen into corruption, by Saint Francis and Saint Dominic. The renovation, he says with superb impudence, succeeded by reinspiring Christian priests to do the worst they can "because they do not fear that punishment they do not see and do not believe in." In plain words, the renovation merely confirmed Christianity in its corruption. But of course it cannot be an accident that the chosen instrument of republican reform, the sensational execution, is also the central mystery of the Christian religion. Nor can we fail to note Machiavelli's particular interest in the executions by Junius Brutus, in which a father kills his sons (*Discourses* I 16; III 3).

It is time to turn to the other obstacle to progress, Christianity. In *The Prince* 12 Machiavelli speaks of Savonarola's prophetic denunciation of Italy and Florence at the time of the French invasion of 1494: "And he who said that our sins were the cause of it spoke the truth. But the sins were surely not those he believed, but the ones I have told of. . . ." This may be taken as representative of Machiavelli's appropriation, for his own project, of Christianity, the sect that conquered much of the world through unarmed prophets. Machiavelli's view of his situation was the following. He saw, first, that the ancients were strong and the moderns are weak. This was nothing but the common perception of the Renaissance applied to politics as well as the arts (and that application was not new). Moreover, he believed that the cause of modern weakness was Christianity—still nothing new. But he went on to ask himself why the strong ancients of pagan Rome were defeated by the weak moderns of Christian Rome. The very cause of weakness appeared in a new light as the cause of strength.

Machiavelli, himself not fearing the punishment he did not see, dismissed divine providence as the cause of the Christian triumph. So he looked for a this-worldly explanation of that success, found it, and took it up for himself to make Christianity serve his end, the liberation of mankind through the use of "one's own arms." For Christianity is strong enough to defeat the strong, but not strong enough, because of its dependence on arms in an otherworldly sense, to be strong on its own. Machiavelli noticed that the unarmed prophets are armed in that sense, that they even speak of a holy war; perhaps they are possessed of the art of war (*The Prince* 14) by which a prince can gain converts. They know how to make a virtue out of weakness—the virtue of humility (*Discourses* II 14). Their militant orders can be described as military orders, which Machiavelli proceeds to do in the second book of the *Discourses*. There Machiavelli describes the three orders of an army—infantry, artillery, and cavalry—with a view to the contrast between the strong ancients and weak moderns who somehow seem superior to the ancients in artillery and cavalry! Manfully Machiavelli struggles to argue that the ancients are nonetheless superior. But only when one applies the analogy between ordinary and spiritual warfare does his argument reveal itself. One sees that the modern superiority in artillery and cavalry and inferiority in infantry (in stubbornness, *ostinazione*, the quality of infantry) refers especially (though not only, of course) to Christianity, and one sees further how Machiavelli's army, the army of the Romans as he reinterprets it, will be better in all three orders. To state these conclusions, to hand them over in a basket, is a far less valuable gift than to prove any one of them in the text, because the highest reaches of

Machiavelli's ambition are to be found in the details, the *cose piccole* (*Discourses* III 33) of his writings.

Machiavelli believes he can carry his enterprise to the point that "another" will have but a brief walk to take it to its destined place (*Discourses* I pr.). He founds the modern impartial republic but leaves something—not so much!—for others to do, according to their competence in perceiving the magnitude of his intention. But he who adds the last bit always seems to have brought the whole thing (*Discourses* III 17); so by leaving a little at the end, Machiavelli leaves most of the glory to his followers, especially to those who do not understand him well and believe that in reading his books *they* are patronizing *him*. Machiavelli's princes belong to his principality, but because they get most of the glory, his principality can also be understood as a republic in the larger sense, the sense in which he speaks of the "Christian republic" (*Discourses* I 12). The difference is that Machiavelli's sect appeals to all mankind. Princes and republics in the usual sense will continue to rise and fall in accordance with their virtue and fortune. The impartiality is in Machiavelli himself and in the indifference he teaches to the partisan principles of Aristotelian regimes.

Thus the "perpetual republic" is both impossible, as Machiavelli says in *Discourses* III 17, and possible, as he says five chapters later. No single state within Machiavelli's system can last forever, but the whole can be perpetual because the various fortunes, or the fates, of its members have been anticipated by Machiavelli. His books will neither be lost nor superseded, though they may be covered over by later books written by princes of similar quality but not of the same priority as Machiavelli, to whom he leaves most of the glory. These authors fill out and develop Machiavelli's enterprise—for example, Bacon and Descartes—so that they can be understood as his captains. Book 3 of the *Discourses* is about the relationship between "one" who commands an army and his captains. (The Roman army in the *Discourses* corresponds to the ecclesiastical principality in *The Prince*.) Machiavelli is in no position to be severe with his captains; he cannot keep his republic uncorrupt with sensational executions. When he says in *Discourses* III 17 that to order a perpetual republic is impossible, it is because of the possible vengeance of an offended captain. But to deal with the difficulty Machiavelli follows the path of Valerius' kindness rather than Manlius' harshness (*Discourses* III 22). By allowing princes to be harsh and cruel, he himself can be kind to them and to mankind; for by allowing them worldly vengeance he prevents the build-up and release of far worse vengeance from an otherworldly captain. So, with the problem solved, his republic will be perpetual.

What distinguishes Machiavelli's idea of progress from following ideas, the ideas of his followers, is the point mentioned at the beginning: he does not appear at the head of a party on behalf of humanity. "Machiavellian" does not refer to a progressive. But for the same reason, a Machiavellian is not a totalitarian claiming to represent all humanity in the name of the universal class or race. Machiavelli's revolution is intended to be irreversible only in regard to the cyclical change of sects or civilizations; revolutions in Aristotle's first two senses of uprising and change of regime will continue. Like any other multitude, humanity needs a head (*capo, Discourses* I 44), but Machiavelli's Valerian kindness requires him to remain concealed. His revolution is partly open because it gives politics a new freedom in new modes and orders, but it is also partly concealed because it appears to continue politics as usual.

Machiavelli accepts the political division of mankind because he wants to retain politics, which is the realm of virtue. Any supposed betterment of mankind at the cost of virtue is no bargain. It is a new virtue to be sure, the virtue of overcoming fortune. But to overcome fortune, virtue is in need of fortune to provide risk and challenge. Machiavelli, the true and only prince, has overcome fortune, but he allows it to his captains and unwitting subordinates. Whether modernity has taken its intended course is doubtful, however. In attempting other, more regular and scientific modes of overcoming fortune, Machiavelli's successors formalized and emasculated his notion of virtue.

4 Kant's Idea of History

SUSAN SHELL

Kant's use of history has long been a puzzle to scholars.[1] First and foremost, as an account that claims to discern rational purpose in history, and that describes a certain trajectory of (the condition of) the human species from worse to better, Kantian history seems to call into question the absolute infinite worth of each human individual, on which Kant also emphatically insists. For as Kant himself admits, a progressive history (history with a happy ending, or history at least with a perpetually improving denouement) condemns those who are born earlier (through no fault of their own) to labor for the advantage of their distant progeny. As Kant himself states, "It remains strange [Kant's word, *befremdend,* also means astonishing or displeasing] that earlier generations seem to carry through their toilsome labor only for the sake of the later . . . [and that] only the latest of the generations should have the good fortune [*Gluck*] to dwell in an edifice upon which a long series of their ancestors had labored without being permitted to partake of the fortune they had prepared" (VIII 20; 14).[2] It would seem, then, that a progressive history is fundamentally unfair or, in the words of Hannah Arendt, at odds with "human dignity."[3] For either it produces *moral* improvement (in which case it seems to undermine the radical moral freedom on which Kant also insists—the absolute obligation of every person, whatever his or her external circumstance, to do right) or it produces *physical* improvement (in which case it seems to treat those of us born earlier not as ends in ourselves but as mere means to the well-being of those to come), or it does both. Kant nevertheless claims that a progressive history, however "riddlesome," is also somehow "necessary."

The riddlesome necessity of a progressive history brings us to difficulty number two: in what sense it is possible to speak—given Kant's strict separation of the realm of nature, in which all is determined by the laws of physics, from the realm of freedom, in which all is governed by the moral law—of a philosophically salient pattern or direction to history in the first place? This difficulty is all the more pressing in the light of Kant's lifelong alertness to the power of nature to cancel any and all human plans. An errant asteroid, as he suggests in a late work, could destroy the world tomorrow. Nothing we know about the world through science gives any assurance that humankind is nature's special darling. On the contrary, the geological evidence, in which Kant took an early and avid interest, suggests that our planet has undergone a series of devastating revolutions in which vast numbers of creatures—perhaps entire species—have been annihilated. In Kant's own philosophic youth, the Lisbon earthquake claimed the lives of forty thousand, thus shattering, many say, the Panglossian optimism of the early Enlightenment and certainly deepening Kant's own temperamental pessimism. Yet despite (and perhaps because) of this pessimism, and an almost gruesome fascination with what he was inclined to call the crucible of nature, Kant insisted that history could, and indeed, must be read as comedy (not farce)—if not for the individual, then for the species as a whole.

To these two difficulties—the moral unfairness of a progressive history and its apparent conflict with what Kant elsewhere says is and can be strictly known of nature—might be added a third: a certain inconsistency that some scholars have discerned between earlier and later treatments of history during Kant's so-called critical period, leading them to treat the early work the *Idea for a Universal History* (published, to be sure, when Kant was sixty, three years after the appearance of the first edition of the *Critique of Pure Reason*) as a less mature, and in some sense precritical version of Kant's brief but significant accounts of history in such later works as the *Critique of Judgment* (published in 1787). I shall not have much to say here about this issue.[4] My own view is that the distinction between Kant's critical and precritical periods has been somewhat overdrawn, and that much can be gained by viewing Kant's later works from the perspective of problems which—I believe it can be shown—exercised an almost obsessive grip on him throughout his philosophic life. This is not the place to make good such claims. But I do hope to suggest ways in which a more rounded, long-range view of Kant's interest in history can tease out, if not entirely remove, some of the more troubling aspects of those later works.

THE *Idea for a Universal History with a Cosmopolitan Intention* (*Idee zu einer allgemeinen Geschichte in weltbürgerlicher Absicht*)[5] appeared in 1784 in a popular journal whose audience Kant could not have expected to have mastered the intricacies of the first *Critique.* And yet precisely because the *Idea* is a "popular" work, the link between the *Idea for a Universal History* and his critical system as a whole remains unstated and, to that extent, all the more puzzling.

The occasion for the publication was the recent appearance, in another journal, of a notice by an unnamed scholar who had apparently visited Kant and reported back the following: "A pet idea [*Lieblingsidee*] of Professor Kant is that the final purpose [*Endzweck*] of the human race is to achieve the most perfect civic constitution, and he wishes that a philosophic historian might undertake to give us a history of humanity from this point of view, and to indicate to what extent humanity in various ages has approached or drawn away from this final purpose, as well as what, in order to achieve it, remains to be done."[6]

This pet idea—*Lieblingsidee* suggests a favorite or beloved—recalls Kant's exemplary discussion, in the *Critique of Pure Reason,* of the "Platonic" idea of the perfect republic, which he defines as that constitution which allows "the greatest possible human freedom in accordance with laws by which the freedom of each is made to be consistent with that of all others."[7] An idea, according to the first *Critique,* is a spontaneous projection of pure reason, a projection to which nothing in experience—nothing, that is, empirically knowable—can be adequate, and yet which is for all that no mere chimera or fantasy.[8] More specifically, a Kantian "idea" is not an object to be contemplated (in which case the charge of fantasy would stick) but a goal to be progressively approached. An idea, in short, is essentially practical, grounded not, as traditional metaphysics would have it, in theoretical knowledge but rather, as German idealists following Kant will insist, in freedom. (What Yirmiahu Yovel has called the eros of Kantian reason—its longing to realize the end(s) that it itself projects—is thus in an important sense autoerotic.) The *Lieblingsidee* of the perfect constitution replaces what Kant elsewhere calls his "first mistress"—the metaphysical dream, with which he was once enamored, of comprehending the universe theoretically.

The occasion of Kant's essay, then, was his need to explain, and perhaps defend from misconstrual, a pet idea that, as Kant knew, could well appear in the most literal sense outlandish. Some years earlier he had written another "cosmopolitan history" that had achieved some notoriety. (Among other things, it gave rise to what astronomers now call the Kant-Laplace thesis of nebula formation; it also inspired Herder's *Ideas toward a Philosophy of the History of Humanity,* published in 1785.)[9] It is one of the fruitful ironies of intellectual history that this work, publicly panned by Kant, yet crucial to the development of nineteenth-century historicism, was written by Kant's devoted former student. The title of Kant's earlier work—Kant at thirty-one did not suffer from false modesty—was *Universal Natural History and Theory of the Heavens* and in it he sought to provide what Descartes and Newton had for reasons of their own refrained from offering—a genetic history, according to mechanical principles, of the universe in its entirety.

About this beautiful, bizarre, and difficult work it is not possible here to say much, except that it was a cosmopolitan effort in the most literal sense. For after sketching out the mechanical principles by which the universe as we know it might have been formed (a sketch that presupposed a sort of second Copernican revolution, in which the Milky Way, traditionally conceived as a mantle encircling the earth, is reconfigured as an ellipse radiating outward from a central areola),[10] and after analogically extending this account of galactic formation to that of the universe as a whole, Kant goes on to speculate about the relation between the suns and planets and the characteristics of their inhabitants (for although it would be dogmatic to assume that all heavenly bodies are inhabited, it would be unreasonable, according to Kant, not to assume that most are or might become so). To the physical constitution of the universe—infinite numbers of galaxies revolving about a central point—there corresponds a spiritual universe—infinite gradations of intelligence ascending upward toward God, and downward toward that point where matter meets spirit and reason borders on unreason. Although not literally giving the lowest rank within this spectrum of spiritual life to human beings (Kant places us, along with Martians, somewhere near the middle) he does suggest us to be the most "degraded"—because of all creatures we seem least to achieve the end for which we were created.

That end, Kant at thirty-one believes, is to contemplate creation. To be sure, the Saturnians, who are made of finer stuff, can do a better job of it. For one thing, they live longer, being farther from the sun that both energizes and destroys the bodily machine. For another, being less dependent on gross matter, they think with greater agility and can thus more quickly unify or combine what we put together more haltingly and with greater pain and effort. Still, we are similarly advantaged in comparison with the slugs—the mental mollusks—of Venus and Mercury. What brings us down is not absolute but relative inability; where lower spirits are sunk in a material torpor from which they cannot arise, and where higher spirits painlessly transcend their bodily coils, we can escape the inertial pull of matter only by the greatest effort. The few willing to make that effort find noble release; the rest remain content to "suck sap, propagate their kind, and die," achieving awkwardly what lower creatures manage with greater decency and finesse.[11] If Mercurians fail to transcend their vegetative condition, they do so without fault. Man's humiliation lies not in his inability but in his unwillingness to rise. Poised between the higher charms of contemplation and the lower ones of animal desire, man finds neither goal conclusively attractive. Within the natural order, man's "end" is uniquely indeterminate—a "freedom" that goes together with the burden of responsibility for his own failure.

All of this, of course, places Kant's own authorial efforts in the *Universal Natural History* in a most peculiar light; for his struggle to assume a truly cosmopolitan standpoint becomes the basis on which mankind—and with it the perfection of the whole which man seems otherwise monstrously to violate—can be redeemed.

A final summary note: Kant's universal natural history, as we have seen, is timely in a special way. The unity of creation is unthinkable apart from the timeless divine schema or plan out of which creation temporally unfolds and in which each creature finds its ground or *raison d'être*. History is a never-ending story whose ending only God knows. Within this framework, man, along with all other created spirits, can only temporally approach as best he can God's immediate comprehension of the whole. In fulfilling this task, however, human beings are especially burdened. Located midway between wisdom and unreason, man finds his material and spiritual entelechies singularly out of sync. Man of all creatures seems least to realize his end because he alone lacks adequate time for the development of his higher capacities. The prospect of an eternal life or, at the very least, perpetual progress, arises from the palpable discrepancy between physical and spiritual perfection, the former obtainable by the individual, the latter, as Kant will much later put it in the *Idea for a Universal History,* only by the species.[12]

From this troubled perspective, Kant's famous confessional note to the effect that Rousseau "turned him around" takes on new meaning. In that note, written in the mid 1760s, Kant claims to be "by inclination" a restlessly desirous seeker after truth. There was a time, he continues, when he had thought that this search alone could constitute the honor of mankind; and he had despised the rabble, who know nothing. Rousseau, however, turned him around (or set him upright) by teaching him to honor man, and Kant henceforth would consider himself more worthless than the ordinary laborer if he did not direct all his efforts to that which gives all else worth—establishing the rights of man (XX 44).

The decisive importance of this moral conversion for Kant's so-called critical turn cannot detain us here.[13] Suffice it to say that the concept of a universal general will, briefly sketched out in Rousseau's *Emile,* becomes in Kant the basis for a new, humanized and moralized version of the "divine schema of creation." The spiritual community that Kant once sought through intellection becomes newly accessible through the idea of a republican constitution of free and equal beings. That this constitution is, at least in Kant's original formulations, explicitly masculine serves only the more emphatically to remind us of the material problem that it addresses. Where Kant once condemned man for the "indeterminacy" of his nature, torn as he is between higher and lower principles of desire, he now exalts in human freedom. The problematic effort theoretically to transcend a metaphorically feminized nature—the exchanges of matter are figured by Kant in abysmally maternal terms—gives way in the face of a practical elevation to the moral world—a community of spirits beyond the flux of time and matter. The only question, for Kant writing in 1766, is how to translate that immediate but merely ideal elevation into real-worldly terms—of how, in other words, to give a wholly spiritual republic political weight and bite.

Kant's *Idea for a Universal History* situates itself in that *intermundia* or space between worlds toward which his early notes on Rousseau experimentally reach. A rational history, Kant insists, requires a plan. The problem of composing a *human* history is therefore unique. "Since men," he writes, "behave, on the whole, not just instinctively, like the brutes, nor yet like rational citizens of the world according to some agreed-on plan, no history of man conceived according to a plan seems possible, as it might be possible to have such a history of bees or beavers."

Kant thus calls for a philosophic history that will discover a "natural plan" for creatures who have no "plan of their own." Kant suggests that he is in part motivated in this effort by a certain "indignation" at the apparently idiotic and childish course of things human, which seem woven together from malice and folly. The eligibility of humanity for membership in a higher world cannot, it seems, wholly eclipse the repulsiveness of a species that (unlike the beavers and the bees) defies purposive conceptualization—an answer to the question "what is man?" (VIII 18; 42).[14] Kant here seeks out a guiding thread (*Leitfaden*) for such a history, leaving it to nature to bring forth the man (*Mann*) in a position (*der im Stande ist*) to compose it. The one who achieves such a history would, like Kepler or Newton, succeed "in an unexpected way," a phrase that calls to mind Kant's characterization elsewhere of genius.[15] The remainder of the work consists of nine theses, intended, perhaps, to recall the famous Ninety-five Theses of Martin Luther, as well as the theses (and antitheses) of Kant's own *Critique of Pure Reason*.

According to the first thesis, *All natural capacities of a creature are destined to evolve completely to their natural end.* Without such a principle, which is confirmed, in the case of animals, by outer and inner (*zergleidernde*) observation, we have a purposelessly playing, rather than a lawful, nature, and unconsoling (*trostlos*) chance takes the place of reason's guiding thread.[16]

In man, however (according to thesis two) *these natural capacities, insofar as they pertain to the use of reason, are destined (or determined) to develop fully only in the species.* Man alone ("as the only rational creature on earth") achieves his destiny not in one life span but only over the endless course of generations. To observe an animal is to attribute to it a purposive cause—a goal toward which its parts seem to aim. In man alone, however, this rule is breached, by virtue of the infinite reach of reason itself. Reason "acknowledges no limits to its projects," for it is itself the power to extend the rules and intentions (*Absichten*) to which its forces are applied beyond the limits of nature. The palpable discrepancy between the shortness of our individual life span and the time needed to develop all our faculties threatens to turn man alone into nature's childish "sport." (*Spiel* in German means play, but also freak.)[17] The purposeless "play" of nature which Kant earlier feared is now connected with man's apparent freakishness or failure to conform to type. A sport of nature is, of course, an offspring differing in form from that of its parent; and man, by virtue of his very freedom, threatens the presumption of natural purposiveness on which judgment and all practical principles ultimately depend. But what does Kant mean by "judging"? Judgment, he elsewhere states, is the capacity to place the individual under a universal concept, as when we judge that this is a tree and that a desk. In the case of man, however, this task is uniquely problematic; for the very concept of humanity, if there can be said to be one at all, is, by virtue of man's freedom, indeterminate and open-ended. What from one point of view constitutes man's glory from another makes him, in the most literal sense, a monster.

It is therefore necessary that man strive toward ("if only in the idea") that point in time at which we reach the level of development which conforms to nature's intention. The idea of history is the guiding thread that leads us out of the labyrinth of man's natural monstrousness—the ideal moment in which nature's leading strings give way to rational self-direction.[18]

To think this moment is to attribute to nature the will that, as Kant puts it in thesis three, *man himself, bring forth everything that goes beyond the mechanical ordering of his animal existence, and that he should partake of no other happiness or perfection than that which he himself, free of instinct, has created by his own wisdom.* Man, in short, is to give birth to himself—all of himself, that is to say, which goes beyond mere physical existence. He is to "bring forth everything from himself" rather than being "guided by instinct." Nature is thus a stepmother to man in the most literal sense: her harshness is linked to a lack of genuine kinship.[19]

Man overcomes the status of contempt in which his monstrousness places him by "working himself up" and thus making himself "worthy of life" itself. Man alone furnishes the *ground* (or sufficient reason) of his own existence (just what Kant's youthful metaphysics vainly sought)—not physically, to be sure, but morally—for man alone of all known creatures can provide out of himself a reason why he ought to exist, and with it a justification or sufficient reason for the rest of creation. Humanity is, as Kant will later say, the final purpose *of* nature and the ultimate purpose or reason *beyond* nature by which creation as such is justified.[20]

Man can so work himself up, however, only historically or as a species; individually, man is of nature born, and nature in the guise of death exacts its due. Hence the "strange" but "necessary" sacrifice of earlier generations (who, to be sure, labor unintentionally) for the sake of later ones—strange, inasmuch as history appears unjust, yet necessary, *if* one assumes that a "species of animals [born to die], should yet have reason." The discrepancy between the physical and spiritual entelechies of which Kant once complained—our inability as natural creatures to develop all the rational capacities of which we find ourselves capable—must be accepted as the fate of a mortal animal endowed with reason. Man's traditional *Bestimmung,* his scholastic definition as the rational animal, rings true only if it is interpreted historically.

Man is born in order to give birth to himself. The means employed by nature to bring this development about is, according to thesis four, the famous antagonism or "asocial sociability" that brings men, driven by vainglory, lust for power, and greed, to conquer their natural laziness or torpor (*Trägheit* also means inertia). (Thus, thesis four: *The means that nature employs to bring the development of all her disposition about* [*zu Stand zu bringen*] *is that of antagonism within society, insofar as in the end it is a cause of low-governed social order.*) Without these inclinations toward evil, man's other talents would remain hidden, and men, effortlessly content, would have no more value than the domestic animals they raise.[21] In such a case, the question Why are there men at all? would remain unanswerable, as Kant insists is actually (almost) the case for such primitive peoples as the putatively happy but lazy Greenlanders and Terra del Fuegans. Evil is thus preferable to natural goodness, and nature is to be thanked for freeing us of the need to thank her (VIII 20; 43; cf. VIII 21; 45). (The paradoxical character of this remark reminds us that even as nature's stepchildren we remain her progeny.)

As a result, the first steps from rudeness to culture are taken by means of a dynamic relation between human forces of attraction and repulsion, that is, from men's desire "for union, a state" in which one feels "more human,"[22] joined with a tendency, arising from well-grounded mutual suspicion, toward self-isolating individuation (*vereinzelnen*).[23]

The greatest problem for the human species, according to thesis five, *to the solution of which we are naturally driven is the establishment of a universal civil society administering law or justice.* In such a perfect civic constitution, in which there is mutual opposition among members, and at the same time the most exact determination of freedom and fixing of its limits so that it may be consistent with the freedom of others, all man's dispositions (*Anlagen*) can develop. To such a state of reciprocal limitation, Kant insists, men are naturally driven by their very love of boundless freedom. Civic union is thus a sort of enclosure or preserve in which wild growth gives way to cultivation—just as trees hemmed in together grow straight and tall through competition for the sunlight, while those in isolated freedom put out branches at random.[24] Though made of crooked wood, man can be made to grow straight through the collective discipline of his own evil inclinations.[25] All culture and fine art, along with the finest social order, are the "fruits" of unsociableness—a deeper and, so to speak, unconscious artfulness by which man's natural seeds are to develop to perfection.

Kant's likening of civil society to an enclosure (the word also means "corral") recalls, however, the domesticated beasts our similarity to which renders us contemptible. How does man, who is, as Kant states, in need of a master, become master of himself and thereby justify his own existence?[26] What is required is that man's merely private will be broken and required to conform to a universal law (i.e., that he be forced to be free). Man can obtain a master, however, only from the human species; hence his master will himself need a master. The Platonic problem of who is to rule is thus, according to thesis six, *the most difficult and the last to be solved by the human race.* Indeed, it is not fully solvable; for from such crooked wood as man is made of, "nothing perfectly straight or upright [the word—*gerade*—also means just] can be built."

That it is the last problem to be solved follows also from the fact that it requires the coincidence of a proper concept of a possible constitution, a great experience of the world course, and, most of all, the good will to accept that constitution—a coincidence of king, philosopher, and saint which will occur, if at all, "very late, and after many futile attempts" (VIII 23; 47). Nature therefore requires us only to approximate this idea, so that the task (which is itself now designated as an idea)—rather than its fulfillment (as Kant had earlier suggested) defines us somehow as a species.

Achieving that goal depends, according to thesis seven, on the solution of a problem involving the relation among states: "*The problem of achieving a perfect civil constitution is dependent on the problem of a lawful external relation among states, and without the latter cannot be solved*" (VIII 24; 47). This result, which reason might have brought about from the beginning, nature achieves by means of the same unsociability and intolerance or *Unvertragsamkeit* that drives individuals to enter a civil compact (or *Vertrag*). In the ensuing devastation, (civic) bodies continually dissolve and reform, until such revolutions (like those from which our solar system arose) bring about a self-maintaining constitution. This tendency toward dynamic equilibrium presupposes (on the analogy of cosmic evolution) a purposive arrangement rather than blind chance. For to accept the latter would be to reduce nature to a lawless treadmill—a revolting eternal return of the same—and thus to renounce altogether the idea of progress—the hope that mankind is moving, by however secret an art, from worse to better.

That war (and its growing threat) ultimately leads to a system of stable peace is the lynchpin of Kant's hope. The same "asocial sociability" that forces men to form civil societies eventually compels the latter—after a course of devastating upheavals and revolutions—to enter into a federation in which the security of each is guaranteed and which maintains itself "automatically." Such a future condition is, we may reasonably believe, no less likely than the cosmic system that has evolved from analogous physical forces of attraction and repulsion:

> Whether, now, one should expect that states, by an Epicurean concourse [*Zusammenlauf*] of efficient causes should enter by accidental [*ungefähren*] collisions (like those of small material particles) into all kinds of formations which are again destroyed by new collisions, until they arrive *by accident* [*von Ungefähr*] at a formation that can maintain itself in its form (a happy chance occurence, that will hardly ever occur!); or whether one should more readily assume that nature here follows a regular course, in leading our species gradually upward from the lowest level of animality up to the highest level of humanity through an art that is man's own, though forced, and hence that nature develops man's original dispositions in an entirely regular manner within this apparently wild arrangement; or whether one would prefer that out of all this human activity and counteractivity in the large, nothing overall, or at least nothing wise, should emerge, that it would remain as it always has been, and that one would thus not be able to predict [*voraussagen*] whether the schism [*Zweitracht*] so natural to our species is not in the end preparing the way for a hell of evils to overtake us, however civilized our condition, in that it again nullifies this condition and all progress in culture made hitherto, through barbarous devastation (a fate one cannot stay [*nicht stehen kann*] under a rule of blind chance [*blind Ungefährs*]—which is, indeed, identical with lawless freedom—if one does not attribute to it [*ihr . . . unterlegt*] a secret guiding thread of nature, a thread tied together [*geknüpften*] with wisdom): all of this amounts approximately [*läuft ungefähr*] to the following, namely, whether it is reasonable to assume the purposiveness of nature in its parts and yet deny it to the whole. (VIII 25; 48)

Kant's repeated use here of *laufen* and *ungefähr,* especially given the latter's multiple meanings,[27] brings Kant's three cosmological alternatives to an ironic and self-reflexive conclusion. The course of Kant's questioning itself leads, in a way that is inexact (and unintentional yet safe?), to a summary question in which both rationality and the purposiveness of nature's parts are already assumed. And yet if this is indeed the issue to which Kant's other questions amount, one is left somewhat perplexed, given the apparent lack of purposiveness in a rational *part* (the human one) which initiates Kant's inquiry and which his essay as a whole is meant to address.

Owing, perhaps, to that difficulty, Kant turns to partiality in another sense—the parts of the political whole, a system that is not without danger (*nicht ohne alle Gefahr*) and yet wholesome (*heilsam*).[28] Just as the state of savagery eventually forced individuals to enter into a civic condition, so the barbaric freedom of civil states "compels our species to discover a law of equilibrium for the opposition of many states toward one another, an opposition in itself wholesome and that originates in freedom, and to introduce a united power to give the former support, and thus also a cosmopolitan condition of public state security. This condition is not without all danger, so that the forces of humanity do not go to sleep, but also not without a principle of equality of reciprocal action and reaction, so that they do not destroy one another" (VIII 26; 49). Like the cosmic system to which he explicitly compares it, Kant's cosmopolitan mechanism will be self-enforcing—a kind of second universe which, unlike the first, is attuned to the requirements of moral culture. Yet:

> Before taking this final step (the union of states), thus when it is just past the halfway mark of its formation [*Ausbildung*], human nature endures the hardest evils under the guise of outward welfare. . . . We are *cultivated* to a high degree through art and science. We are *civilized* to the point of excess. . . . But for us to consider ourselves *moralized* much is lacking. For while the idea of morality already belongs to culture, the use of this idea, which only extends to the similacra of virtue in honor and outward propriety, constitutes mere civilization. So long as states apply all their forces toward vain and violent aims of expansion [*Erweiterungsabsichten*], unceasingly obstructing [*hemmen*] the slow effort toward the inner formation [*bilden*] of the way of thinking [*Denkungsart*] of their citizens—even removing from them all support for this aim—nothing from this way is to be expected. For the former demands a long inner elaboration [*Bearbeitung*] of each commonwealth for the formation/education [*Bildung*] of its

> citizens. But everything good that is not grafted onto a morally good mentality [*Gesinnung*] is nothing but empty appearance and glittering misery. The human race will probably remain in this condition until it has worked its way out of the chaotic state of its state relations in the way I have described. (VIII 26; 49)

The problem, then, is roughly this. Human history "according to a plan" has seemingly started to take shape, with human nature just past the mid-point of its formation. (Is that mid-point Kant's own explication of the moral idea as a system-constituting ground?) That moral idea, Kant says, already belongs to culture, but is used by states in ways leading to only the similacra of virtue. Hence the hardest evils lie ahead, evils consisting in states' unceasing obstruction of the formation/education of citizens.[29]

How then is the education of citizens to go forward, barring a coincidence of philosopher, king, and saint that is (almost) as unlikely as the emergence of self-maintaining order from Epicurean chaos?

Thesis eight indicates a way out of this seeming impasse, if only by way of a hint that nature furthers reason's goal: "*One can in the large see the history of the human race as the fulfillment of a hidden plan of nature to bring about an inwardly—and for this purpose also outwardly—perfected constitution of states, as the only condition in which she can fully develop in humanity all her dispositions*" (VIII 27; 50). Unlike the chiliastic expectations of revelation, the fulfillment of philosophy's goals can be hastened by awareness of the idea they are based on, this fact being sufficient to distinguish such goals from fanatical illusions.

But distinguishing ideas from illusions is not enough; one must, it seems, also secure the thread by which the ideas of reason connect with nature. Or so one is led to understand by Kant's claim that "it comes down only to this: whether experience discovers *something* of such a course of nature's intention."

What, then, of nature's intention does experience discover? Kant says (*Ich sage*): "a *little bit*" (*etwas Weniges*). And the fact that "human nature" cannot "be indifferent" to the most distant epochs in which our species treads, combined with the fact that in our own case (*in unserem Falle*) we may be able to accelerate this happy point in time for our descendants through our own rational organization

(*Veranstaltung*), suggests a naturally supported, albeit ideal, closing of the circle by which the species is to be determined.[30] In any event, our natural inability to be indifferent to the certain future of our race (an inability heightened by our present awareness that we can consciously act to further a happy end) makes even weak traces (*Spuren*) "extremely important to us," so that the faintness of the track is, in effect, offset by its potential significance.

Kant locates those traces in the relations among states, which find themselves in so artful (*künstlichen*)[31] a condition with respect to one another that none can neglect inner culture without losing power and influence over the rest. Given the combination of nature and art arrived at in the current moment, the selfish tendencies of rulers are no longer (or need no longer appear as) an implacable obstacle to the articulation of history according to an idea. First, the ambitious intentions of states tend all by themselves in such a condition to secure the "maintenance of nature's end." Beyond this, state power comes actually to *require* the freedom of citizens. For to hinder the citizen from doing what he will so long as it is consistent with the freedom of the rest "obstructs the vitality of ongoing business [*durchgängigen Betriebes*]"[32] and thus impedes "the forces of the whole." It follows that personal limitations (*Einschränkung*), including restrictions on religion, grow ever weaker; and there thus gradually arises, with intermittent delusion and crankiness, *enlightenment*, a "great good that the human race must reap even from its rulers' self-aggrandizing intentions if only they know their own advantage. At the same time, the sympathy (*Herzensantheil*, literally, heart sharing") enlightened persons feel for anything good they fully comprehend, will gradually spread upward to heads of state. In the meantime, rulers, even if they do not actively support education, find it in their own interest not to impede citizens' own efforts. And war itself, by virtue of a growing commercial interdependence that makes a tremor in one state felt by all the rest, becomes increasingly costly and hence counterproductive.

The upshot of these remarks is to suggest the emergence of a great state body (*grossen Staatskörper*) the stirring of whose members (*Gliedern*) is already (nearly) visible: "Although this state body is discernible for now only in very rough outline [*Entwurfe*], it seems as if, so to speak, a feeling is rising in all members for maintaining the whole: and this gives hope that after many revolutions . . . what nature has for its highest intention will at last come to pass—a universal cosmopolitan condition, as the womb [*Schoos*] in which all original dispositions of the human species will become developed" (VIII 28; 51). It is as if, in human history's case, the revolution of the heavens gave rise—as it were, spontaneously—not just to a mechanism of dead nature but to a *living being*, a being, moreover, whose body Kant characterizes as a *Schoos*, or womb, in which all the natural dispositions of mankind can develop. This womb is both the visible trace of history's unfolding and the site out of which humanity emerges, the only individual (so far as we know) of its kind—a child, so to speak, without a parent. In short, mankind (by virtue of this conceit) gives birth to itself and, in doing so secures, however paradoxically, an otherwise dubious natural affinity. The secret tie that binds nature and reason thus stands exposed, or promises so to do to the extent that such a tie is humanly conceivable.

Kant's ninth and final thesis posits his essay as its own sought-for sign: a philosophic attempt to work out (*bearbeiten*) a universal history of the world according to a plan of nature which aims at a perfect civic union of the human species must be regarded as possible, and even as furthering this intention of nature (VIII 29; 51).

The possible success of such an attempt is sufficiently established, it seems, by the attempt itself. For by so linking the observer and the observed, such an attempt is itself the sought-for trace of reason's natural embodiment, and hence the strongest indication available that such a plan exists. Kant is thus able to establish that the philosophic effort to work out a planful history is not itself unreasonable.[33]

He is to this extent able to defeat (at last) the apparent "strangeness" or "absurdity" of the design (*Anschlag*) of wishing to compose (*abfassen*) history—as distinguished from romance (*Roman*)—according to an idea. The *utility* of that idea, as long as we may assume that nature, even in the "play of human freedom," does not operate without a plan, distinguishes it decisively from an illusion, and this despite the fact that, unlike (other) rational ideas, the idea of history *is inseparable from* nature. Unlike other rational ideas, which belong to all rational beings, the idea of history, in other words, belongs peculiarly and especially to man.

But what exactly does it mean to assume that nature does not operate without a "final intention"? Is this to presume that nature acts intentionally? Or is it merely to reject the claim that intentionality on nature's part is lacking? (Might it be the case that nature does not operate either with intention or without it?) In any case, *if* we may make that assumption:

> And even though we are too near-sighted[34] to penetrate the secret mechanism of [nature's] organization [*Veranstalltung*], this idea may yet serve as a guiding thread to represent an otherwise planless *aggregate* of human actions as, at least in the main, a *system.* For if one starts out with Greek history—as that in which all earlier or contemporaneous histories are preserved, or at least must be authenticated [*beglaubigt*]; if one follows the influence of Greek history on the formation and misformation of the state body of the Roman people, which swallowed the Greek state; again, if one follows down to our own times the influence of the Romans on the Barbarians, who destroyed the Roman state in turn; if one then adds episodically the state histories of other peoples, insofar as knowledge of them has gradually come down to us through these enlightened nations; one will then discover a regular course of improvement of state constitution in our part of the world/continent (which will probably one day legislate for all others). Further, one must always attend [*Acht hat*] only to the civil constitution and its laws, and to the relations among states, and notice how both, through the good that they impart, served for a time to lift up peoples for a time (and with them also arts and sciences). But we should also attend to how their defects . . . led to their overthrow, but in such a way that a seed of enlightenment always remained over, developing further through each revolution. (VIII 29–30; 52)

One would in this way, Kant believes, discover

> a guiding thread that can serve not only for explaining the confused play of human things, or for political prophesying of future political alterations (a use to which human history merely as the disjointed effect of rule-less freedom has already been put!); rather, it would serve to open up a consoling prospect into the future (that we, without presupposing a plan of nature, cannot hope for), a prospect in which

> we are shown from afar how finally the human species works its way up to a condition in which all the germs that nature has placed in it can fully develop and its destiny be here on earth fulfilled.

In the case of humanity alone, the divine schema, to which we can otherwise, according to Kant's critical teaching, only figuratively appeal, becomes accessibly our own—and the figure of a perfect machine purposively united, by which we metaphorically—but only metaphorically—conceptualize all other living things, is actualized in the earthly incarnation of a community of moral beings. In the case of humanity, too, the vexed "problem" of generation—of how the intercourse of two living individuals can produce another—is, if not overcome, at least set aside; for qua species in the determinate sense, humanity is one individual, whose "natural history" ceases at the moment in which men consciously unite, thereby becoming pregnant with their own future.[35]

The discarded traditional ideal of knowledge as an apprehension of the inner essence or perfection of a thing is in this manner newly, and uniquely, revived. For in mankind alone knower and known are, or can be, one. Mankind unites through the idea of such a union which each member shares. It is in this crucial sense that mankind, unlike the race of dogs and horses, literally creates itself—not just as an aggregate of individual living beings but as a whole, a species that is not only worthy of membership in the cosmos (which the current state of affairs might lead us to doubt) but which also justifies the rest of creation. In humanity so conceived, Leibniz's question of sufficient reason—why is there something rather than nothing?—finds its only humanly adequate response.

Unlike Alexandre Kojève, the twentieth-century Hegelian who worried that the end of history—the universal rational state—would spell the end of human negativity and thus the end of man, Kant sees it as the dawn of the first truly human, if not Saturnian, age. Prior to its emergence from the new and happier womb, mankind would presumably remain a sort of fetus, inwardly developing the organs of ethical culture which would allow it to be reborn at last as a fully determine species.[36] Mankind would at last transcend the monstrousness adherent to its hybrid status as an animal endowed with reason.

Man, one might be tempted to conclude, is a historical being. But Kant, unlike Hegel, does not go so far. For to the extent that history depends on nature, whose ways we can interpret but not entirely control, progress remains a hope rather than a realized certainty. Qua moral being, man's full humanity is assured, albeit only in another world to come. Qua natural being, on the contrary, man's full humanity is merely an idea, distinguished from a fantasy or romance only by the fact that that idea, to the extent that it is propagated, can become a self-fulfilling prophecy.[37] This, and man's "natural" interest in the most distant epoch that our species may encounter, if only he can anticipate it with certainty, creates a sort of ideal union of mankind—a common humanity, so to speak, before the fact.

The result is an authenticated *Buildungsroman* whose hero is the learned (*gebildet*) public at large, a community of letters unbroken by the course of time. The authors of history—those who tell its tale—are thus in an important sense its subject matter as well. History, according to Kant, begins with the "first page" of Thucydides—written about and for the first people capable of perpetuating the story.[38] Only with the Greeks, in other words, does mankind achieve continuous self-awareness—a sort of communal equivalent of the transcendental unity of consciousness on which Kant pegs individual human identity. Once one accepts this collective consciousness, one has only to grant the survival and further development (however slight) of the "germ" of enlightenment in each subsequent political revolution—and perpetual progress is assured.[39] Add thesis one—that all natural dispositions of a creature are destined or determined to evolve completely to their end—and the earthly fulfillment of the human race, however distant, becomes a certainty. This "consoling" prospect is at once Kant's "guiding thread" and his most important "motive ground"—the "end" of history in both senses of the term. Man reconciled with nature is man literally remade—man as the author of himself.

We are not, it seems, very far here from the "self-developing self-consciousness" of Hegel's world spirit—from the historical *Weltgeist* under whose wheels many a (mere) individual is crushed. But Kant is not Hegel. The "strangeness" of a history that holds the fate of some hostage to the well-being of others cannot be entirely suppressed. Kant's historical totalization of humanity thus remains incomplete. Man's historical evolution leads up to, but does not include, his full emancipation or rebirth, for which a new moral "grafting" (*pfropfen*) is required. The tension between nature and reason—and with it man's hybrid or bastard status, his failure to conform to type—cannot be fully resolved.

Thus Kant does not offer the consoling prospect of man's full development on earth, and with it nature's "completed rational intention," but only his belief (*Glaube*) that such a prospect is possible, and this despite the fact that without such a prospect the history of the human race is not only a "constant reproach" to the putative wisdom embodied in the rest of nature, but actually forces us to "turn away our eyes" in revulsion.

His idea of a world history has, then, an a priori *Leitfaden* only "to a certain extent" (*gewissermasse* or, alternatively, "only in a manner of speaking"). It would, Kant insists, be a misunderstanding of his intention (*Absicht*) to think that with that idea he would wish "to displace the working out [*Bearbeitung*] of history [*Historie*] proper, which is composed merely empirically." His idea of world history is rather

> only a thought [*Gedanke*][40] of what a philosophic head (who must also be very artful historically) might be able to attempt from another standpoint. Besides, the otherwise praiseworthy detail with which one now composes the history of one's time must naturally bring about concern as to how our remote descendants will cope with the burden of history that we bequeath to them some centuries from now. Doubtless, they will value the history of the oldest times, of which the original documents would have long disappeared, only from the view point of what interested them, namely, what peoples and governments have done to help or harm a cosmopolitan intention. To consider [look back on] this so as to direct the love of honor of heads of state and their servants to the only means by which their fame can spread to later ages: this can be a minor motive ground for attempting such a philosophic history. (VIII 30–31; 53)

Kant's own intention and the intention of world history mentioned in the title of his essay, then, both do and do not coincide. The announced goal of the essay—to "see whether we can succeed in finding a guiding thread" to human history according to a plan—issues in the discovery of a guiding thread, but one that goes only so far, and thus remains ambiguous at best. (Is a thread that leads Theseus only part way through the labyrinth better than none at all?) Kant's idea cannot authenticate itself historically. It is not, however, for all that useless, for it supports the hope that nature will produce another, more historically artful philosophic head in which such an authentication might be accomplished. With that authentication, the composition of a human whole (articulated according to an idea of which its members were aware) would, it seems, also be achieved, but for the reliance of such composition on art rather than philosophy. Given that reliance, the articulation of human history—which combines reason's guiding thread and nature's leading string—must remain equivocal. In any case and in the meantime, Kant's own attempt overcomes blockages to human self-formation which are imposed by (otherwise) misguided states.

IN HIS ESSAY *What Is Enlightenment?* Kant dares mankind to "sever" its "leading strings."[41] But what sort of guiding thread can replace those leading strings—nature's stepmotherly chord—without evicting us from nature entirely?

What Kant elsewhere calls the object of practical reason (or happiness conjoined with worthiness to be happy) does not here suffice; for while that object can deliver us into a moral world to come, it cannot determinately indicate the path we are to tread on earth.

In the end, Kant's idea of history does not and cannot answer the question with which it begins, that of how a species as *eingebildete*—the word means conceited, but also imaginary—as ourselves is to be conceived at all. This failure points at once to the marginality and to the centrality of history to Kant's project as a whole, whose three basic subjects of inquiry—what can I know? what ought I do? what may I hope? reduce, as Kant elsewhere observes, to the single question—what is man?[42] It is, ultimately, Kant's insistence on human dignity—on the absolute moral worth of every individual—which prevents, or saves, him from taking the Hegelian plunge, in which philosophy and history ultimately merge in the self-conceptualization of a spirit that is no longer, for that very reason, altogether human.[43]

We thus return to the simultaneous necessity and strangeness, by Kant's own account, of his historical idea. The necessity of that idea arises not so much from its moral utility—the spur to worldly action for which it is generally taken, though there is surely something to this—but from a deeper imperative on Kant's part—a desire, or need, to figure the relation between reason and unreason. The ensuing exercise in spontaneous generation (or what Herder called spiritual self-birthing) escapes the charge of fantasy (of which Herder accused it) only by virtue of history's strangeness—the unrelievable tension between man as a progressive or "species-being" and the infinite value of the individual—a value that sets an absolute limit to both nature's and history's reach. It is this strangeness, I believe, that ultimately prevented Kant from writing a true philosophy of history, forcing him to rely instead on the pure postulates of practical reason—God and the immortality of the soul—to stave off the inertial despair that would otherwise weigh down our moral action.[44]

But Kant's insistence on human dignity, which he would like to be the final word, is itself both philosophically and historically entangled—bound up with his own lifelong effort to come to terms with nature's infinite fecundity, a fecundity that constantly threatens to swallow up again the progeny to which it gives rise. (Kant's humanity is itself, as Nietzsche might say, all too human.) It is this tangled root of Kantian thought which partially resurfaces in Heideggerian historicity and being-toward-death—that other great shaper, along with Hegelian spirit, of historical consciousness in the twentieth century.

It is today difficult—even more difficult than in Kant's time—to find consolation in the hope of perpetual progress, a hope that has been all but blasted by the totalizing politics to which Kant's idea of history indirectly contributed. Still, that Kant's call for philosophic history has borne some bitter fruit should not be held entirely to his account. For like the antidotes that—according to Kant—nature conveniently places next to toxic mushrooms so that the species who consume them may survive, Kantian morality—and in particular his account of human rights—may well offer the best prospect of relief from the political afflictions for which his thought is also, in some sense, responsible. If this is so, Kant's idea of history may provide strangely redeeming comfort after all.

5 The End of History in the Open-ended Age? The Life Expectancy of Self-evident Truth

JOSEPH CROPSEY

Whether history has ended is a question subordinate to several other questions: Is history a thing? If it is a certain something, of what kind is it? Is it of the kind capable of having an end? What could be the meaning of "end" as applied to such a thing as history? And does "Now" have the character that would satisfy the definition of "end" of history if history proved capable of having an end? Other questions will arise, but these will serve to start the inquiry.

We know that for the present purpose it is not possible for history to mean the succession of events or the record of that succession and at the same time "end" to mean "nothing thereafter," for that would presuppose the extinction of the world, which is not contemplated. It follows therefore that What is history? is really subordinate to the question What must history be if it is to fall within the class of things having an end, whatever that word proves to mean, without presupposing the annihilation of everything? Now we have progressed far enough to see that we need one word that means "end as last one of all" and another that means "end in another sense that we have not yet been able to define." Let us use "terminable" for the former and "perfectible" for the latter.

If at least one thing, namely, the Whole, is not terminable, then history cannot be absolutely comprehensive but must be a part of something larger. It would be a finite part of the infinite Whole. Some things would fall within history and some would not. But before knowing what kind of "thing" history is, we can scarcely know what it includes or pertains to, what kind or kinds of things it *can* include or pertain to. The mutual dependence or "coprimacy" of the fundamental questions need not paralyze the inquiry, but it will compel us to make a beginning that is arbitrary. Let us begin with ends.

Whatever other meanings may attach themselves to the word "end," there is one meaning that no other can exclude or replace: an end is a "toward which," in time or space or being. That a thing has a "toward which" is a sign that it is either terminable or perfectible or both. "Toward" implies movement or change. Bodies move toward a place where they are not but where in some sense they ought to be. Young plants and animals "develop." Minds "grow." Why is there such a thing as a "toward which," and how far is it affected by "ought"? We know that a body on a slope moves down, it has a "toward which" imposed on it by a truth inherent in matter. Living things develop in obedience to a truth imposed on them by obscure necessities. Minds grow to some extent in spite of themselves. It is clear that the "ought" that goes with "toward which," in the examples that have come to mind, is an ought of necessity, not of freedom, choice, or good. The necessity is of the nature of truths. Truth is necessity, necessity is truth—thus far. So an end is a place or a state in which something subject to change must find itself by reason of truth.

Where is that truth or necessity? We will not know whether, in speaking of the "where" of truth, we must continue to flounder in the language of metaphor until we know whether a truth is a something that can be "somewhere." In the meantime, we will ask whether the truth that dictates its end to a thing is within the thing or external to it. Where is the principle of gravitational attraction, and where are the truths of genetics which govern the development of living things? We are inclined to say that the truths are incorporated in the individuals that they govern, but this is to beg the question, because what we would like to know is exactly whether there is a truth that "is" (using "is" as the verb that corresponds with "being") independently of its "incorporation." But what would be the mode of being of something—truth—that "is" without any existence in which to express itself, so to speak; for the being or end of the truth of gravitation seems to be to induce certain states in bodies. Can—indeed, must—a truth have an end, a toward which or consummation? Or is its being its only consummation, its perfection and its satisfaction? In the latter case, we human beings would have to ask ourselves how we could become aware of a truth that need not and does not manifest itself in an existent? Our only answer would have to be provisional: by our power of ratiocination, we come to conclusions whose existence lies in the logic that dictates their absolute necessity. We prove the necessity of their government of things by the necessity of their own being as demonstrated to ourselves by ourselves, we having informed ourselves that there is a question to be answered because we have taken note of existent things whose behavior puzzles us: from the existent things to the necessity governing them, which is the truths, then back to the existent things. But this exactly avoids the question whether there is truth, and if so whether we human beings could be aware of it, if it were absolutely and in every way detached from empirical, existent manifestation. What is a truth that is not "about" something capable of coming within experience, not restricting experience to sense perception but in any sense however wide? This is not the place to rehearse the Socratic doctrine of Ideas or the Kantian critique of the pure reason, but rather to return to the problem of a possible end of history, making use of whatever aids we have gained along the way. To justify the foregoing as helping us toward our goal, it should be said that the proposition "history can end" implies that there is a truth in the world of our experience.

Before leaving this area of troubling questions, all of them attached to the thesis that history can end, one further formulation of our problem should be considered. If there is an inner truth in the whole, is it of such a nature that it *must* come forth, or rather that it *might* come forth and be manifest, or even that it absolutely *cannot* come forth as empirical? Otherwise put, is there a *logos* that is immanent in and thus inseparable from the material in which it must utter itself; is the *logos* such as to be brought to actuality only if aided by fortuitous chance; or is the *logos* of such a nature as exactly, by virtue of its nature, to be in a state of opposition to the material in which it would utter itself, as would be the case if blind and stupid matter were an insuperable frustration to reason? Will there be an apodictic demonstration that one of these describes the condition of truth in the whole? The very question whether there can be such a demonstration is likely to remain in contention indefinitely. But until such enigmas are replaced by conclusions, history itself will not be brought to a conclusion, for history, which is human history, is lived in the mind as well as in the city. The attainment of admirable politics is a true marvel, but it does not exhaust human experience.

Suppose now, to resume, that there is no truth, certainly no truth accessible to us human beings, that is not incorporated, that is, that is not in principle manifest or brought to our mind by a thing or things that exist. (Let us set aside the truth of the moral law, which may or may not be known to us with certainty and without experience as a ground.) Suppose conversely that there is nothing that comes within our experience which is not the expression of a truth that has the force of a governing necessity by which it controls what we have experienced. What must we suppose next in order to give a ground to the thought that history has an end, apart from whether the end is at hand? We would have to suppose that history is one thing like every manifest thing; that it is not only or essentially the conglomerate of occurrences but that it is itself an occurrence; that although it encompasses things or parts, and so belongs to the class of wholes and not parts, it behaves like a part in the relevant respect, namely, that it is under the influence of a necessity that is a truth and that compels it toward its perfection; that it signals its partiality by its having to progress toward its perfection rather than eternally to be in possession of it; that there is not one order of explanation, truth, or being for Whole and another for Part, but one order for both, meaning thereby that "toward which" is intelligible when applied to a true whole just as it is when applied to a true part. Can "toward which" bear a meaning that is applicable to the Whole and also to a part? What can change mean with respect to the literal Whole, if not simply rearrangement of its parts? It could mean much more: the growing disclosure of the interior truth of that Whole, an act that is either the actualization of the truth of the Whole at the initiative of the Whole—the supposition of Revelation—or the growing presence of that truth in the minds of the only intelligent beings capable of knowing it, namely, man. Then the unequivocal end of the Whole, its perfection, would be the completion of its self-disclosure and the perfection of the intelligence of the intelligent being.

Perhaps we have gone far enough to venture a definition of the end of history and its conditions. The conglomeration of human experiences, itself having the character of a perfectible entity, has been propelled by a truth, which is the necessity of its being, to a consummation that expresses that necessary truth in its totality. The attainment of the absolute human "toward which" is the end of history.

In order for that consummation to be veritable, it must be known as a consummation to the being whose perfection is asserted in and through the fulfillment of truth in him, that is, the completion of his understanding. His understanding of what? First and foremost, of himself, which means of his human condition; but it is absolutely impossible to understand his human condition without understanding his position within the Whole of which the human is only a part. The exhaustion of knowledge of the human is impossible without exhaustion of knowledge of the Whole, for without the latter we do not know conclusively how important we are, or where we stand in relation to the Whole that conditions us, that is, in the end, our condition. The limit on our knowledge of the Whole is, in another guise, the limit of our knowledge of ourselves, as will be clear to anyone who wishes absolute knowledge of the fate of the soul. In brief, for human history to end, we must have conclusive knowledge of the Whole; but the only settled knowledge of the Whole that has ever come to the mind of man is the knowledge that what we face when we confront the Whole is alternatives, not resolutions. The human contemplation of the Whole is the history of the human contemplation of the Whole, a history without end. Revelation provides not a refutation but a confirmation of this thought, for what Revelation reveals is the inscrutable God. Neither reason nor revelation discloses to man fully and without residue of mystery whether or why the truth of the Whole is a power rather than an object, an efficient rather than a formal cause. Without such knowledge, every supposition that the end is accomplished is veiled in uncertainty because the ground of the end lies in doubt.

But why may it not be argued that man is indeed in possession of the absolute knowledge that is the condition for the completion of his history, for he possesses the knowledge that ultimate knowledge is knowledge of the intractability of the alternatives—say, for convenience, reason and revelation, or ancient and modern philosophy. Suppose in brief that to know the reason that lies in one's doubt is to replace the doubt with the decisive wisdom. Let us accept that argument and suppress the question whether nothing new can come hereafter to the mind of man. How can we move from the speculative absolutization of knowledge, which is the knowledge that absolute knowledge is knowledge of intractable alternatives, to the conclusion that constitutional democracy is the best regime—and let there be no doubt that the end-of-history thesis is a modern transform of the ancient best-regime thesis. Is there any need to say more than that the end-of-history thesis is essentially modern, that is, that it itself belongs to one branch of the intractable alternatives and that its universality or absoluteness is ipso facto destroyed? There is indeed a need to say considerably more, for its "essential modernity" might be its strongest defense rather than its fatal weakness, its demonstration of progress. If, as is obvious, it connects a disclosure of truth-within-the-Whole and the passing of time, it may be vindicated by its very insight, of which it is its own decisive evidence. By what then might it be overthrown, its premises being defended by their abstractness, if not by the falsification of its concrete conclusion, which is that a certain political order is the best regime?

Our task is twofold: first, to bring to light the premise of the end-of-history thesis that the truth within the Whole is a cosmic conspiracy for the good of man, a power that disciplines the enormous reticulation of causes and effects to cooperate in the achievement of the human state of rational freedom, thus apparently implying that everything that has hitherto represented itself as a free act of man was an unselfconscious movement on the part of a figure in a clockwork—there has been no freedom until "now." And second, that the regime of constitutional democracy, of rational freedom, is so incontrovertibly the best political order that the truth of the Whole, in causing it to materialize, becomes visible as a force for accomplishing the predestined consummation of man's life in society.

The first part of our task has been addressed in the foregoing sketch of a critique of the end-of-history thesis as a metaphysic of politics. It remains to attempt a critique of the thesis as a political philosophy of the best regime which identifies liberal constitutional democracy as that very regime. Fortunately, it will not prove necessary for the present critical purpose to describe the best political order, but necessary only to consider the arguments that trouble the identification of our own as that apex of social evolution.

Support for the special distinction of the liberal regime should not be drawn from recent events in the communist world, partly for the trivial reason that these events are sure to be followed by others that are unforeseeable, partly for the reason that the turn from socialism is a turn of *faute de mieux* with an economic rather than a moral meaning, and partly for the reason that the intelligible as such is not confirmed in its truth by the empirical but is simply made visible to us thereby; it is rather the empirical that is explained by the intelligible, for intelligible implies exactly an appeal beyond the empirical.

That the turn from socialism might move in retrograde or other vagrant directions is only too obvious. That the turn would not have occurred at all if socialism had generated prosperity is at least likely. That socialism is incapable of generating prosperity is no more than likely, but so far as it is credible it seems, but only briefly, to accord with the end-of-history thesis qua political theory. For history, rather than imposing capitalism as the scourge for which socialism was to be the remedy, appears to have ordained socialism as the failure destined to precede liberal capitalism in order to attest the truth and goodness of the latter. How curious, if the socialist regime whose only speculative support lay in the end-of-history thesis were to be consumed for the strengthening of that fickle theory, which now sets its seal not on the removal but on the robustness of the institutions that promote rivalries within society. The theory of history and the socialist regime that served each other as support and corroboration have parted ways because the theory has changed its mind about what is to be understood as progress.

The Soviet leader has admonished the West not to gloat. His advice is sound for a number of reasons, not all of which are merely political and some of which come to view when we look, for this invidious purpose, at our own innermost composition.

We begin with the thousand-times rehearsed birth of modern liberalism out of the philosophy of the sixteenth and seventeenth centuries, with additional impulses contributed in the eighteenth century. Unable any longer to share in the prevailing belief that the Whole is informed by a truth that exerts itself on our behalf in exchange for man's abasing himself before it, the bold spirits began a revision of the inner springs of the world. In fact, they reinvented nature, with famous effects on human life through technology and political science. The greatest power in the universe proved to be not man's master but his slave. To know this was the beginning of wisdom. But the emancipation, the empowerment, and the enlightenment came at a singular price: man had to give himself over to nature as completely as, theretofore, he had been required to give himself over to his erstwhile master. That this was a new bondage came eventually to be seen, first when it became clear that man supine in nature was a frightened wretch, and later when the plenitude of accommodation to nature, could man be capable of it, was interpreted as the loss of freedom and therewith morality on the part of an automaton. Modern liberalism, whose claim to be the best regime we are now testing, was born out of the philosophic struggle to order man's relation to nature in such a way as to avoid any confrontation with it as our master while extracting every service from it as our servant. It would be a fatal mistake to consider those services to be limited to technology. As important are the enormous practical benefits conferred through the cunning of nature, by whose agency our freedom is sustained and our prosperity enhanced as by an invisible hand. Mastery of nature is as profoundly dependent on obedience to it as was ever the case between man and his master in the Age of Faith; only in those days the sovereign laid down a moral law while at present the imperial order is that of cause and effect.

In the light of its genesis, how may we describe our liberal regime with a view to judging its eligibility to be known as best of all and apex of history? It is the regime of freedom and reason. It is the regime of reason because it acknowledges no power superior to that which joins cause to its natural and naturally knowable effect. Knowledge is the knowledge of that conjunction. Wisdom is the prudence that exploits that knowledge. Freedom is the actualization of wisdom in private and public practice. Modern liberal society is framed in freedom, and thus in reason.

How has liberal life in fact unfolded? It would be impossible to answer that question without taking note that the liberal societies have existed like cells with a penetrable wall. Human communities have long proved to be permeable by alien influence, but the liberal societies are unique in incorporating their permeability in their definition. They cannot do otherwise while remaining faithful to their commitment to freedom. If there is a tension between liberal dedication to freedom and liberal openness to whatever threatens it, the perfect resolution of that tension has yet to be found. Fortunately, perfect resolutions are not necessary in practice, but they are indispensable to a theoretical showing that the object is an epitome of reason, where contradiction is intolerable.

The freedom that is the pride of liberal constitutionalism is well understood as both limited and confirmed through autonomous acts that are, as autonomous, testimonies to freedom. These free acts of self-restraint take place on the plane of government and law by the mediation of representatives, but they cannot take place on that plane only. For the true perfection of the freedom of the liberal society, its individual members should be disposed to will what is worthy to be willed as that is made known to them by reason itself. In borrowing the language of Hegel in order to round out the notions of Rousseau, we engage in an exaggeration that helps to reconnect freedom and reason: if there is something fatuous about demanding that each member of the liberal society will the rationally attested willworthy, in what more moderate sense is the demand met that freedom and reason pervade the ultimate community? The petty reason of individuals who participate in affairs and the myopic volition that collaborates with their shrewdness must surely be overridden by a Reason and a Will that dignify the best political order by raising it to levels of which its denizens are unaware. Granting the power of the benign *logos* with its invisible hand, it follows that the true reason and freedom that endow the lives of the beneficiaries of liberal life are as remote from the knowledge of those human beings as if the latter were drones toiling in a commune of bees. Where reason lit the active mind of every citizen and disclosed to him the truth that ennobles him in defining his freedom and guiding his will, the regime that truly perfects history would be in place. Is there no education, no concert of art, religion, and ordinary schooling, that could equip the members of liberal society to recognize their own dignity? The higher and lower culture of the West would by itself be enough to suggest a discouraging answer. The actualities of freedom in liberal society have not accorded with the idealities of reason contemplated by the end-of-history thesis. Too many influences that the thesis can dismiss as merely adventitious or marginal, historical in the humble sense, such as the migrations of peoples, the developments of technology, the discovery and dissemination of substances that console and accelerate demoralization, all these and more—irresistible by liberal society, partly because it is in principle permeable by everything from without and partly because it understands its freedoms in a way that makes it vulnerable to everything within—all seem to mock the allegation that we are at the peak to which man is predestined by cosmic truth.

We might be in danger of imposing an unrealistic and unnecessary condition on the end-of-history thesis, which after all does not itself use the language of "best regime." Why should not the ultimate political society be the best possible rather than the best simply? Because attributing the power of governing history to a force that *must* stop short of procuring the best is to conjure a contraption whose oddities accuse it of makeshift. Truth moves through the world with a benign purpose using nature as its instrument. Then it encounters nature in the form of human nature, and the very truth itself finds its beneficence halted at the point of second-best for humanity. How might one verify this affirmation of an obdurate nature in revolt? When we encounter the inborn contumacy of man in Scripture, it appears as the mysterious product of a creator whose truth is not the cosmic principle that the world must rise to its peak in human freedom and reason but rather that the world will end in blessings for those who live in obedience and faith. Understandably abjuring the support of revelation, and barred by its rationalism from invoking mysteries it cannot dispel, the end-of-history thesis is exposed to the suspicion that it stealthily divides nature against itself and then conveniently assigns contrary roles to the mutilated parts in order to accommodate overwhelming ignorance to the absolute knowledge that rules over it. So doing, the thesis can only lose its authority to proclaim the millennium.

What critique of western civilization would contribute to a judgment on the apotheosis of the liberal state? What weight should be given to the growth in liberal societies of masses of residents, citizens in only the most technical sense, for whom the common standards of civil life have lost their meaning: for whom imprisonment is no disgrace, matrimony no prerequisite to procreation, usefulness no qualification for support; for whom positions of trust and power are passports to plunder and oppression, as they were in the most benighted of times; of hypocrites, fanatics, and swindlers in what remains of religion, just as in all the ages since the first false prophet was exposed? What are we to make of the inner harmony of a society in which the overwhelmingly prevalent religion teaches a love so high as to take precedence of faith itself, while the supreme rule of private and public affairs is the friction of selfish interests? Are these influences indispensable mutual antidotes or are they contradictions that reveal weakness in the framework? Are the arts controlled by mediocrities in whom the insufficiency of genius is compensated by twitchings of solipsism accompanied by stale political ruminations, whinings of neglect, mumblings against philistinism, and perhaps outpourings of tedious smut? In a spasm of fair-mindedness we might wonder whether the arts are a stronghold of resistance against the bourgeoisification of everything, a protest against the rule of greed in affairs and banality in leisure, and an expression of the will to be more than the epigoni of dead masters. Let us rather persevere in comfortable self-mortification in the company of Nietzsche, who has done much of the work for us, believing himself to have confounded Hegel. But Nietzsche has not disposed of the issue of the Ultimate Regime by drawing in gray the likeness of the Ultimate Man. Why not find repose in the analgesia of the sheep who may safely graze, and why shake little fists against the eternal return that spares us the absolute sunset? The evocation of the will to power rings indeed with the dignity of man, but it smacks also of theater, of *Menschenmorgendammerung*, part of a transparent myth, *jeu d'esprit* of a hyperthermic spirit. Do Nietzsche's and our own disparagements of liberal life, or discovery of what is problematic within it, suffice to discredit the theory of history which brings everything important to a culmination in us? Not any more than the events in eastern Europe suffice to confirm it. In plain language, we do not know whether our discontent with our civilization has the force of the jeer that sends the actor from the stage or is the admission of flaws that become insignificant when measured by the blessings they accompany. Nor do we know whether the collapsed regimes of the East and any others of their kind which may admit their bankruptcy will become examples of reason and freedom or of some squalid compromise between repression and grumbling.

Whichever way we turn, we find the critique of the end-of-history thesis troubled by the difficulty of determining whether the decisive test of it is empirical or theoretical. If merely empirical, then history must have the unpretentious meaning it has always had and the oceanic character it has been thought to have, exhibiting long ground swells like the many-centuried movement toward democracy proclaimed by Tocqueville, the tidal accessions and recessions in the lives of dynasties and nations, and the transient undulations that agitate the decades. It is true that something better than confusion may grow from these perplexities, as becomes clear to us when we consider that the difficulties of the critic of the thesis shed a light on the thesis itself, for the difficulties of the critic are identically the same as those of the proponent: the difficulty of corroborating a hypothesis belongs precisely and in the same degree to the propounder of it and to its critic, for its propounder is its first and most urgent critic. But all of this has as its premise that the decisive test of the end-of-history thesis is empirical. What if the test is speculative?

With some regret, we are pushed to the level of metaphilosophy, of some reflection on the history of speculations. The philosophy of history out of which the end-of-history thesis has grown could be depreciated without malice as an episode of nineteenth-century reaction to political and intellectual currents of the day. This by itself would not deprive that philosophy of history of its right to claim that the circumstances that prepared it were exactly those preclimactic conditions that were foreordained to usher in the climax. But there has been philosophy in the meantime which has changed the terms of speculation about history to such an extent that the transitions of states from socialist to liberal would have anything but the character of a testimony to some great cosmic intervention, and assuredly would not mark an ascent to the peak of social possibility for mankind. Were Heidegger to be believed, the liberal democratic constitutionalism of the West and the socialist communitarianism of the East do not differ sufficiently to make any transitions between them in either direction important enough to excite a deep thinker. And this not because they do undeniably have a common genealogy in the tradition of thought that runs from Hobbes, Locke, Spinoza, and Hume to Adam Smith on one side but to Rousseau, Kant, and Hegel on the other. Rather, Heidegger's philosophizing comes to a point in some reflections on technology and the dehumanizing of man's relation to the natural ground of his existence. It is safe to assume that Heidegger is not covertly repeating the Marxist thesis that the conditions of production govern everything human. Without going further into his larger purposes, we cannot doubt that he had receded so far from merely empirical or political considerations and advanced so far into abstraction from them—let us say for the present purpose emancipated himself from them—as to illustrate for us the problem that would be faced by an end-of-history theorist who wished to transcend the plane of merely phenomenal history. Heidegger's contemplations enabled him or perhaps compelled him to dismiss as irrelevant the difference between the daily misery of entire peoples and their sufficient satisfaction. That he looked for light as if there were no truth in the visible is of interest to us now only because it helps us to think about the relation between the status of the speculative in a context that is unavoidably political and empirical. How should we choose between the ascent into the heights and subsequent return with the ultimate political order as performed by Hegel on the one hand and by Heidegger on the other, to say nothing of Plato? There is no way to know them by their works, for they have none except their very own intellectual selves.

After having asked ourselves what an end of history might be, we have had to ask how human beings could recognize one—whether through living it or through being persuaded by the force of the argument that announces it. If the former, then we are to count our blessings, which are in truth very many but also mixed enough to make us pause. If the latter, then the philosophy of history must be unique and preeminent in the relevant respects. Let us see if the case can be made for its uniqueness and preeminence.

The end-of-history thesis finds the materialization of the truth of the Whole in the final reality of reason and freedom in a political order. Reason rules in that the will of all is directed to purposes that are free from contradictions or from contradictions that are not themselves fruitful, according to a logic that is fertilized by contradiction rather than offended by it. In some sense, reason rules. But on this showing, end-of-history philosophy is not purely unique. Plato too demonstrates that reason rules by right. To speak briefly, Hegel argues that reason must rule, must rule through institutions of popular freedom, must rule because of the power of flawless and therefore irresistible cosmic reason that enlists itself as the cause of human good and reveals itself as well in politics as in philosophy. Plato argues that if reason ruled in men's affairs, in political life, it would rule through the monarchy of philosophy, but that far from ruling inevitably, it can scarcely ever rule, for the active hegemony of reason, as distinguished from its title to rule, is hindered by the irremovable presence of reason's antithesis in the construction of the Whole. Philosophy of history cannot claim to be unique in the decisive respect, which is an affirmation of reason's title to rule. In every other particular, philosophy of history, and therewith the end-of-history thesis, is no more than one among a number of conceptions about reason, the standing of reason in the universe and the bearing of it on human life. But the end-of-history thesis has no special authority if it does not have preeminent standing, for its claim is to be climactic and absolute. To this date it remains an unconfirmed and probably unconfirmable speculation.

We return to the political realities of the late twentieth century, which gave new life and unaccustomed plausibility to the end-of-history thesis through the collapse, as was said before, of the socialist regimes descended from the philosophic source of that thesis. Before we pronounce the Western democracies to be the true inheritors of the earth, we should be aware of certain facts about their character which would bear on their eligibility for the role. Those facts emerge when we look within and ask ourselves what we truly are, or what is found by one who looks for Western constitutional liberalism. Is it free-enterprise economy? Freely elected responsible government? Equality before the law? The organization of social existence under the natural right to life, liberty, and the pursuit of happiness? It is all of these and more of the same kind. But these conditions have prevailed, say, to take an example, in the United States for two centuries, a period during which the lives of Americans have undergone great changes that have been paralleled in the other Western liberal countries. The American who fought and did not fight in the Civil War is hardly recognizable as the ancestor of the one who, a hundred years later, went either to Vietnam or to Canada. Or to take another example, the Oxford of 1850 must seem like an object of paleontology to an undergraduate of our time. In both cases, one sign of the encompassing change is the altered presence of religion in the two eras. The documents of the Civil War and the impossibility of imagining John Henry Newman in present-day Oxford help us to see this change, but they do not explain it to us. Can it be attributed to the progress of reason through the world, somehow if not exactly as philosophy of history declares? The Western liberal societies have certainly not become godless, but they have just as certainly become secular. Is there not enough of the Enlightenment in our composition, in a moderate mode, to establish a common ground with the communist scheme of dogmatic atheism which grew out of participation in the same Enlightenment? Every consideration of common sense and decency would have to be subverted in order to accommodate these facts to the conclusion that the one system is the moral equivalent of the other. One need not adopt that wrong-minded view in order to perceive the latent or partial pacifism, the automatic anti-imperialism, the welfare elements of social democracy, the gender and family reformations inspired vaguely by the revolt against bourgeois institutions, all these and more that are part of our existence for better and worse and that have modern roots in the ideology of class war. Enough of Marxism is present in our constitutional regimes, through either shared ancestry or hybridization, so that the termination of history in us would have an element in it of perpetuation of what we are to bury.

And what are we to make of the inclusion within the end-of-history thesis of the continued presence of warfare among men in the posthistoric period? Whatever else it signifies, it inevitably draws attention to the fact that the envisioned consummation of the human experience would be an affair of a minority of the human kind. The rejection of this prospect as "elitist" would be as inane as it is inevitable, but there is a weighty reason for giving it some thought. By what principle of selection would the reason of the universe elect these rather than those communities for promotion to the ultimate state? And for that matter, what causes it to be true that the end for man is not also the end for most men? The end-of-history thesis serves us well by reminding us of this question in all of its antiquity, a question answered in one way and on a very different plane in the theology of a chosen people and in another way in the theology of grace and predestination. Those answers are not available to the Enlightenment theory of the end of history, which seems to be pushed toward conceding that reason strikes the earth like lightning—illuminating and energizing but entirely by chance, unless recourse be had to an infinite regression of causes which explains everything in principle by mechanizing the whole. Can the freedom of the Ultimate State of man be understood as an irony of the absolute necessity that we slaves to that necessity call the ground of our freedom? If the saying that we cannot escape history means that we cannot escape necessity, the mind finds itself in doubt. It would seem that the end-of-history thesis has to share the weight of this difficulty, or at least to consider whether humanity's being forced into freedom poses a problem that is more than a quibble based on play of words. Resolved in a certain way, this question would point toward the answer to another question, namely, What might God be? God might be that thrusting power in the universe which expresses itself in the irresistible progress of man toward and into his ultimate-highest condition. God so understood would have the ineffably philanthropic disposition to bring humanity to fulfillment not in spite of man's errant nature but precisely through and because of it. That is to say, the providence of the scriptural God would be replaced by the cunning of nature. That the end-of-history thesis is an implicit theology is neither news nor bad news, and that it might be, from the scriptural point of view, a blasphemy that replaces God with a nature that no longer acts as God's instrument is a thought that must be faced. My purpose is not to blame the end-of-history thesis for being a theology or for being a blasphemous one, if such it were, but only to suggest the heavy burden of clarification which it bears in making good its claim to draw its very attractive conclusions from the current state of world events.

It must be said that the politics, both domestic and international, of the late twentieth century quite properly encourage us to think in terms of the end of history. At a time when the culture of the West gives cause for concern and the centers of its civilization are in disorder, thinkers could be excused for wondering what lies ahead, and especially whether liberal society has resources within itself to remedy what is in disrepair. If it has, then we *might* be the end of history. If it has not, we cannot possibly be the end of history in any but the most melancholy sense. If the present constitutional regime is to look within for the means of cleansing itself, it must look first of all into the Constitution that defines it, in order to discover those means. In plain language, can the Constitution be read in ways that are conducive to confronting the influences that threaten liberal life? It goes without saying that there is so much disagreement about what is threatening liberal life that that issue must be faced before any other can be reached. Is it criminality and the militant decay of traditional standards or is it brutal contempt for rights and prejudiced adherence to traditional standards? There is no assurance that all such problems will be disposed of in ways conducive to the perpetuation of the regime. This is not to cast into doubt the goodness of the liberal society but rather to suggest that its difficulties are considerable enough so that its friends can scarcely avoid thinking about what might follow it if it proved incapable of curing itself by means that lie within itself. What would it turn into? What is available for it to turn into?

In the middle of the seventeenth century, England turned itself briefly from a monarchy into a parliamentary republic, as a preparation for the conversion of its monarchy into a constitutional regime. In the eighteenth century, France transformed itself under the influence of ideas that were actively critical of monarchy. Our own founding was accomplished in the same atmosphere of hostility to monarchy, the affirmative side of which was the assertion of the natural rights of all human beings equally. It is not necessary to recur to the oscillations of Greek cities between democracy and monarchy, the Roman conversions to and from republican forms, and the European drifts into and out of the feudal institutions, in order to be reminded that history is the history of constitutional forms, which are the expressions of the urgencies and thoughts of the times. What are the urgencies and thoughts of our time? The convulsion of eastern Europe, which gives rise to the immediate version of the end-of-history thesis, lets us know that in the West our problem is not the repression of individual liberty, for we embody the social arrangements being adopted in the places where the failures are traced to the reality of that repression. Eastern Europe had us to contemplate as a model. What do we have that could serve us in the same way? Although thinkers have spoken about the decline of the West and particularly of the United States, to what place or idea have they drawn attention as an inspiration for reform? National socialism proposed itself for the role and was dismissed in loathing and blood. International socialism has dismissed itself. Perhaps we must look beyond any empirical paradigms, which means looking into the realm of pure speculation on the best regime, abstracting from the questionable argument that we are it. The most fully elaborated philosophy of our time, on behalf of which one might claim that it could form the basis of a new political dispensation, is Heidegger's temporalized metaphysics. To what political form does it attach itself if not to that of the Third Reich? To the regime of the ongoing self-disclosure of *physis*, under the auspices of "another god"? The seer has not yet appeared who could look into that formula and describe, to say nothing of recommend, what it betokens politically. Have we strengthened the end-of-history thesis by arguing that nothing reveals itself to us as replacement for our regime? We have, unless we can satisfy ourselves that it is merely our blindness or complacency that obscures a future without us. Otherwise, we must accept the great truth that we are the future because the truth is us. We denizens of the liberal West are in the curious position of cherishing our institutions, of not being able to see beyond them to anything more true or beneficent, of resigning ourselves to an uncomfortable life within them, and of being loath to believe that the progress that has brought us our rich estate can do anything but march on forever.

Can we believe that we are the children of progress, that part of our endowment from progress is the conviction that ethnocentrism and anthropocentrism, like geocentrism, are the mistakes of people who cannot distinguish a mirror from a telescope, and believe at the same time that the whole progress of progress can come to a halt anywhere, even in the political society that enshrines government of, by, and for the people under the self-evident truth that all men are created equal and are endowed by nature with the right to life, liberty, and the pursuit of happiness? Perhaps it is impossible for us to believe with perfect faith both in progress and in ourselves. As theorists we might incline to believe in progress, as citizens to believe in the self-evident truths that support our liberal constitutional regime in freedom and official rationalism. The end-of-history thesis can claim to have the power to reconcile the theoretical and the civic understandings if it understood itself to maintain that there is indeed a prospect of indefinite progress in the sciences other than political, a progress that will be fostered by, or to the extent of, the perpetuation of the free society beyond which there is no civil progress. If there is an objection to this reconciliation of progress and completion, it might lie in the demonstrated fact that repressive and even wicked regimes are not as such incapacitated for high technology, which they are more likely to use for violent purposes than are the liberal countries as such. Must this depressing empirical truth be included in the truth of the whole as an ingredient of it which recalls as it accuses the grand optimism of the end-of-history thesis?

There remains one resource that might save both the end-of-history thesis and the constitutional regimes of freedom and reason. The end-of-history thesis proclaims the superiority of liberal political life, its status as end, certainly in speech, less certainly in deed. An age-old question arises: is the goodness of the regime impeached if durability is missing among its excellences? If not, then why did Socrates, who knew about the best regime, characterize conflict as the doing of the good city in its typical act? (See *Timaeus.*) We follow Socrates in this, and suggest that the liberal countries adopt the end-of-history thesis as their ruling theoretical dogma alongside their belief in their self-evident truths, never mind any of the apparent contradictions suggested earlier. But it should be understood that the end-of-history thesis is to be made an article of patriotic faith when put in the following hypothetical formulation: liberal constitutional society has the responsibility of proving the truth of the end-of-history thesis; and that thesis would be falsified if empirical history disclosed an opening rupture between the goodness of free society in speech and its goodness in deed, which is its durability. It therefore behooves us to vindicate the goodness of the truth of the whole by securing the prosperity of the political society in which that truth is manifest. If this be thought to imply that the end-of-history thesis can be made useful even if it cannot be made demonstrable, and if it be thought further that this suggestion seems like an Erastian conversion of old theology to new purposes, the propounder of it might take refuge in a privilege sacred to liberal constitutionalism and decline to incriminate himself.

6 Nietzsche and Spengler on Progress and Decline

WERNER J. DANNHAUSER

I

Nostalgia ain't what it used to be, say the wags, but they are wrong. It abounds all around us, leading one to think that it abides *herrlich wie am zweiten Tag,* "splendid as on the second day," to misquote Goethe's *Faust.*[1] One imagines that the first day of Creation soon became the first of the good old days, days that will never come again. Even cynics and atheists, who grumble that the good old days were never here in the first place, have been known to yearn for the past. The rest of humanity, pondering the biblical depiction of the beginnings as good or very good or blessed, reacts predictably to a present that is bad or very bad or accursed. Most of us yearn for a vanished golden age; we have nostalgia in our bones.

One of the ways leading thinkers differ from most of us is in refusing to glorify the past at the expense of the present; they are above nostalgia. For example, Thucydides states that one can find "nothing on a great scale, either in war or in other matters" in "remote antiquity."[2] Aristotle also has his doubts about the beginnings, remarking that "the laws of ancient times were overly simple and barbaric" and that "whatever . . . ancient ordinances still remain are altogether foolish."[3] Skepticism about the worth of origins can be said to increase in modernity; suffice it to point to the description of the state of nature in Hobbes and the influence of that description on Locke, Rousseau, and subsequent philosophers.

Nevertheless, nostalgia remains what it used to be. It predominates as the nonphilosophical or subphilosophical response to the past and the passing of time. It is the unthinking man's way of coming to terms with history. Conversely, any thinker worth his salt believes in the possibility and actuality of some sort of progress, of change for the better. That belief brings us to our common inquiry.

It does not help much to know that all serious thinking affirms belief in some sort of change for the better. *What* sort occurs? Change for the better can be limited or unlimited, for example. Aristotle comes to mind again, as a believer in limited progress. Thus, he testifies to the progress of Athenian tragedy, but only upto the attainment of its nature, its limits,[4] after which comes either a plateau of greatness or decline, a change for the worse. The idea of progress necessarily involves its contrary, the idea of decline. Aristotle's sober view should be contrasted with the onward-and-upward view of the arts, with its faith in novelty.

One must also distinguish between partial and total progress. One can think of a total improvement in the quality of life, in which case one could follow Claire Huxtable of the Bill Cosby Show and talk about "the bad old days," or one can think of a progress in some areas which involves or entails decline in others. The arts may flourish while manners and morals degenerate. A country as a whole may decay as daily life becomes more comfortable and charming. Mediocrity may weaken a nation even as a genius towers above a dreary scene.

The possible coexistence of progress and decline raises further questions. Could decline be just a glitch in the world's gradual unfurling of goodness? One can argue that prophecies of doom reached their height before the advent of Hitler. Many saw fascism in the future but few foretold the fall of the Third Reich after a "mere" twelve years. One might thus hope that decline is reversible and progress the more fundamental phenomenon. One can also argue, however, that the world is going to hell even though a few points of light adorn the scene.

By raising such questions, we attest to the advisability of consulting such major thinkers as Spengler and Nietzsche, who have grappled with them. A different problem also justifies this procedure. Any given moment in history may be part of a decline or an ascent. Given the general fashionability of prophets of doom, how can we know whether they are catering to nostalgia or telling it like it is? In other words, one must distinguish between warranted and unwarranted nostalgia, between the nostalgia of someone living during the decline of the Roman Empire who experiences it as such, and the nostalgia of someone who pines for by-gone days mainly because he loves to pine. We need the help of Nietzsche and Spengler, skilled at providing criteria for recognizing progress and decline. It is reasonable to violate chronology and begin with Spengler, who can serve to introduce Nietzsche.

II

Few people today read Oswald Spengler (1880–1936), at least not in the United States. No book of his can be found in paperback, though *The Decline of the West* remains in print in two bulky hardback volumes.[5] Americans like gloomy books about the crisis of our time, but such volumes can make do without Spengler, whose name cannot be found in either Paul Kennedy's *Rise and Fall of the Great Powers* or Allan Bloom's *Closing of the American Mind.* Spengler has suffered the fate of others who impinge on the public consciousness without really informing it: he has become an adjective enabling us to sound more precise than we are. "Spenglerian" means something like "gloomy and apocalyptic" or "German and bombastic," as when one mocks Henry Kissinger's views. Nobody finds it necessary to read Spengler to talk in Spenglerian terms. He can be encapsulated in a formula: "The West has seen better days, and if you think things are bad now, you ain't seen nothing yet."

Spengler did not always suffer from such neglect. In the early days of the Weimar Republic he was all the rage, and he commanded the more or less respectful attention of such people as Max Weber, Thomas Mann, and the young Heidegger. He was translated into English and gathered his share of admirers in this country. In the 1930s, to be sure, he fell into disfavor as he came under suspicion of being a Nazi, though he wasn't. Spengler did advocate a kind of national socialism, but he thought of the iron rule of a Prussian aristocracy imbued with a love of the common good. He had contempt for Hitler and the Nazis, who courted him briefly but soon felt the same way about him. Spengler was too intelligent and decent to fall under the sway of Hitler, and he could not easily become a mentor of the Third Reich because no hatred of Jews ever consumed him. A single but representative sentence from *The Decline of the West* proves the point: "The Jews are a peculiar phenomenon in world history only because we insist on treating them as such" (2:205). That utterance has a benign ring to it when one considers the whole history of pronouncements by Germans about Jews.

Nevertheless, I have neither the wish nor the power to exonerate Spengler from all responsibility for the fatal development of German history in this century. His frequent references to the profundity of blood and the superficiality of reason, occasionally rhapsodic predictions of a coming Caesarism, and above all his distinction between the vitality of culture and the decadence of civilization, all these combined to render him a pernicious influence. Indeed, the culture-civilization distinction alone seduced a number of Germans—especially young Germans, and more especially the "best and brightest" among them—to antisocial casts of thought. The feeling spread among them that the West was stultified beyond redemption and that Germany was not truly part of the West, which stood for mechanical petrification, the emptiness of technology, the sterility of denuded rationalism. By contrast Germany was music, art, blood, and soil; Germany owned a special destiny; Germany was promises.

Spengler may have deserved the eclipse of his renown in the 1930s, but he survived it. At the end of World War II, the victors suffered from a failure of nerve. Triumph seemed bereft of meaning because everything seemed bereft of meaning. Spengler was taken seriously again. Thus, when I began my studies at the University of Chicago's Committee on Social Thought in the 1950s, he was widely studied. He was never "up there" with Plato and Aristotle as an author for whom one was thought responsible, but he gave the likes of Mill and Burckhardt a run for their money. That is no longer the case.

I doubt that Spengler's latest fall from grace has much to do with the discovery of his true stature or lack of it. To some extent, it is simply that he has been popularized, vulgarized, trivialized so much that one thought one could dispense with his enormous masterpiece, so hard to read even though Spengler often wrote with grace and beauty. To some extent he was simply displaced by Arnold

Toynbee, more congenial to the English-speaking world because he comes across as both more empirical and more spiritual, though one could argue—and I would argue—that Spengler is superior to Toynbee.

Will there be a third wave of enthusiasm for Spengler? His own views argue against it. After all, he wrote a serious book that argues that the time for serious books has come and gone. The hour is too late, the year 2000 being the time either for a vigorous Caesarism or for utter chaos and dissipation.

But of course Spengler may have been wrong. We honor him by frequent references to the "decline of the West," but we preserve our critical distance from him, putting a question mark after the title of his book, whereas Spengler himself would surely have preferred an exclamation point. The mean between paying homage to Spengler and dismissing him turns out to be revisiting him, which is what I am doing. I shall indulge myself as I reminisce a bit about my first visit to Spengler, more than forty years ago. (More than my private nostalgia is at work here, for my memories will help provide a better sense of Spengler's work.) *The Decline of the West* was the second book about which I wrote a whole paper as an undergraduate, the first being Thorstein Veblen's *Theory of the Leisure Class.* Even at twenty, I had a taste for quirky books.

I came across Spengler in a seminar at the New School for Social Research, "The Crisis of Our Time" taught by Eduard Heimann. Other readings included Ortega y Gasset, Paul Tillich, and Georges Sorel. I chose to work on Spengler because he stood for history, my friends and I being convinced that history was the key to practically everything: to understand anything was to understand its origins. In my youth, H. G. Wells and Henrik Willem Van Loon were required extracurricular reading. Yet that kind of reading left me dissatisfied. The books either painted with too broad a brush, such as Wells's *Outline of History,* which I had trouble finishing, or they were too detailed, such as Albert Matthiez's history of the French Revolution, which I could not penetrate. Unbeknownst to myself I was seeking a philosophy of history full of specifics. I was looking for Hegel and found Spengler.

The Decline of the West bowled me over. The very first sentence of Volume I enthralled me with its boldness: "In this book is attempted for the first time the venture of predetermining history" (1:3). The second volume begins just as strikingly: "Regard the flowers at eventide as one after the other, they close in the setting sun" (2:3). These sentences point to two poles of Spengler's thought I found equally attractive. On the one hand, Spengler promised to be scientific, so that not only could one comprehend the past with certitude; one could predict the future without guesswork. On the other hand, Spengler rivaled poets with his evocation of moods and his rich metaphors. Some of his depictions stamped themselves on my mind indelibly, as when he called Berlin an "autumnal city" (1:79).

Most dazzling of all to me was the fact that the first volume came with three magnificent charts plotting what Spengler called "contemporary" cultural, spiritual, and political epochs, as each culture—called a growth—made its way from the springtime of its birth to its death as a civilization. These charts permitted one to enter a magical world in which the *Niebelungenlied,* the *Iliad,* and the Gospels were contemporary events in the lives of different cultures, even as Mohammed was the spiritual twin of Oliver Cromwell. Pythagoras was the Greek Descartes; Locke was the Faustian Socrates; Plato "equaled" Goethe; Kant "equaled" Aristotle—and so it went.

As an undergraduate, I was, of course, interested above all in my own time and place. Reading Spengler, I did not care much about his meditations on, say, the fate of the Chinese; I wanted illumination about the winter of our Western, or Faustian, discontent. Poring over the charts, I found a description of Western decline which became for me the most memorable sentence of the book. In a culture's winter, according to Spengler, "Life itself becomes problematical" (II, App. Table 1).

III

Returning to Spengler after many years, I feel grateful to him. If I now find him less profound than I remember him, it is largely because since then I have studied greater thinkers with whom Spengler helped put me in touch. He is not famous for his modesty, but in his 1922 preface to *The Decline of the West* he names two men to whom he claims to owe "practically everything," Goethe and Nietzsche. He owes his "method" to Goethe. Spengler always had the courage of his eccentricity, and was one of the very few who thought of Goethe as an even greater scientist than poet. He preferred Goethe's emphasis on the organic to Newton's mechanistic physics, and he attempted to apply Goethe's morphology of plants to cultures.[6] He did so with a scary literalness: to Spengler cultures have a kind of vegetable vitality; their groping toward sunlight means more than any possible awareness of that groping; Spengler litters his book with such adjectives as "unwitting," "unintentional," and "unconscious."

Spengler asserts that he took his "outlook" and his questioning faculty from Nietzsche. Traces of Nietzsche's influence abound in *The Decline of the West,* from its deprecation of democracy to its praise of the Dionysian, from its distinction between master and slave moralities to its radicalization of perspectivism. If one finds Spengler wanting, one is likely to be judging him by standards gleaned from writers he eloquently presented as proper standards.

Revisiting Spengler, I noticed something else in the preface that helps us understand him. He expresses gratitude to Goethe and Nietzsche but he fails to mention Hegel, in some ways Spengler's natural predecessor. The book's references to Hegel tend to dismiss him. This neglect of Hegel tempts one to think that he is Spengler's silent enemy. For Hegel, history manifests the cunning of reason; for Spengler, cultures have destinies, but they manifest neither rational origins nor ends. Spengler can be said to have written a hymn to the cunning of *un*reason. For Hegel, history is progressive despite its dialectical twists, culminating at the zenith of the post-Napoleonic world and of the mind to comprehend it, Hegel's own. Hegel's narrative of the triumphant march of reason adorns the Whig interpretation of history with metaphysical splendor.

By contrast, Spengler finds no progress in world history. He considers Hegel an optimist and he characterizes optimism as cowardice.[7] What is more, Spengler finds no continuities in history. Hegel sticks to the traditional division of history into ancient, medieval, and modern. Thus, according to Spengler, he fudges three completely different cultures and civilizations: the classical world of Greece and Rome; the Magian or Arabian culture, which includes

Judaism, early Christianity, and Islam; and our own Faustian culture, whose reign began around the year 1000 and which will end right about now.

Spengler's divergence from Hegel illustrates the oddness of his scheme and points to various facets of his thought we must neglect. Suffice it to say that for Spengler we moderns are not the spiritual heirs of either Athens or Jerusalem. Our Christianity has nothing essential in common with its Magian pseudo-origins, ours being the faith of infinite striving. Similarly our classicism is doomed to a profound misunderstanding of the Greeks. No culture can understand another culture; each is a lonely growth without real antecedents in a previous culture or genuine influence on later ones.

Spengler's book teems with oddities for which he has had to pay a heavy price. For example, there can be no Renaissance for Spengler, no rebirth of the classical spirit in a Faustian setting. How then *does* Spengler explain what others call the Renaissance? He tries to explain it away, first by confining it to Florence and then by dismissing it as a countermovement to counterpoint, a Gothic dream or nightmare of the classic.[8] To one who knows something about a topic, Spengler can be most unpersuasive. Thus a student of the *Theologico-Political Treatise,* impressed or oppressed by Spinoza's rationalism, will not be greatly helped by Spengler's characterization of Spinoza as a misfit, a Magian "fossil"—a kind of Kabbalist in drag (2:228, 241, 321). Nor is it all that illuminating to be told that during the Crusades the Jews were persecuted because they were in "the wrong phase" (2:318–21). Spengler can remind one of Nietzsche's view that a will to a system makes one seem more stupid than one is. To learn from Spengler today, one must discard the excesses that accompany his rigid scheme of classification. Moreover, one must overlook his combination of relativism and historicism, which he calls his Faustian skepticism and which continually strains one's credulity. Here I shall only indicate its contours.

To begin with, one is struck by Spengler's habit of pluralizing key words. There is for him no such thing as philosophy, only philosophies; no truth, only truths; no science or art, only sciences or arts; there are even botanies and chemistries. What is more, he denies the existence of any way to establish the superiority of one philosophy, or any systematized thought, over another.

As a radical relativist, Spengler becomes fair game for the standard refutation of relativism. If one says everything is relative, one can be accused of incoherence: if everything is relative, what one asserts is also relative, in which case not everything may be relative. I do not exercise that option now, it being more useful to point to some of the ways Spengler grapples with the problem of self-contradiction, though such grappling is not his strong point.

At times, he employs the strategy of humility, suggesting that while no scheme of the kind he articulates can be simply true, his scheme is the best one available. At other times he seems to employ an instinct strategy: reason leads to relativism, but Spengler relies on intuiting reality. He reaches the truth by virtue of his strong feelings. At still other times, Spengler presents himself as somebody who merely develops a morphology of culture which has little substantive content; there may be absolute truths but they are formalistic, methodological, and more or less trivial.

More often than not, Spengler posits an absolute moment when the absolute truth first becomes available; notwithstanding Spengler's disdain for Hegel, we may fairly call this his Hegelian strategy. Oswald Spengler, strategically situated in history, becomes the first thinker able to pronounce the final truth. Faustian culture is the first culture to have a historical sense, and Spengler is the first thinker in whom that sense is fully conscious of itself. This means that Faustian culture is the absolute culture—a situation of momentous consequences to which we shall return.

Right now, I concern myself with bracketing certain aspects of Spengler's book. I omit from consideration the considerable portions of the work which have been conclusively refuted, usually by critics who lack Spengler's lavish gifts. Moreover, I pass over the vast stretches of *The Decline of the West* which are not about the decline of the West. Spengler writes at length about prehistory, about the rise of the West, about non-Western cultures, and about historiography. My neglect of these parts does not mean they are negligible. Spengler can be fascinating on a vast number of topics, including burial customs, modern excellence in music, and the role of the window in Faustian culture. His opinions can stimulate even when they prove untenable, as when he overestimates the literary merits of George Bernard Shaw.[9]

IV

My main concern, to which I return at last, is Spengler's depiction of the decline of the West and the adequacy of that depiction. To repeat, for Spengler a culture is a spiritual entity and an organism. Its growth and decline follow iron laws and take about one thousand years. Every culture Spengler studies features the same movements, especially the following five:

1. from intuitive and rural societies enveloped in myth, to a bloated urbanism accompanied by a practical, materialistic outlook;
2. from a poetically and mythically expressed sense of community to a prosaic individualism;
3. from a spring of dream-like feelings of fullness through a summer of consciousness in which philosophy displaces religion, to an autumnal rationalism that leads to a winter of utilitarianism;
4. from a vigorous cultural primitivism through a period of great masters, to a formalistic pretentiousness;
5. from a politics of patriarchal chivalry through aristocracy, to a decline into economism and democracy.

Near the end, a kind of reinvigoration occurs in the form of Caesarism and imperialism. A rough politics triumphs over money. But the rejuvenation rings hollow, what with barbarianism at the gates, and a second religiousness that resembles senility.

All this has a certain rough plausibility about it, so that one can turn with great interest to Spengler's description of our own culture, which begins with the *Niebelungenlied* and the appearance of Saint Francis of Assisi. In its youthful exuberance it produces the splendors of Gothic architecture, the imposing work of Saint Thomas Aquinas, and fertile tension between popes and emperors.

The Faustian summer brings with it the Protestant Reformation and the philosophy of Descartes. Science and mathematics flourish, while oil painting adorns the arts. Politically, an era of great statesmanship culminates in the phenomenon of Napoleon.

Autumnal ripeness follows, marked by the Enlightenment, Rousseau, and German classicism. The arts favor music, and social life witnesses the reign of the great cities, especially Paris. Throughout these three "seasons" Faustian culture manifests infinite yearning.

In his own time, Spengler sees mostly decay. Materialism ensnares both the left and the right. Philosophy has become both mathematical and purely academic. Religion is in a state of degeneration which is only partly masked by the kind of inauthentic faith Spengler calls second religiousness. The whole culture lacks an inner sense of form; instead, one finds aimless nervousness. Democracy in one form or another reigns supreme, and with it mediocrity. Everyone seems to share a shallow belief in progress, and everyone denies that human beings are still beasts of prey. The advent of journalism is but one sign of general artistic decay.

This is the picture Spengler draws of his time, which in significant respects is our time as well. Probity compels us to admit that in some important ways Spengler tells the truth and that he is useful in helping us to define our situation. But one cannot read Spengler's account of the crisis of his and our time without realizing that he has been anticipated and excelled by Friedrich Nietzsche (1844–1900). We therefore do well to turn briefly to the Nietzsche of *Thus Spoke Zarathustra, The Use and Abuse of History,* and other writings, in which he reveals himself as a superb diagnostician of our problems.

V

We can be briefer about Nietzsche than about Spengler, whose views are not well known today. Nietzsche has never fallen into oblivion, though like Spengler he was tarnished because he had something to do with the rise of fascism. For various reasons, Nietzsche was easier to "denazify." Many poets loved him and served as his character witnesses, while philosophers testified to his greater depth compared to Spengler. After having been abandoned by the right, Nietzsche became a favorite of the New Left, which was bored with Marx and found Nietzsche's bourgeois-bashing incomparably more eloquent and profound.

Moreover, the absence of impending collapse as we approach the year 2000 is more of an embarrassment to Spengler than to Nietzsche, whose views allow for a total rejuvenation within each cycle of history (see below). For Spengler, present decline is inevitable, but for Nietzsche the crisis of our time means that humanity faces a critical choice. It may degenerate into the era of the "last man," who abandons all goals except comfortable self-preservation, who is despicable because he is no longer able to despise himself, and who blinks as a prelude to dozing off.[10] But the same crisis may herald the advent of the superman, the Roman Caesar with the soul of Christ, a new synthesis of saint, poet, legislator, and philosopher.

Nietzsche's philosophy thus admits of the possibility of present progress. One must, however, hasten to add that Nietzsche distinguishes his own hopes from those who usually preempt the term "progressive" for themselves. The latter, the advocates of what Nietzsche calls modern progress, strive for a socialist utopia. Working for equality and peace, they wittingly or unwittingly favor the coming of the last man. Nietzsche's references to progress are usually derogatory, and it may be useful to quote what amounts to his last word on the subject, an aphorism from *Twilight of the Idols:*

> *Whispered to the conservatives.* What was not known formerly, what is known or might be known, today: a reversion, a return in any sense or degree is simply not possible. We physiologists know that. Yet all priests and moralists have believed the opposite—they wanted to take mankind back, to screw it back to a former measure of virtue. Morality was always a bed of Procrustes. Even the politicians have aped the preachers of virtue at this point: today there are still parties whose dream it is that all things might walk backwards like crabs. But no one is free to be a crab. Nothing avails: one *must* go forward—step by step further into decadence (that is *my* definition of modern "progress"). One can *check* this development and thus dam up degeneration, gather it and make it more vehement and *sudden:* one can do no more.[11]

An apocalyptic era of crisis is inevitable, according to Nietzsche, but its outcome is subject to human willing. The crisis humanity is fated to confront in our time is the death of God. That statement refers primarily, by no means exclusively, to the Christian God, who no longer compels belief, so that religion can no longer serve as a binding glue for society. With the disappearance of God from the scene, our moral anchor disappears as well. We no longer know what is right or wrong: if God is dead all is permitted. All substitute standards die with God; *all* gods are dead. We have lost our moorings, strangers and afraid in a world we never made. Mankind as defined by its reverence must disappear, for there is nothing left to revere.

If man must cease to be man, he may decay into the above-mentioned last man, but the death of God could just as well usher in a great age of great politics in which man can become more than man, the superman. The death of God is an ambiguous datum that Nietzsche seeks to interpret creatively. God's existence dampened human aspirations by judging them by standards that belittled man: why should God be mindful of him? The death of God can be understood as the revelation of human creativity. God did not create man but man created God. The final stage of humanism arises in which there is nothing above man except perhaps what he can still become.

Such a historical moment demands a new doctrine, for now the unconscious creator of God has become a conscious creator. Nietzsche articulates the doctrine of the will to power to accommodate this unique historical situation. A human being is one who is privileged or doomed to try to overcome everything he encounters. Life is will to power; indeed, everything is will to power.

Nietzsche's doctrine of the will to power, developed by him in *Thus Spoke Zarathustra*[12] and all the books following it, plainly allows for progress. It proclaims that if God is dead, everything is possible. Conscious creativity puts unconscious creativity to shame. God, nature, and truth itself are now revealed as human constructs, subject to human mastery. The will reigns supreme; the future is promises.

The doctrine of the will to power raises very serious problems, which Nietzsche's integrity would not allow him to ignore. To begin with, if it is the creation of Nietzsche's own will to power, it is not simply true, and thus cannot overcome the relativism that Nietzsche strives to resolve. Then too, it seems impossible to assign limits to the will to power. If everything can be overcome, humanity will decline because it lives in a world without challenges, yet if not everything can be overcome striving will sooner or later turn out to be vain. Even at present, the supremacy of willing might be meaningless, for "meaningful" might mean "beyond one's power to will." Finally, can the past be overcome, and if not, are we not finally impotent?

Unable to leave things at the doctrine of the will to power, Nietzsche developed his enigmatic vision of the eternal return of the same, according to which the will peaks in affirming the world exactly as it is and always has been and always will be. The will wills life as a kind of utterly meaningless Rube Goldberg contraption designed by nobody for no purpose. The doctrine of the eternal return of the same overcomes nihilism by taking it to its uttermost extreme and beyond. It embraces the irrational and the impossible, as *Thus Spoke Zarathustra* makes clear.[13]

With the willing of the eternal return, progress reaches its zenith as the man who wills it becomes a superman. But the time of the superman will vanish. Decline follows progress, so in the last analysis progress turns out to be illusory. Ultimately, Nietzsche outdoes Spengler in regard to gloom. He sings a song to the effect that "all is in vain." That is Nietzsche' formula for the nihilism he seeks to transcend and fails to transcend.[14]

VI

We must now distance ourselves from both Nietzsche and Spengler and dwell a bit on our own troubles. Surely those troubles are real; they cannot be explained as a simple yearning for the good old days, as the nostalgia with which we began our inquiry.

To repeat, feelings of decline and nostalgia can be found everywhere and anytime, but they are not always unwarranted: we may really resemble the Romans who wished in vain for things Greek. Nor do our troubles stem from external threats. The Soviet Union has vanished and the threat of nuclear war abated, but many of us, perhaps most of us, continue to feel a certain malaise. There is something spiritually wrong with us, even as Spengler pointed out.

It does not, or should not, take a Spengler to familiarize us with the idea of decline. We know, or should know, that all the works of man come into being and are destined to perish. The great books we study teach as much with perfect clarity. Thus Thucydides, who wrote his history as a "possession for all times" educes our sadness by making it clear that time is running out for Athens as well as for Sparta. Thus, too, many of us who read Tocqueville's *Democracy in America* experience sadness because it is obvious to him that some day there will be no United States of America. As a philosopher, he faces that eventuality with a composure we find hard to emulate.[15]

Of course, we do not need books at all to meditate on decline. We know a good deal about it in our bones, and the older we get the more we discover about it—we know we will die.

All of us, even the young, are occasionally beset by intimations of mortality which interrupt our feelings that it is good to be alive, though we do not know *why* we are here. No matter what pessimists, nihilists, and their kin tell us, we feel we belong here, that we are part of some whole. But we also know that we won't be around forever, that our hold on life is tenuous. Philosophy may teach us how to die, but the fact that we will die puts a question mark after all philosophical endeavor, after all human endeavor.

How do we deal with the fact of our own inevitable decline? Usually we do not deal with it at all. When it crosses our minds, we change the subject. We go to lunch or to sleep; we make trouble or love; we play or we work. We are all virtuosos of what Pascal calls diversion;[16] and to some extent our virtuosity serves us well, guarding us from morbidity.

But the subject won't stay changed, so what do we do? Some find a refuge in faith, which usually involves a belief in immortality. But ours is a bad time for faith, what with Nietzsche's emphasis on the death of God and Spengler's even more rigid atheism. Both contribute to the difficulty of believing in the immortality of the soul, or in the satisfaction of the yearning for eternity which characterizes even those who profess no belief in immortality but simply long for the existence of some kind of being beyond all becoming. Both assert that there is only becoming and having become, that all is flux. It is useful to recall that Spengler wrote his doctoral dissertation on Heraclitus and that Nietzsche exempts Heraclitus from most of his strictures against previous philosophers.

Yet even those who doubt that the thirst for eternity can be quenched can live with a measure of composure and dignity, though their lives may merely exemplify what Freud called ordinary human unhappiness. How do they manage it? Let us not fear triteness in such weighty matters. We make do with the feeling that what we do matters, that it makes a difference, that we make a difference. We labor to produce what will survive us, whether it be children, or students, or poems. We dedicate ourselves to what is beyond us, and that is enough; it will have to be enough.

There is however, no denying that what is at work here is the yearning for eternity in disguise. Returning to Spengler after our detour into Nietzsche's ultimate gloom, we find that Spengler too makes our future seem bleak. What he tells us is, to be sure, confusing, and possibly confused. Thus the first volume of *The Decline of the West* ends with a reference to coming cultures: life will go on after our Faustian culture (1:428).

We must be sketchy about Spengler's prognostications. At times, he thinks of America as the future, as has been common in German thought at least since Goethe wrote a little poem beginning "*Amerika, du hast es besser*"—America, you're better off. More often than not, however, Spengler condemns the United States for its soulless materialism. At other times he looks to Russia, the Russia of Dostoevsky rather than Tolstoy. Incidentally, in Spengler's arcane racialism Russia is part of the "colored world" (2:192–96).

At times Spengler agrees with Nietzsche in seeing a special fate for Germany, the least Western and hence the least domesticated part of the West, the most distant from modern degradation. Spengler, to repeat, cannot be exonerated from all responsibility for national socialism, though he met Hitler only once and was not impressed.

None of the continuities Spengler envisages provides more than cold comfort, for they are not genuine continuities. Spengler's biological metaphor breaks down: the cultures he likens to plants have no seeds. Whatever the future will bring, it will be not Western culture but a culture that will grow and thrive in oblivion of us, or else in utter incomprehension of us.

Moreover, there may be no future at all in any meaningful sense. For Spengler, a culture is a losing battle with nature; the plant withers but the earth abides. Because, however, Faustian culture has tampered with the earth, one has to face the possibility that after this plant withers nothing will be left to abide. Faustian culture has also been the absolute culture in a spiritual sense, the culture striving to understand all other cultures and to reach infinity. Perhaps the absolute culture will die the absolute death.

Nothingness may lie ahead, but Spengler has recommendations for the immediate future. He abhors whining and counsels dignified resoluteness, lest we be dragged demeaningly into what will come inevitably. The days ahead will feature engineers rather than artists, politics rather than poetry, but we can learn to live with that. We can cope with the Caesarism just around the corner. Spengler denies he is a pessimist, thinking that his stance of manly acceptance guards him against that charge.

One may well be attracted to such a stance, but one must conclude yet again that it is cold comfort. We want to matter, and on the deepest level we do not matter and nothing we do matters. A sense of futility envelopes us whether there is no future at all or a future with no understanding for all we have striven to accomplish. If Spengler is right, he orchestrates Nietzsche's dirge that all is in vain.

But is Spengler right? I cannot refute him, but can only advance some reservations, most of them based on some "idiot faith" that we can catch glimpses of meaning in our world, for we find in it wonders beyond our powers to make. On more solid ground, I can point to the tarnishing of Spengler's determinism by the failure of his timetables to be precise. We have survived the tyrannies of Hitler and Stalin. We may still be headed for disaster, of course, but I am reminded of a German popular song of the 1950s: "The world will end on May 30, but nobody knows in which year, and that is really wonderful."

We may also take comfort in the fact that to this very day in the United States, and elsewhere as well, decline has remained voluntary to an appreciable extent. We may not be able to save Faustian culture but we can try to save our immortal souls, and if they are not immortal we can try to save our mortal souls, and that may be enough because it will have to be enough. We must try to live an honorable life and die an honorable death.

Attempting to do so, we can draw on the unswerving courage of both Nietzsche and Spengler. Nietzsche's courage is well known, so it is only fair to end on a positive note about Spengler. In spite of his forays into the wilderness of modern thought, he never lost his old-fashioned conviction that the one thing that cannot be taken from a man is an honorable death. For this, and for much else, he deserves our respect and even our gratitude.

Part III

CONTEMPORARY REFLECTIONS: WHERE IS HISTORY GOING?

7 Political Conflict after the Cold War

SAMUEL P. HUNTINGTON

What are the implications of the collapse of Marxist-Leninism and the end of the Cold War for international conflict? Will this new era in world affairs be characterized by more conflict, less conflict, or different conflict than occurred earlier in this century?

In 1989 and 1990 two brilliant social scientists advanced two very different answers to these questions. Francis Fukuyama's imaginative essay, which attracted so much attention, was titled "The End of History?" He puts a question mark at the end of his title, but the argument of his essay left little room for doubt as to what he means. "We may be witnessing," he says, "the end of history as such: that is, the end point of mankind's ideological evolution and the universalization of Western liberal democracy as the final form of human government." To be sure, he says, conflicts will continue to occur in the Third World, but the global conflict is over, and not just in Europe. "It is precisely in the non-European world" that the big changes have occurred, particularly in China and the Soviet Union. The war of ideas is at an end. Believers in Marxist-Leninism may still exist "in places like Managua, Pyongyang, and Cambridge, Massachusetts," but overall liberal democracy has triumphed. The future will be devoted not to great exhilarating struggles over ideas but rather to resolving mundane economic and technical problems. And, he concludes somewhat sadly, it will all be rather boring.[1]

Part of this essay was first published in *Foreign Affairs* 72 (Summer 1993), 21–47.

A year after Fukuyama presented his image of this placid future, John Mearsheimer, chair of the Political Science Department at the University of Chicago, came forth with an equally dramatic but very different prediction. "Many observers now suggest," Mearsheimer says in an obvious reference to Fukuyama, "that a new age of peace is dawning; in fact the opposite is true." The end of the Cold War means the end of what John Gaddis has labeled the Long Peace, the longest period of time in modern history—forty-five years—without war between the major powers. This Long Peace of the Cold War, Mearsheimer says, was the product of bipolarity, the rough equality in military strength between the two superpowers and the alliances they led, and the existence of nuclear weapons. If we in the United States want to preserve the peace, he argues, we ought to preserve the Soviet threat and prolong the Cold War. We cannot do that, however, and hence the probability of war in Europe—and he focuses almost entirely on Europe—will increase dramatically. With the decline of the superpowers, Europe will return to where it was in the 1930s, the 1920s, and the nineteenth century. The title of his essay, indeed, is "Back to the Future." The old national rivalries and antagonisms will manifest themselves and war in Europe becomes a high probability. To lower that probability he recommends that Germany acquire nuclear weapons. But even that step is not likely to prevent conflict. "The next decades in a Europe without the superpowers would probably not be as violent as the first 45 years of this century, but would probably be substantially more prone to violence than the past 45 years."[2]

What are we to make of these two conflicting arguments? Both cannot be true, but both could be wrong. In my view Fukuyama is 75 percent wrong; Mearsheimer is 50 percent right.

Fukuyama is only 75 percent wrong because of one very important fact, to which he never alludes but which does support his argument. That is that while liberal democracies fight just as many wars as other types of states, they do not fight each other. Modern democratic states emerged in the nineteenth century, and for 150 years now no wars have occurred between democratic states. The only exceptions to this generalization are trivial: during World War II Finland was for a while technically at war with the Western democracies but it was forced into that by the Germans, and no fighting occurred between the Finns and the Western democracies. Fifteen years ago, a silly little affair, the so-called Cod War, occurred between Britain and Iceland, in which warships exchanged a few shots in a dispute over fishing rights. Both the British and Icelanders quickly said this is ridiculous and went to the negotiating table to resolve the dispute. The absence of war between democratic states is, consequently, an extraordinary and very important phenomenon. It is particularly important now because during the past fifteen years more than thirty countries have shifted from authoritarian to democratic regimes. If this wave of democratization continues, the number of possible wars is significantly reduced.

If one looks about the world, the no-wars-between-democracies principle appears still to be operating. Note the problems Britain has had with its last remaining outposts of empire. It had to fight a war with Argentina over the Falklands; it had to deploy a significant military force to Belize to protect that former colony against Guatemalan aggression; it was involved in a major confrontation with Spain over Gibraltar. These disputes occurred when Argentina, Guatemala, and Spain had nondemocratic governments. All three countries now have democratic governments, and the likelihood of violence in these disputes has virtually disappeared. Britain and Argentina have reestablished diplomatic relations and said that they will not use force to resolve the Falkland Islands question. Guatemala has promised not to invade Belize, the British have reduced their troops in that country, and Guatemala and Belize have established diplomatic relations. The border between Gibraltar and Spain has been opened. The king of Spain has visited the queen of England in London. Democracies do not fight democracies.

The argument is made that the absence of wars between democracies has been an artifact of history and geography. Historically wars have occurred most often between neighboring countries. Until the mid-twentieth century there were relatively few democracies in the world, and by and large they did not abut each other. Hence the absence of propinquity was responsible for the absence of wars between democracies. This hypothesis is now being tested in the Subcontinent. During the past forty years, India and Pakistan have fought three wars when Pakistan had nondemocratic governments. In 1990 tensions between India and Pakistan escalated over Kashmir and nuclear weapons. Like India, however, Pakistan now has a more or less democratic government, and war has not occurred. If war does not occur, this fact will be evidence against the propinquity argument and support for the broader principle that democracies do not fight each other.

Why should this be the case? One can think of several plausible reasons. First, the leaders of democracies are accustomed to resolving issues not by force but by negotiations and compromise. That is the way of democracy in domestic politics; it is natural that it should also extend to international politics. As they do at home, the leaders of democratic states will work out their differences between them or learn to live with those differences. Second, because democratic societies are open societies, they interpenetrate one another. The interests and views of one democratic state will be articulated in another. For one reason or another some groups in one state are very likely to be sympathetic to or even to espouse the position of the other state. Cross-cutting cleavages thus moderate the intensity of interstate differences. Third, in order to go to war, democratic governments must not only secure public approval but also must mobilize public support for and public participation in the war effort. These steps usually require portraying the enemy as a true villain or devil. It is easy to paint tyrants in this way. Democratic publics will rally to a war against the Kaiser, Hitler, Japanese warlords, Stalin and Godless Communism, Saddam Hussein. It is much harder to arouse democratic publics against states led not by military juntas or ideological fanatics but rather by bumbling mild-mannered politicians rather similar to their own leaders.

To the extent that these factors render unlikely wars between democracies, there may be some truth to Fukuyama's argument, and the spread of democracy in the world will mean the expansion of a zone of peace in the world. Yet that quite clearly is not the whole story. Fukuyama is a Harvard doctor of philosophy and a man of ideas. He identifies the history of history with the history of ideology and historical conflict with ideological conflict. This is a distinctly modern, Western, and intellectual view of conflict. The twentieth century, as Fukuyama says, has been characterized by a "paroxysm of ideological violence." Ideology is a modern phenomenon, a product of the nineteenth century. Yet there were violence and conflict for centuries before the French Revolution. Was there no history before the French Revolution? There certainly were an awful lot of wars. Ideological conflict is not the norm in history but the exception in history. Most history has been the history of struggles between tribes, races, nationalities, peoples, and religions. Even since 1945 the bloodiest wars have been civil wars between ethnic, religious, and racial groups in the same societies. The end of ideological conflict does not mean the end of conflict. Indeed, it may well mean the reinvigoration of other types of conflict.

That, of course, is Mearsheimer's argument. And there is a core element of truth in that argument. A variety of old antagonisms has erupted in Europe. Ethnic consciousness has dramatically emerged, particularly over the treatment of minority populations. Mearsheimer is a structural realist, and structural realism does provide an insight into international politics. But it is a limited insight. Mearsheimer totally rejects two key factors. First, domestic politics and institutions: the democracies-don't-fight-democracies fact. This is the domestic political constraint on conflict. Second, he totally pooh-poohs the effects of international institutions. This whole complex structure of European institutions—the European Community, the Council of Europe, NATO, the Western European Union, the European Parliament, the Conference on Security and Cooperation in Europe CSCE—is to him of no consequence. These institutions will wither before the reemergence of national rivalries and fears. He assumes that nation states in Europe are what they once were. He refuses to recognize that many of the decisions national governments used to make are now made by bureaucrats in Brussels, that the distinguishing characteristics of nation states in terms of borders, passports, and citizenship are disappearing, and that the probability of war between France and Germany is somewhere between the probability of war between the United States and Canada and the probability of war between Michigan and Indiana.

Paradoxically, Fukuyama focuses his principal argument on the Soviet Union and China, where he is wrong, rather than on Europe, where he is right. Mearsheimer focuses his argument on Europe, where he is wrong, and ignores the Third World, where his argument clearly holds true.

Moving beyond the dramatic but overly simple arguments of Fukuyama and Mearsheimer, what would be a more realistic and more complex picture of future conflict?

First, for the immediate future, ideological conflict between states will not be significant. Ideological conflict within states will also decline in importance: revolutionary ideologies are likely to be increasingly restricted to a few Western intellectuals with minds locked in the 1930s or the 1960s and to the remaining peasant movements active in Central America, Peru, the Philippines, and perhaps a few other places. Economic development will gradually undermine the basis for these movements, and the era of Marxist-Leninism and its offshoots will come to an end.

Second, among industrialized democracies interstate military conflict is highly unlikely. Economic competition among the major industrialized countries, however, will be more intense than it has been because no longer will it be subordinated, as Edward Luttwak has emphasized, to the "strategic imperative of preserving alliance cooperation against a common enemy." Economic competition will generate political conflicts "fought out with the weapons of commerce: the more or less disguised restriction of imports, the more or less concealed subsidization of exports, the funding of competitive technology projects, the support of selected forms of education, the provision of competitive infrastructures, and more."[3] Among these states, "economics," in Daniel Bell's phrase, "is the continuation of war by other means."[4]

Third, military conflicts among less-developed countries are likely to be more prevalent than they were during the Cold War because of the weakening of the restraints imposed by the superpowers, who did not want Third World conflicts to escalate into superpower conflicts. The sources of conflict in the Third World include the uneven economic development of countries, the growth in economic and military power of countries, unresolved border disputes, the rights of ethnic and religious minorities, access to resources including oil and water, the proliferation of sophisticated weapons, and the feeling on the part of some states that they may have the right and perhaps even the duty to establish regional security systems in which they are the hegemon.

Some parts of the Third World are much more conflict-prone than others. The Middle East and southern Asia, but also Africa and southeast Asia, are areas where international conflicts of the traditional sort over territory, resources, power, and armaments are probable. International or interstate wars could occur in the Balkans. Conflicts also exist where governments have forcefully seized the territory of other peoples against their will. Many of these situations have, however, been resolved in recent years. The Soviets got out of Afghanistan; they withdrew from eastern Europe; they recognized the independence of the Baltic states. The South Africans are out of Namibia. The Vietnamese are out of Cambodia. The Iraqis are very definitely out of Kuwait. In mid-1991 the Israeli occupation of the West Bank and Gaza was virtually the only remaining case in which military forces had been used to invade and occupy a foreign territory against the wishes of its inhabitants.

The Gulf War was a unique event. The American leadership, military commitment, and diplomatic coalition that characterized the response to the invasion of Kuwait will not be repeated. Yet that war clearly makes less likely forceful challenges to the existence of states and forceful challenges to existing international boundaries. Even in the Third World territorial aggression may be less likely in the future than it has been in the past. Intervention may be more likely. Aggression is the effort to change boundaries by force. Intervention is the effort to change governments by force. In the new era, boundaries are likely to be more sacrosanct than governments. It is hard to think of examples in the 1970s and 1980s in which efforts to change boundaries by force have succeeded. In the 1980s, however, the United States twice successfully intervened to overthrow governments. If instead of annexing Kuwait, Saddam Hussein had simply intervened in that country, thrown out the al-Sabah family, established a government there more to his liking, and then withdrawn his forces back to Iraq, the world might have said tut-tut but would have accepted the new situation and gone on doing business with Iraq and with the new government of Kuwait.

The 1980s have seen a growth in the economic capacity, political cohesion, and military power of many Third World states. A central element of this process has been acquisition by several states of sophisticated weapons and efforts by some states to acquire nuclear, chemical, and biological weapons. In the Middle East, south Asia, and on the Korean peninsula, these efforts have created highly unstable and fragile balances of power. It seems likely that in the future some states could be tempted to take preemptive military action against rival states that appear on the verge of acquiring new levels of weaponry. In addition, the United States itself might in some circumstances find it in its interests to destroy the unconventional-weapon capabilities of another state, acting either unilaterally or under authorization from the United Nations or some other international body. Classical interstate wars, particularly those over territory, thus may be less likely in the future because of the spread of democratic regimes and the acceptance of an international norm on the inviolability of borders. Military interventions, on the other hand, may be more likely in order to change governments or to prevent weapons proliferation.

Fourth, as ideology and class decline as sources of political and social identity, ethnicity and religion are likely to become more important in both developed and less-developed countries. In some instances, these identities will coincide with loyalties to existing nation states. More frequently, they will provide alternative sources of identity which will lead to challenges to the authority of existing states. Most countries in the world are not homogenous. They are riven by ethnic, racial, and religious differences. Such rivalries have given rise to the bloodiest wars in recent decades: in Lebanon, Iraq, Sri Lanka, Burma, the Sudan, Ethiopia, Rwanda, Burundi, Nigeria, Uganda, Liberia. Frequently no participant in these conflicts is strong enough to win a definitive victory; hence the conflicts go on indefinitely. Negotiations arrive at truces or understandings; these hold tenuously for a short period, then they are broken and the wars resume. This scenario has been dramatically the case in the Sudan between the Muslim Arab population in the north and the black population in the south. It has been the history of the Kurds in Iraq.

The end of the Cold War and the loosening of the alliances led by the superpowers have thus permitted and encouraged the eruption of long-suppressed ethnic and religious hostilities, particularly in eastern Europe and the former Soviet Union: Hungarians and Romanians, Slovaks and Czechs, Croatians and Serbs, Poles and Germans, Balts and Russians, Armenians and Azeris, Georgians and Russians, Bulgarians and Turks. With the decline in the need for external unity, internal differences reassert themselves.

Within states the opportunities for communal conflicts are expanding rapidly. The collapse of nondemocratic ideologies is stimulating a revival consciousness and ethnic demands. Apartheid ideology in South Africa and Ba'athist ideology in Iraq provided justification for authoritarian rule and for the dominance of one ethnic group over others. The weakening or collapse of these ideologies opens up a new ball game. This opportunity is most clear with the collapse of Marxist-Leninism in multiethnic communist states. It is not so much liberal democracy but ethnicity that is replacing communist ideology. Marxist-Leninism provided justification for an East German state. Take away the ideology, the justification for the state disappears, and it goes out of business. Marxist-Leninism also provided justification for the Yugoslav state. Take it away and the Yugoslav state goes out of business. The same is true in Czechoslovakia. And it is, of course, most dramatically true in the former Soviet Union.

The Soviet Union was the last of the large, multinational, continental empires. The Hapsburg, Hohenzollern, and Ottoman empires came to an end in World War I and were replaced by a large number of successor states. The Russian empire also came to an end, but it did not break up as others did. Instead, the Russian Revolution brought a group of extraordinarily able, ruthless leaders to the fore who had a new doctrine and who in the name of that doctrine recreated the Russian empire and gave it a new lease on life for seventy-five years.

With the bankruptcy of that doctrine the empire is now coming apart. Each of the fifteen republics has declared its own sovereignty. Six have made it clear they want full independence and three have achieved it. Within republics, autonomous regions and nationality groups are also asserting sovereignty and demanding autonomy. Where does this process stop? Within the extraordinary ethnic mosaic of the Soviet Union, there was always a minority within a minority. This ethnic heterogeneity greatly complicates movement toward democracy in the former Soviet Union. Many years ago, Sir Ivor Jennings pointed out that "the people cannot decide until someone decides who are the people." The identities of the peoples of Lithuania, Armenia, Georgia, and Russia are now at issue. Who is a citizen of Latvia: only ethnic Latvians or also the many Russians resident in Latvia? As long as the Soviet Union was a unified state, such questions were not important; now they are of central importance and a prime source of conflict. Historically, the relations among ethnic groups have been sorted out in a variety of ways, through accommodation between groups, by the assimilation of one group by another, by subordination of one group to another, through voluntary but often violent migration (reportedly there are already one million refugees within the Soviet Union), through forced migration, and by extermination or genocide (which unfortunately appears not inconceivable among some of the groups in the Caucasus).

History shows that the decline of empires is almost invariably messy, conflict-ridden, and prolonged. Professor Stephen Peter Rosen of the Olin Institute at Harvard has directed a study of the decline of eight historical multinational, continental empires, from the Spartan empire to the Austro-Hungarian Empire. At least four generalizations emerge from this study. Empires usually do not collapse purely from internal causes, because the imperial regime has the bureaucratic, police, and military means to suppress or contain internal disruption. The decline of empires is also usually a very prolonged process, with reform elites at times attempting (like the Young Turks) to bring new life to the imperial system. The external environment is usually supportive of the empire: other governments do not rush in to tear apart the decaying empire but instead tend to prop it up. The final collapse of the empire is then brought about by a war or other external event. These historical patterns may or may not hold up in the Soviet case. They do, however, suggest that what has been the Soviet Union is likely to be a scene of political instability and violent conflict for years to come.

Fifth, the end of the Cold War may open the way to conflict on a broader level beyond the nation state and ideology. The principal lines of conflict in the modern, Western world have changed over time. For a century and a half after the emergence of the modern international system with the Peace of Westphalia, the conflicts of the Western world were largely conflicts among princes—emperors, absolute monarchs, and constitutional monarchs attempting to expand their bureaucracies, their armies, their mercantilist economic strength, and, most important, the territory they ruled. In the process they created nation states, and with the French Revolution in 1789 the principal lines of conflict were between nations rather than princes. This nineteenth-century pattern lasted until the end of World War I. At this point, as a result of the Russian Revolution and the reaction against it, the conflict of nations yielded to the conflict of ideologies, first between fascism-nazism and liberal democracy and then in the second half of this century between Marxist-Leninism and liberal democracy. During the Cold War, this latter conflict became embodied in the struggle between the two superpowers, neither of which was a nation state in the classical European sense and each of which defined its identity in terms of its ideology.

With the end of this ideological conflict, if not the end of history, what will emerge as the predominant basis for conflict in international affairs? Both Fukuyama and Mearsheimer focused on past forms of conflict: Fukuyama on the ideological conflict of the mid- and late twentieth century, which is ending, and Mearsheimer on the nation-state conflicts of the nineteenth and early twentieth centuries, to which he sees the world returning. The predominant form of conflict in the twenty-first century, however, is unlikely to be either of these. It will be the conflict between tribes which, at its highest level, is the conflict between civilizations.

What is a civilization? A civilization is the largest cultural grouping of people below that of the human race. Villages, regions, ethnic groups, nationalities, religious groups—all have distinct cultures at different levels of cultural heterogeneity. The culture of a village in southern Italy may be different from that of a village in northern Italy, but both also will have common elements of an Italian culture which distinguish them from German villages. A civilization is the broadest level of cultural identity short of that which distinguishes humans from other species.

Civilizations may involve a large number of people (China) or a much small number (Anglophone Caribbean). A civilization may include a large number of nation states (as in Europe, Latin America, the Arab world) or only one state (Japan). The lines between cultures are seldom sharp—obviously there is overlap and blending—but they are real. Civilizations also are dynamic; they rise and fall; they merge and divide.

After World War II the world was thought of as divided into three parts along two dimensions. On an east-west axis, there was the "free" world of the Western allies and associated states, the communist bloc led by the Soviet Union, and the nonaligned nations. On the north-south dimension, substantially the same three groups of nations were labeled the First, Second, and Third worlds. In the post–Cold War world these tripartite divisions will lose much of their relevance. The east-west dimension has already disappeared; the north-south dimension is becoming blurred as many Third World countries move towards the First World.

In the future it seems likely that the most salient lines of division in world politics will be between civilizations: between the European, North American, and Latin American components of what at a broader level is Western civilization, between Europe and the Arab Islamic civilization to the south and the Orthodox Slavic civilization to the east; between Orthodox Slavs and Turkic Muslims in the Balkans and along the southern areas of the former Soviet Union; across Africa from Dakar to Zanzibar between Arabs and black Africans; within the Subcontinent between Hindus and Muslims; between Indians and Chinese; between Chinese and Japanese; and between Japanese and North Americans. Conflicts between nationalities and ethnic groups will be most frequent and most intense when the nationalities and ethnic groups belong to different civilizations. In these instances, lower levels of identification reinforce the higher levels of identification.

In some instances the higher level of identification with a civilization may in part supplant lower levels of identification with a nation state. This process is probably most advanced in western Europe, with people increasingly thinking of themselves as Europeans rather than as Germans or Belgians. Different levels of identification need not conflict with one another, but instead will reinforce one another. Identifications depend on context, and as peoples from different civilizations increasingly interact with one another, identification with one's own civilization becomes increasingly salient. Frenchmen react negatively to massive North African immigration and begin to see virtues in the movement to Paris of fellow Europeans (and Catholics) from Poland. In a similar way, as Donald Horowitz has pointed out, "An Ibo may be . . . an Owerri Ibo or an Onitsha Ibo in what was the Eastern region of Nigeria. In Lagos, he is simply an Ibo. In London, he is a Nigerian. In New York, he is an African."[5]

The interactions among peoples of different civilizations enhance the civilization-consciousness of people, which, in turn, may reinvigorate traditional differences and animosities stretching back deep into history.

The consequences of the end of the Cold War for the stimulation of conflict between civilizations is most notable in Europe. The Cold War began when the Iron Curtain came down across central Europe, dividing Europe politically and ideologically. The Cold War ended with the removal of the Iron Curtain. As the ideological division of Europe has disappeared, however, the cultural division of Europe between Western Christianity, on the one hand, and Orthodox Christianity and Islam, on the other, has reemerged. The most significant dividing line in Europe, now, as William Wallace has suggested, may well be the boundary of Western Christianity in the year 1500.[6] This line runs along what are now the boundaries between Finland and Russia and between the Baltic states and Russia, cuts through Belorussia and the Ukraine separating the Catholic western Ukraine from the Orthodox eastern Ukraine, swings westward separating Transylvania from the rest of Romania and then goes through Yugoslavia almost exactly along the line now separating Croatia and Slovenia from the rest of Yugoslavia. In the Balkans this line, of course, coincides with the historic boundary between the Hapsburg and Ottoman empires. The peoples to the north and west of this line are Protestant or Catholic; they shared the common experiences of European history—feudalism, the Renaissance, the Reformation, the Enlightenment, the French Revolution, the Industrial Revolution; they are generally better off economically than the peoples to the east; and they may now look forward to increasing involvement in a common European economy and to the consolidation of democratic political systems. The peoples to the east and south of that line are Orthodox or Muslim; they historically belonged to the tsarist or Ottoman empires and were touched only lightly by the shaping events in the rest of Europe; they are generally less advanced economically; they seem much less likely to develop stable democratic political systems. The Velvet Curtain of culture has replaced the Iron Curtain of ideology as the most significant dividing line in Europe. As the events of 1991 in Yugoslavia have shown, it is not only a line of difference; it is also a line of conflict and at times of bloody conflict.

The breakdown of communism ended a seventy-five-years' ideological struggle. The downfall of Marxist-Leninism, however, does not necessarily mean the triumph of liberal democracy. The prospects for democratic regimes emerging in the republics of the former Soviet Union vary considerably. They are very high in the Baltic republics; they are probably very low in the central Asian republics, Georgia, and Azerbaijan. They are uncertain in Armenia, Belorussia, the Ukraine, and, most important, Russia itself. As has happened in the past, a struggle is under way for the soul of Russia between Western concepts, tendencies, and desires and more traditional, nationalistic, authoritarian ones. A Russia that developed in accordance with these latter influences is unlikely to have easy or harmonious relations with Europe or America. The conflict between liberal democracy and Marxist-Leninism was, in a sense, a civil war between two Western ideologies that, despite their major differences, ostensibly shared common goals of freedom, equality, and prosperity. A traditional authoritarian, nationalist Russia could have quite different goals. Marxism was thus in some ways a link between the Soviet Union and the West. As the Russians stop behaving like Marxists and begin behaving like Russians, the gap between Russia and the West could widen. A Western democrat who could carry on an intellectual debate with a Soviet Marxist would find it virtually impossible to do so with a Russian traditionalist.

Conflict along the fault line between Western and Islamic civilizations has been going on in seesaw fashion for thirteen hundred years. After the founding of Islam, the Arab and Moorish surge west and north ended only at Tours in 732. From the eleventh to the thirteenth centuries the Crusaders attempted with temporary success to bring Christianity and Christian rule to the Holy Land. From the fourteenth to the sixteenth centuries, the Ottoman Turks reversed the balance, extended their sway over the Middle East and the Balkans, captured Constantinople, and laid siege to Vienna. In the nineteenth and early twentieth centuries, as Ottoman power declined, Britain and France established Western control over most of North Africa and the Middle East. After World War II, in turn, the West began to retreat; the colonial empires disappeared; Arab nationalism and Islamic fundamentalism manifested themselves; the West became heavily dependent on the Persian Gulf countries for its energy; and the oil-rich Muslim countries became money-rich and, when they wished to, weapons-rich. Intermittent wars occurred between Arabs and Israel (which had been created by the West). British and French forces invaded Egypt in 1956; American forces invaded Lebanon in 1958; subsequently American forces returned to Lebanon, attacked Libya, and engaged in various military encounters with Iran. Then in 1990 the United States sent a massive army into the Persian Gulf to defend some Arab countries against aggression by another. This action divided the Arab world between those governments allied with the United States and portions of their own populations, which joined other Arab governments in opposing the American action. Saddam Hussein and anti-Western Muslims, however, attempted to define the war as a war between civilizations. "It is not the world against Iraq," as Safar Al-Hawaii, dean of Islamic Studies at the Umm Al-Qura University in Mecca put it in a widely circulated tape. "It is the West against Islam."[7] The outcome of the war left many Arabs feeling humiliated and resentful at the dependence of Arab countries on the West for their security and at the superiority of Western military power.

The military interaction between the West and Islam, which has gone on for centuries, seems unlikely to decline in the future. It could become more virulent. Many Arab countries, in addition to the oil exporters, are reaching levels of economic and social development in which autocratic forms of government become inappropriate and efforts to introduce democracy become stronger. Some openings in Arab political systems have already occurred. The principal beneficiaries of these openings to date have been Islamic fundamentalists. In the Arab world, in short, Western democracy seems to strengthen anti-Western movements. This may be a passing phenomenon, but it surely also complicates relations between Islamic countries and the West.

Those relations are also complicated by demography. The spectacular population growth in Arab countries, particularly in North Africa, has led to increased migration to western Europe. The movement within western Europe to the minimization of internal boundaries and controls has sharpened political sensitivities with respect to this development. In Italy, France, and Germany, political reactions against Arab and Turkish migrants became more intense and more popular in 1990 and 1991.

Historically, the other great antagonistic interaction of Arab Islamic civilization has been with the pagan, animist, and now increasingly Christian black peoples to the south. In the past, this antagonism was epitomized in the image of Arab slave dealers and black slaves. During the Cold War, it was reflected in the ongoing civil war in the Sudan between Arabs and blacks, the fighting in Chad between Libyan-supported insurgents and the government, and the recurring riots and communal violence between Muslims and Christians in Nigeria. The slow modernization of Africa coupled with the rapid spread of Christianity is likely to enhance the probabilities for violence along this fault line. Further east, on the Subcontinent, India is increasingly shaking off the Western secularism of its British rulers and their Nehru-generation successors and returning to its Hindu roots. This trend exacerbates both its relations with Pakistan, increasingly sensitive to the appeals of Islamic fundamentalism, and the problems posed by its own huge Muslim minority. In central Asia, it is quite possible that the boundary that did exist between the Soviet Union and its neighbors will give way to boundaries drawn more on cultural, linguistic, and religious lines. Turkey is developing its contacts with Azerbaijan and the five central Asian Soviet republics with primarily Turkic-speaking populations. This cohesion could intensify conflicts between these people and the Orthodox Slavs, as well as possibly with the Chinese to the east.

In eastern Asia, Japan is clearly the dominant economic force, and other societies have to determine to what extent they wish to be absorbed into a Japanese-led prosperity sphere. As China develops economically, however, it will increasingly challenge Japan for regional leadership and, possibly, the United States for global leadership. As a region, east Asia is one of the three economic powerhouses of the post–Cold War world, and it is the only one of the three that is highly deficient in conflict-reducing democratic political systems and almost totally lacking in conflict-reducing regional international institutions. China is not a pariah state, but unlike the other major states of the post–Cold War world (the United States, Britain, France, Germany, Soviet Union or Russia, Japan), it remains detached from the central core of the world community. Isolated nations, when powerful, are dangerous nations. China is increasing its power, and unless it becomes democratic and/or coopted into the world establishment, it will become dangerous, even as did Germany—another isolated, excluded, and undemocratic nation—when it became more powerful in the 1930s.

Violent conflict, as has been indicated, seems unlikely among the industrialized democracies. Yet economic competition, as has also been suggested, seems likely to intensify. Economically the developed world is clearly moving in the direction of three major economic blocs, which are largely identical with European, Japanese, and North American civilizations. The increasingly difficult relations between Japanese and Americans in the late 1980s and early 1990s reflect the reinforcing overlay of economic conflict and cultural difference. People on each side allege racism of the other, but at least on the American side the antipathies are much less racial than cultural. The basic values, attitudes, and behavior patterns could hardly be more different. The economic issues between the United States and Europe are no less serious than those between the United States and Japan, but they do not have the same political salience and emotional intensity because the differences between American civilization and European civilization are so much less than those between American civilization and Japanese civilization.

In a world where the differences between civilizations and the conflicts between civilizations assume greater importance, some countries and peoples will be caught in a schizophrenic position, not sure to which civilization they do or should belong. The late-twentieth-century leaders of Turkey, for instance, have followed in the Attaturk tradition and defined Turkey as a modern, secular, Western nation state. They allied Turkey with the West in NATO and in the Gulf War and they applied for membership in the European Community. At the same time, however, important elements in Turkish society have supported an Islamic revival and have argued that Turkey is basically a Middle Eastern Muslim society. In similar fashion, beginning in the 1980s Mexico's leaders increasingly liberalized the Mexican economy, promoted the NAFTA agreement with the United States, and defined Mexico as a North American rather than a Latin American country. As in Turkey, significant elements in Mexican society resisted this definition of their country's identity. In Turkey, Western-oriented leaders had to make gestures to Islam

(Turgut Ozal's pilgrimage to Mecca); so also Mexico's North American–oriented leaders had to make gestures to those who held Mexico to be a Latin American country (Carlos Salinas de Gortari's Ibero-American Guadalajara summit). In some instances, most notably in Yugoslavia, the conflict of civilizations can split apart nation states erected across the boundaries between civilizations.

In a broader sense, many but not all of the potentially more serious conflicts between civilizations in the post–Cold War world will be a new phase in the continuing interaction between the West and the non-West. Western civilization is both modern and Western. The peoples of non-Western civilizations generally wish to share in the benefits of modernity, but they are ambivalent about adopting the values and institutions of the West. They can react to the West in one or some combination of four ways: by substantially abandoning the values and institutions of their own civilization and adopting those of the West (Westernization), by attempting to insulate their civilization from penetration or "corruption" by Western values and institutions (isolation), by attempting to adapt their values and institutions and integrate them with those of the West (reformism), or by reacting against the West and attempting to revitalize and give new meaning to the values and institutions of their non-Western civilization (fundamentalism). The conflict between civilizations will thus go on within as well as between nation states (including within Western states, as a result of immigration). In the post–Cold War world, the ideological conflict between communism and democracy will no longer exist, conflicts between ethnic, religious, and national groups will predominate, and the conflict between Western and non-Western civilizations will hold center stage.

8 Enlightenment under Threat

CONOR CRUISE O'BRIEN

The first point I should like to make is that the heritage of the Enlightenment is not confined to the Western capitalist, politically democratic world. The Enlightenment was a most complex and partly ambiguous phenomenon, and not all parts of it are to be thought of as benign. Both the Western system and the Marxist-Leninist system descend from the Enlightenment: different aspects of the Enlightenment, coming down to the twentieth century through different channels.

Broadly speaking, our own Western system descends from the early phase of the Enlightenment, beginning in England in the late seventeenth century and coming down to us through England's Glorious Revolution of 1688 and through the American Revolution.

The Marxist-Leninist system descends from a later phase of the Enlightenment, centered in France, and came down through the French Revolution, the Revolution of 1848, and the Paris Commune to the modern communists.

The two traditions and systems have in common a secular emphasis and a common commitment to science and reason. But even the things that they have in common in principle are twisted apart, in practice, by the great differences, of both origins and channels, between the two sets of heirs of the complex heritage of the Enlightenment.

What we may call the Anglophone tradition, deriving from the early Enlightenment and passing through the two Anglo-Saxon revolutions, is pragmatic and limited—a matter of rooting out certain specific abuses, and continuing a process of piecemeal reform, under reformed institutions whose stability is not merely respected but surrounded with deliberate veneration. In matters of religion, the emphasis is on tolerance and mutual respect, combined with the separation of the secular and religious spheres.

The other branch, deriving from the later Enlightenment in France and descending through the French Revolution, is anti-Christian, utopian, arbitrary, and unlimited. It takes its anti-Christianity, which is also anti-Judaism, mainly from Voltaire. The anti-Christianity and the abolition of limits are connected with the utopian dimension. Man, liberated by enlightenment and revolution, will build his own heaven on earth. The new incarnation is Rousseau's General Will.

What may be called the Francophone and Anglophone branches of the Enlightenment heritage were thus very different. During the French Revolution, Edmund Burke, defending the Anglophone branch against the Francophone, did more than anyone else to establish the magnitude and profundity of the divergence. He had been aware of that divergence even before the French Revolution: "I feel an insuperable reluctance," he wrote, "to destroy any established system of government, upon a Theory." He wrote that in 1783, six years before the fall of the Bastille. It is a convincing illustration—one among many—of the consistency and continuity of this thought.

By the second half of the twentieth century, the world appeared as divided between the two branches of the Enlightenment tradition, with the heritage of the English and American revolutions established not only in all the English-speaking countries but also in western Europe and Japan. The utopian-arbitrary heritage of the French Revolution appeared as dominant, and exclusively articulate, in the Soviet Union and what was then its eastern European empire, and also in China. The Third World was divided between the two tendencies, with the utopian-arbitrary one having a greater intrinsic attraction, at least from the fifties through the seventies. The greater intrinsic attraction was at first partly set off by the material influence of the West—known to a part of the international Left as "neocolonialism." Later the prestige of the utopian prospects faded after the failures of various socialist experiments, ranging from the drab but not inhumane failure of Ghanian socialism to the horrors of Equatorial Guinea and Pol Pot's Cambodia.

Then, five years ago, came the crisis of Soviet communism, which still continues. At the end of the eighties, in the euphoria that accompanied Soviet withdrawal from eastern Europe, this crisis appeared as almost wholly benign. It was widely assumed, in the media, that Soviet tyranny must automatically and everywhere be replaced by Western-style democracy. In terms of our present discussion, the branch of the Enlightenment that stems from the English-speaking revolutions would supersede the utopian-arbitrary branch, derived ultimately from the French Revolution. And I believe that that is the transition that Mikhail Gorbachev and the companions of his perilous journey did genuinely intend to make. They may indeed have put the eastern European countries—or some of them—on that road. But as far as the Soviet Union itself is concerned, it is now obvious the great reforming effort is in deep trouble. To many in the Soviet Union it looks as if the ghastly choice may lie between on the one hand the disintegration of the Soviet Union in a turmoil of multiple civil wars, based on local ethnic and religious conflicts, and on the other, the restoration of some kind of neo-Stalinist dictatorship. The recent "bankers' plot" speech by the prime minister of the Soviet Union, recalling the "doctors' plot" of Stalin's last months, is suggestive of rather rapid regression in that direction, which is the direction in which both the KGB and the highest ranks of the Soviet military establishment clearly wish to move.

We are all rightly apprehensive about that particular tendency, with its implied threat of a renewal of the Cold War, and the ominous possibility of delays in implementation of the withdrawal of Soviet troops from Germany and Poland. Yet we should not allow our apprehensions about the real threat coming from that direction to blind us to the hardly less horrendous threats coming from the opposite direction, the direction of the disintegration of the Soviet Union. And it is in that direction, most particularly that there lies, in its most acute form, the threat to *all* Enlightenment values which would be inherent in a general return to ethnic and religious traditions in the forms in which these prevailed before the dawn of the Enlightenment in *any* of its forms.

Let me now, to illustrate what I have in mind, come down from the level of abstract generalization and consider the fate of a particular section of a particular Soviet people with whom I happen to have had some contact. The people I speak of are the Tadjiks, and the section I have in mind, among the Tadjiks, are the educated women.

The Tadjiks are a people of central Asia. Tadjikistan borders on Afghanistan. When my wife and I visited Tadjikistan, in the early eighties—pre-*glasnost* days—the Afghan war was still in progress. The Tadjiks are akin to the Afghans and speak the same language, Farsi. Yet the Tadjiks we met did not identify with the Afghans. They regarded the Afghans as backward and barbarous, themselves as modern and civilized. The image of Enlightenment was vividly present in their minds. They contrasted the condition of their principality—Dushanbe—brilliantly lit by electricity, with the unrelieved darkness of the Afghan borders. They did not want to go back to that. Yet these same Tadjiks were intensely proud of their own cultural tradition, and in particular of the rich poetic heritage of the Farsi language. My wife is a poet, and many of the Tadjiks we met were poets and intellectuals. About half of them were women. They came from Muslim families, but did not think of conforming to Muslim rules. They dressed in Western style and talked with males on a basis of equality. They all had jobs.

That was nearly ten years ago now. Times have changed, and horribly for the worse, for people like that. Both for geographical and cultural reasons, news about Tadjikistan does not often reach us through the Western media. But what has reached us is not reassuring. One item, last year, told us of eight Tadjik women who had been raped by a Muslim mob. Their offense was that they were wearing Western dress as they walked down the streets of Dushanbe. That may or may not have been an isolated incident. But it is clear that in the event of Tadjikistan's seceding from the Soviet Union, and becoming an Islamic republic, women will be forcibly returned to the Middle Ages. And were there to be a plebiscite on the subject in Tadjikistan, women would probably not be allowed to vote.

I should not like to be a citizen of the Soviet Union. But I should prefer to be a citizen even of today's Soviet Union than to be a citizen of an independent Tadjikistan. And women have much stronger direct reasons for entertaining that preference than men do.

When I noted just now the presence of Enlightenment in Tadjikistan, that language may well have seemed strange to some at least among you. After all, such Enlightenment as reached Tadjikistan came there courtesy of Moscow, and came first in the days of Lenin and Stalin. To describe Stalinist Moscow as the source of *any* kind of Enlightenment may well seem to some of you a perversion of language. I don't think it is so, provided we keep in mind the distinction proposed in the opening part of my remarks. The kind of Enlightenment which radiated out from Moscow to places like Taskken or Samarkand or Dushanbe was not the kind of Enlightenment that most in the West cherish. It was a much harsher version, filtered and distilled through the French Revolution and then the nineteenth-century Russian revolutionary movement and then the Russian Revolution itself and the multiple civil wars through which the Russian empire was remolded into the Soviet Union, in the aftermath of the Russian Revolution. It had the characteristics of what was originally the Francophone branch of the Enlightenment-revolutionary tradition. It was—and is, for it is not dead yet, though it is in possibly terminal crisis—absolutist, utopian, dogmatic, and militantly antireligious.

Now it may reasonably be argued, from a Western point of view, that this particular tradition has no real title to the honorable term Enlightenment. Yet there are certainly features in it which would commend themselves to some of the leading figures of the Siècle des Lumières. Voltaire would have preferred the antireligious militancy of the Marxists and Bolsheviks to the wishy-washy live-and-let-live approach favored by the western democracies. Rousseau, like Robespierre, would have liked the putatively secular version of dogmatic absolutism which sustained the long-unchallengeable authority of the Communist party of the Soviet Union. The authority of a Lenin or a Stalin is foreshadowed in the role of the "guide" or "legislator" who makes his somewhat mysterious debut in chapters 6 and 7 of the second book of *Du contrat social.* The function of the guide/legislator was to interpret the General Will, not merely to others, but even to itself. As Rousseau wrote: "The General Will is always right [*droite*] but the judgement which guides it is not always enlightened." So the guide/interpreter stood to the General Will in the role of a tutor, and an equivocal sort of tutor at that. It was the job of the guide/interpreter "to see objects as they are, sometimes as they ought to appear to it." Historically, the first avatar of Rousseau's guide/interpreter was Robespierre, who, during the Terror of 1792–94, told the French exactly what the General Will wanted them to do. Robespierre reduced Rousseau's teaching to the lapidary formula: *"Notre Volonté C'est La Volonté Generale."*

The relationship in which Lenin and Stalin stood to "scientific socialism, Dialectical Materialism, and the Dictatorship of the Proletariat" was identical to that of Robespierre to the General Will.

As we look toward Moscow from the West, it is almost inconceivable to us that anyone could identify Moscow with any form of Enlightenment. But the view from the east has been different. To many young people in archaic and totally pre-Enlightenment environments, intellectually dominated by mullahs or shamans, Russian communism, with its militant and confident antireligiosity, appeared to bring a liberating message. That phenomenon has much to do with the astounding success of Lenin and Stalin in reconstituting the Russian empire, right out to Vladivostok, in the aftermath of a local revolution in Petrograd. The appeal of the Red army in the vast benighted areas of that empire was similar to the appeal of Bonaparte to the stagnant and stiflingly devout cities of northern Italy, as described by Stendhal in *La Chartreuse de Parme*. Now all that is threatened with reversal. In many areas, the authority of the mullahs and the shamans appears to be on the way back. The men and women who had distanced themselves from that authority are now threatened, especially the women.

The repercussions of the failure of the Soviet version of Enlightenment are not confined to the Soviet Union. They resound throughout the entire Third World. In that context, it must be remembered that the Soviet version of Enlightenment was always more intelligible in the Third World than the Western version is. The Western version is generally not proselytizing: the European countries, for example, never seriously tried to disseminate it to the masses in their Asian and African dependencies. Those who did acquire it—and they were a significant minority—generally did so in spite of their rulers, rather than with their encouragement. A typical comment, toward the end of the nineteenth century, was that of a governor of the Gold Coast, who spoke of "the educated African, the curse of the

West Coast." Much later, in what is now Zaire, I heard a Belgian mercenary declare, "I *like* the natives—that is the ones who are not polluted by the towns."

Both the education and the pollution to which those two statements referred were those of the Western Enlightenment, deemed unsuitable for export. On the other hand, both the Soviet Union and its Western admirers were very anxious to spread *their* version of the Enlightenment, with its utopian and antireligious components. The elites who came to power in the Third World through decolonization, early in the first half of the twentieth century, generally carried in their heads, along with their native inheritances, a confused and confusing mixture of both Enlightenment traditions. They had acquired something of the Western version, almost by osmosis, usually in periods of residence in Paris or London. At the same time in these same cities they had acquired, from left-wing intellectuals, a diluted version of the tradition that was common to the French and Russian revolutions. A common feature was faith in socialism as the key to liberty, progress, and the future.

Socialism was the faith of those Third World elites which were most affected by the Enlightenment tradition, in both its branches. And this fact put Enlightenment values at risk whenever professed socialists were in power and required to deliver the utopia to which socialism was supposed to be the key. The religious have the advantage there. They speak of Heaven, but they don't actually have to deliver it here on earth. You can't disprove religion. But you can disprove a terrestrial credo by trying it out and finding its working to be even more unsatisfactory than what had preceded it. In most cases, in the Third World, the terrestrial credo happened to be socialism, and its failure was universal. Indeed, the failure of the utopian version of the Enlightenment tradition was inherent in its very nature. Utopia literally gets you no place.

The failure of socialism, wherever it was tried in the Third World, has now been followed by the almost-declared bankruptcy of Soviet communism. Because what has failed is the version of the Enlightenment tradition which is most readily intelligible, the tendency of these developments has been toward the discredit of Enlightenment ideas generally. The train of thought runs: "It is a foreign idea. We tried it out and it didn't work. For the future, let's stick to our own ideas." That train of thought can be heard rumbling away in much of the Third World, and also in the Soviet Union and even in eastern Europe. "Our own ideas," now apparently in the ascendant, turn out to have a great deal of religion in them, and a great deal of miscellaneous xenophobia, including intensified anti-Semitism.

Most of the failures were under the banner of socialism. But capitalism and democracy—the most conspicuous institutions of the Western branch of the Enlightenment—are also at high risk in the measure that they penetrate into the Third World, and at some risk also, I believe, in eastern Europe.

The most conspicuous failure of capitalism, and the most resounding and comprehensive rejection of Enlightenment values was, of course, the Iranian revolution. The shah was not exactly an incarnation of the finest values of the Western Enlightenment, but he was attached to certain of these values, crudely interpreted, and he was generally seen as having adhered to those values, in preference to those of Islam. In failing to dissimulate the contempt he felt for the Muslim teachers of the Law, the shah appeared to be treating his own people with contempt, while he fawned on the foreigner. He paid the penalty for having violated a basic maxim of Machiavelli's: "The Prince must cultivate an appearance of piety."

That is a maxim which Western Princes, even in the very capital of the Enlightenment, have always prudently observed. To get away with being enlightened, you have to be polite and considerate toward those who are not. Those who are not are not confined to the Third World.

The Iranian revolution should be carefully studied, and whatever lessons become clear from it should be learned. There was certainly a spectacular advance there, by what is loosely called fundamentalism, against a crude version of Enlightenment. Yet the fundamentalist gains in this case may not be permanent: in fact, they seem to be eroding at present. The ayatollahs may have overplayed their hands by setting up a Rule of the Saints. They were, in a sense, repeating the error of the socialists, by appearing to promise the undeliverable: Heaven on earth. As a result Iran, in the future, may prove a more fertile seed bed for Enlightenment ideas than other countries in the region.

The relativity and instability, under Third World conditions, of categories like "fundamentalist" and "enlightened" appear from the recent history of Iran and Iraq. In theory, Iraq is among the most enlightened countries of the Middle East. Its enlightenment derives from the French left, through the left-wing Christian Syrian intellectual Michel Aflaq, and it belongs in consequence in that branch of the Enlightenment which descends from the French Revolution, and is cognate with the Russian one. The fact that Iraq is, in practice, a despotism in no way flaws its legitimacy within that particular branch of the Enlightenment. Both Voltaire and Diderot cultivated enlightened despots, and Saddam Hussein, until very recently, was content to appear in that role. During the Iran-Iraq war, Iraq appeared as a bastion of secular enlightenment against the fundamentalist theocracy to the east. Yet as soon as the enemy ceased to be Iran and became the United States, Iraq promptly switched off its Enlightenment. Saddam proclaimed, and continues to proclaim, the jihad for the protection of the holy places of Islam, allegedly threatened by the infidels. Iraq's "enlightenment" of yesterday had not penetrated very deep, and it may be that Iraq's "fundamentalism" of today does not go much deeper.

In terms of Enlightenment values, the general pattern that can be discerned, worldwide, is roughly as follows: One branch of the Enlightenment—the one that descends through the French and Russian revolutions—has lost ground, mainly to pre-Enlightenment forces, both religious and ethnic. Within the Soviet Union the struggle between these forces is oscillating between the poles of anarchy on the one hand, and a restoration of despotism on the other. Similar though not identical struggles are going on in eastern Europe. These are dangerous conditions, by their nature, and there are signs that the era of good feeling between the United States and Gorbachev's Soviet Union may be drawing to its close.

The Western branch of the Enlightenment, derived through the English Revolution of 1688 and the American Revolution, has outlived the other branch, enormously influential though that branch once was. The Soviet Union itself may indeed be knitted together again, painfully and bloodily, by a coalition of centripetal forces in and around the Communist party cadres, the armed forces, the KGB, and the minorities inside various republics. If that happens, the communist ideology, is likely to be dusted off and restored, at least to some extent, if only as a sort of conceptual lingua franca of the Russian Empire, after its second restoration. The same ideology serves a similar uniting function in China. But communism no longer exerts a magnetism, internationally. It is those institutions of the Western Enlightenment, capitalism and democracy, which do exert such a magnetism.

In general, it would be well if the leaders of the Western world would allow these institutions to exert their inherent attractiveness in their own way, and allow them to find their own balance, along with the local pre-Enlightenment forces in different parts of the Third World. Vocal, missionary exhortation about spreading democracy, for example, probably does more harm than good, by stamping democracy, in the eyes of all kinds of nativists everywhere, as an alien idea.

Let me conclude by a word about the Charter of the United Nations, and about the Gulf War. The Charter is a classic Enlightenment document, owing something to both branches of that tradition. It stands for the principle of collective security against aggression. But how much that may mean, in any given set of circumstances, depends on the major powers, at the given time. The League of Nations also stood for collective security, but Britain and France, the leading relevant powers at the time, let Mussolini get away with his annexation of Abyssinia, thus dooming the League to extinction, and starting the world on the slide to the Second World War.

When Saddam Hussein, in August 1990, annexed Kuwait, that was the first time in history that one member of the United Nations had annexed another. The United States took the lead in determining that that annexation would not be permitted. The United States was admittedly motivated, in so doing, not only by its commitment to the charter but also by its own perceived interests in that oil-rich region. But the interests of the United States also require a certain minimum of order in international relations, and Saddam Hussein's course of action was a denial of that basic minimum. The war in the Gulf is not only formally, but also in substance, a war in defense of the charter. All small countries with powerful and greedy neighbors will be the safer for it.

The Western reaction to Saddam's annexation of Kuwait was both legitimate in principle and solidly based in terms of interest. But

Western promises about a new order in the region, after the Gulf War, are a serious mistake. Neither the United States nor any of its Western allies is capable of such prodigies as bringing about stability in an inherently unstable region or bringing about reconciliation between Israel and those Palestinians who cheered Iran's SCUD missiles on their way to Tel Aviv. The records of both British and American diplomacy in the Middle East are very poor indeed—and that holds good of American diplomacy right up to the end of July 1990, when signals were still being sent to Saddam Hussein which he interpreted as a green light for his invasion of Kuwait.

Let us put all that within the framework of our present topic. Minds formed within a post-Enlightenment culture find difficulty in communicating with minds formed within what is still largely pre-Enlightenment culture. Communication will, nevertheless, have to be attempted. But the more modest and the more readily intelligible the objectives, the more effective the communication will be. Efforts to attain grandiose objectives, such as stability for the Middle East, are bound to fail, and amid recriminations that will leave things even worse than before.

On the plane of ideas, the leaders of the post-Enlightenment world cannot determine how fast or in which modes the Enlightenment can spread to the Third World. Conscious efforts to spread it will defeat themselves by stimulating xenophobia. Left to themselves, certain Third World countries already find themselves at home with one institution of the post-Enlightenment: capitalism. In general, Enlightenment has to spread itself, through minds eager to receive it. Governments should stick to less ambitious projects.

Afterword

This lecture was delivered on February 20, 1991. It shows clear marks of its date of composition and I am content on the whole to leave it like that. That is how events looked then and on the whole it is still, I believe, relevant to what has gone on since and is still going on.

There are just two points on which I have second thoughts: one concerns the relatively benign effects of the French revolutionary tradition of the Enlightenment as it reached certain Third World areas. I still believe this is generally so, or has been so as regards the former Soviet Union. But I have become convinced after reading Kanan Makiya *Cruelty and Silence* (London, Johnathan Cape 1993) that certain versions of modernization claiming descent from the Enlightenment (specifically the French Enlightenment) are even worse than fundamentalist Islam. Specifically, modernization as practiced in Saddam's Iraq and Assad's Syria (though we know less about the latter) is more oppressive than the conservatism of Jordan and Saudi Arabia and possibly even than the Iranian theocracy.

I also need to revise my remarks on Tadjikistan—not for their general tendency this time but because of the course of events since they were written. The fundamentalists do seem to have tried to take over there, but their opponents called in and received aid from Russia and are now holding off the fundamentalist exiles based in Afghanistan. In this particular case, sticking to Russia seems to be preferable, at least where women are concerned, to the alternative that the exiles and the Afghans have to offer.

9 "What Then?": The Irrepressible Radicalism of Democracy

ALAN GILBERT

Radicalism as an Avatar of Liberalism

Since 1989, democratic revolutions and movements have swept eastern Europe, the Soviet Union, and China. Though some of these movements have yet to succeed, they have signaled the end of authoritarian, one-party socialism. Many politicians and social scientists who had seen these systems as unchangeable enemies of the capitalist democratic West have now discovered the death of Marxian radicalism ("outside of Cambridge and Managua") and the end of history in a "free"-market, parliamentary regime. Francis Fukuyama, for instance, alleges that such regimes realize classless democracy. That supposition mirrors Hegel's defense of nondemocratic liberalism, a notion that history has reached completion.

Since the revolutionary inception of liberalism, democratic struggles, often led by radicals, have extended the insight that no one may own the body or compel the conscience of another. At each juncture—the emancipation of serfs and slaves, the extension of suffrage, the organization of workers, the women's movement, the struggles against colonialism, racism, and fascism—the advantaged have proclaimed the end of history, the achievement of a sufficient common good, and sought to lay specters to rest. Yeats's "What then?" questions a complacent academic life that attempts to force completeness. The chorus, "But louder sang that ghost: what then?" also haunts Fukuyama's account, which seeks to trim history to the often-harmful workings of the capitalist market.

This argument will give ethical reasons to support Fukuyama's position—*if* he is empirically right—and suggest two rejoinders. First, radicals maintain that major political and social changes are needed to further democratic individuality and deepen moral progress. Thus democratic theorists have long emphasized the primacy of equal liberty, the notion that each person has basic rights—including freedoms of conscience, speech, and association—which constrain justified state policies. Yet inequalities of wealth tend to transform parliamentary regimes into oligarchies.[1] The reign of the free market—and even the welfare state—may conflict with equal freedom. Second, radicals argue for the moral and social theoretical deepening of liberalism. For, as a modern Hegelian might ask, who are we to cut the restless concepts of democracy and individuality to current circumstance? A regime that furthers individuality—the idea that each may pursue a good life, revising her conception in the light of experience as she sees fit, so long as she does not harm others—may rule out hierarchical individualisms.

This essay identifies what is common in core Aristotelian, liberal, and radical *political* theories and sketches social theoretical debates between sophisticated liberals and radicals—ones responsive to each others' objections—over democratic institutional changes. The last three sections focus on the potentials for democratic internationalism and peace, the role of "intelligence" testing and eugenics in renewed repression, and the role of transformed conceptions of individuality in the design of radical democratic institutions.

Political Theory and Moral Progress

As Aristotle's *Politics* reveals, the Greek city marked the discovery that even the divinely sanctioned rule of a monarch is not political, not adequate to a publicly created good life for humans.[2] To put Aristotle's argument in a modern idiom, (those regarded as) humans have an equally sufficient capacity for moral personality or public freedom. Free regimes contrast with the defective rule of earlier Persian and Greek despotisms: "The most natural offshoot of the village appears to be that of the colony or offshoot from a family. . . . This, it may be noted, is the reason why each Greek polis was originally ruled—as the peoples of the barbarian world still are—by kings." Once a free politics emerges, so do distinctive conflicts about justice. Thus Aristotle depicts the domination of rich and poor, oligarchy and democracy, as the most common regimes and sketches institutions that might sustain a common good. Aristotle thus advances three theses that will prove central to political theory: (1) that a regime characterized by equal freedom for at least some humans is possible and desirable (the free-regime thesis), (2) that class conflict for domination ordinarily characterizes political life within free regimes (the class-struggle thesis), and (3) that political institutions that benefit all and offset the power of an otherwise predominant class are possible (the common-good thesis).

Modern political theories extend and transform these insights. In Hegel's words, Aristotle's conception, though marred by the justification of slavery, registers the moral discovery that "some [Greek males] are free." Yet Hegel's theory of individuality deepens Aristotle's notion of freedom: "The Greeks not only had slaves, on which their life and the continued existence of their beautiful freedom depended, but their very freedom itself was in part only a contingent, undeveloped, transient, and limited flowering and, in part, a hard servitude of all that is human and humane."[3]

If, along with Aristotle, we consider ethics and political science to be theoretical projects that proceed through contrasts of the leading contemporary arguments—"opinions"—in the light of evidence, then we may think that the best explanation for the decline of slavery and the emergence of institutions in which all—women as well as men, "barbarian" as well as Greek—"are free" is that preliberal political and social institutions, by and large, conflict with a good life for humans.[4]

Hegel articulates a legal structure that furthers individuality and freedom of speech; he was, however, no democrat.[5] In this regard, both an Aristotelian conception that values public deliberation—ruling and being ruled in turn—as an intrinsic good and modern democratic views have political and institutional resources that an unmodified Hegelian theory does not. More important, however, Hegel defends modern individuality: "the substantive aim of the world spirit is achieved through the freedom of each individual." For the core notion of democratic individuality is, once again, that each person can pursue a good life as he sees fit, revising his conception in the light of experience, so long as he does not harm others.[6] But the notion of democratic individuality is also social and political. Thus, for Hegel, the idea of free self-consciousness has three moments: the particular decisions of the will, the objective realization of the will in a regime of equal freedom, and the insight that the regime as well as the agent is free. In fact, despite Hegel's protests against the misapplication of notions of contract to politics, his notion of self-consciousness resembles Rawls's democratic contractarianism: in an uncoerced setting, each must be able to affirm that the basic social and political structure is genuinely cooperative. We may reformulate the project of democratic theory in a Hegelian idiom: to forge the political and social institutions, organized around a *common good* of mutual recognition among persons, which further—or at least do not obstruct—the individuality of each. We might call this explicitly transformative notion of a common good characteristic of liberalism the project-of-politics thesis. In this context, Marx's conception of an association in which "the free development of each is the condition for the free development of all" is a variant of liberalism.[7] Thus modern liberalism and radicalism each extend and, in some respects, revolutionize Aristotle's conception of a free regime.

In *Marx's Politics* and *Democratic Individuality,* I have argued that sophisticated radicalism emerges out of the unfolding of democratic revolutions. Adapting Aristotle's conception of class struggle, radicals note that oligarchy cannot sustain the freedom of each; an "extreme democracy" or "red republicanism" arises when the free, who are many, seek to dispossess the wealthy. As Marx puts it.

> The first manifestation of a truly active communist party is contained within the bourgeois revolution, at the moment when the constitutional monarchy is eliminated. The most consistent republicans, in England, the Levellers, in France, Babeuf, Buonarroti, etc., were the first to proclaim these "social questions." *The Babeuf Conspiracy,* by Babeuf's friend and party comrade Buonarroti, shows how these republicans *derived from the "movement" of history* the realization that the disposal of the social question of rule by princes and republic

> did not mean that even a single "social question" has been solved in the interests of the proletariat.[8]

Unlike Aristotle, for whom, "by Zeus," the rebellious poor are a "herd of beasts," or Hegel, for whom they are a victimized but misguided "rabble," radicals offer a contrasting causal theory and transvalue moral assessments.[9] Yet their critique adapts earlier arguments.

For liberals also recognize that slaves have the capacity for moral personality; in Hegel's words, "the status of slaves is an outrage against the concept of a human being."[10] Like radicals, he suggests that the capitalist system harms the poor—subjects them "through no fault of their own"—and undercuts the ethical universality of the modern state. Unlike radicals, however, Hegel envisioned no novel political and social alternative. Instead, he sought to head off the class struggle he glimpsed in England through the preservation of estates and monarchy.[11] One might see these institutional claims as Aristotelian attempts to secure a common good. Hegel's defense of monarchy is, however, defective. One cannot affirm freedom of conscience in religion but deny it in politics, or insist on enlivening individuality in civil society yet constrict political individuality to kingly caprice.

Radicals often mainly criticize the exploitation of wage workers as well as slaves. In the new capitalist setting, however, radicals also stress Aristotle's and Hegel's critique of oligarchy—the corruption of *equal* freedom which arises from inequalities of wealth. For radicals may more tellingly criticize unjust wars or racist and sexist ideologies than narrower forms of predatory economic advantage. Thus, in the *Grundrisse,* Marx insisted, from the moment slaves recognize their potential as humans—that they are not "the property of another"—slavery has only "an artificial, vegetative existence."[12]

Liberal theory is close to the radical one that sees "wage slavery," understood in its full ramifications as oligarchy, as a further "outrage against the concept of a human being," to rephrase Hegel. In fact, the version of radicalism most difficult for a liberal to repel is precisely one that starts from a common revolutionary moral insight, the project-of-politics argument, then criticizes inegalitarian institutions and practices and suggests democratic alternatives. We might call such arguments *equal-freedom-* or *democratic autonomy-driven egal-*

itarian ones in which egalitarianism is understood not just in terms of economic distribution but of democratization of social and political institutions. Liberalism promises that on the most important issues—those of persecution, war, and distribution—a deliberative *political association* can control or even become the state; a radical view seeks to deliver on this promise.[13]

Thus, in upholding mutual regard among persons across differing views, liberal affirmations of moral progress resemble, at least broadly, radical claims. This argument counters widely held misimpressions of both political theories. For instance, some think that liberals hold no historical view at all, that they build society out of asocial individuals ("atoms") or "aggregate" containers of putatively natural, exogenously determined preferences. But these spurious facsimiles of liberal conceptions fail to capture the central importance of equal freedom, of the moral personality of each, let alone of individuality, to liberalism. Equal freedom as an ethical and political property cannot exist as a characteristic of isolated individuals; in addition, psychologically, such freedom is not one preference among others comparable to that for rutabagas. For a coherent liberalism, freedom refers to an underlying capacity to form and act on authentic "preferences." On a similar misunderstanding, some hold that, for Marxians, "moral" stands vary with modes of production or social class.[14] But these relativist or reductionist metaethical claims do not capture the complexity of radical moral judgments and are self-refuting. Thus, Marx praises communist association for abolishing war, racism, and exploitation; yet these metaethics suggest that the opposite conditions would be equally "justified."

Well-argued theories of moral advance—Aristotelian, liberal, and radical—have three features: (1) conflicts of intrinsic human goods characterize the initial period(s) of human history or what Marx refers to as "prehistory"; (2) common occurrence and mutual reinforcement of major goods characterizes a subsequent stage—fully human history—even though some important ethical and spiritual qualities may be lost; and (3) these two phases involve overlapping but shifting understandings of the self—in prehistory, the prevalence of comparatively deficient selves, at least ones not fully characterized by mutual recognition and individuality; in history, comparatively self-aware, democratic individuality.

On a modern understanding, Aristotle's political theory also identifies conflicts of goods, for the initial despotisms at best preserved existence—security against foreign attack—at the expense of freedom. But Aristotle identifies a *political* regime as one that furthers not mere life but a good life.

Kant's and Hegel's philosophies of history, however, sketch a distinctively liberal account of ethical advance. On the first feature, as Kant puts it, "Only later generations will in fact have the good fortune to inhabit the building on which a whole series of their forefathers (admittedly without any conscious intention) had worked without themselves being able to share in the happiness they were preparing."[15] Initially, as Hegel suggests, the Greeks purchased their beautiful freedom at the expense of slavery. But a modern regime joins wide political freedom with the search for individuality. For the earlier phase(s), liberals recognize conflicts of goods—say the emergence of freedom, philosophy, and science at the expense of mutual recognition—as characteristic of moral advance. If the modern creation of free institutions is, to some degree, a self-conscious enterprise, we might consider the Greek case—and perhaps a number of others—*necessary* to the progress of political and individual self-awareness, but inadequate. Once a vision of cooperative arrangements that further individuality emerges, we might doubt whether such conflicts of goods continue to be necessary; at some, perhaps quite early, point, they become contingent.[16]

Marx's judgments about initial, alienated progress stress similar moral conflicts. His accounts of original capitalist accumulations do not praise the advance of science and mechanization; instead, he speaks of the "blood and fire" of English enclosures, the "hothouse transformation of Africa into a commercial warren for the hunting of blackskins," the rending of the innocent Indian village: "Has the bourgeoisie ever affected a progress without dragging individuals and peoples through blood and dirt, misery and degradation?"[17] Given such conflicts of goods, Marx offers no overall assessment of precapitalist and capitalist regimes. But cutting against the grain of instrumental progress to empathize with the suffering of ordinary people, Walter Benjamin's insight that *the angel of history looks backward* captures the moral tenor of radical—and well-argued liberal—theory.

At a certain historical point, the second feature of moral progress, a concordance of goods—the concomitant realization of diverse intrinsic goods in a wider common good—becomes possible. Thus, for Aristotle, the polis realized political goods (freedom, military prowess, virtue) and nonpolitical ones (friendship, contemplation, science, the arts). But modern liberals such as Montesquieu would contrast ancient warrior republics, which fused military egalitarianism and slavery, to the English commercial republic, which would abolish torture and slavery, tolerate religious differences, promote commerce, industry, and gentle manners, and achieve peace. According to Montesquieu, that republic's greatness arose from modern individuality as opposed to the ancient virtuous, but fierce and often mindless, attachment to what is common.[18]

On the third feature, the understanding of the self, for both Kant and Hegel new political and social conditions facilitate the emergence of less-domineering conduct. In "prehistory," passionate individuals, driven by what Kant calls the "asocial sociability" of narrow self-interest, spur *historical* change. Transformations occur "behind the backs" of the actors; outcomes contrast with intentions. Yet such liberal accounts do not rule out the Aristotelian concern for a healthy person to be a self—a concern for what we would call individuality—as distinct from being selfish; they maintain only that selfish actions or ones lacking self-awareness mainly drove the first economic and political transformations. Thus a liberal—and radical—view of progress requires no startling transformation of human motivation, no prevalence of impersonal altruism; rather, under favorable conditions, a free regime elicits ordinary psychological possibilities for mutual regard and individuality, which have been blunted by hierarchical institutions.

Similarly, for Marx, a free regime sustains diverse goods such as political deliberativeness, peace, the abolition of wage slavery, the arts and sciences, leisure, and individuality. As the *Manifesto* insists, the proletariat and its allies must "win the battle of democracy."[19] Marx commends the institutions of the Paris Commune, characterized by public debate, the payment of only a skilled worker's wage to officials, immediate recall of corrupt officials, and a citizen army, as "the *political* form at last discovered in which to work out the economic emancipation of labor."[20] More sharply than those liberalisms that tolerate class and status differences, a radical conception emphasizes a plurality of comprehensive *individual* views about the good.

In contrast to classical liberalism, Marx thought that self-aware individuals would create communism; like Wilhelm Wolff, to whom Marx dedicated *Capital,* such individuals would find (a significant part of) their self-realization in working to achieve a better society. For Marx, democratic argument requires some transparency of political and social structure. But as Will Kymlicka puts it, today's liberal theorists also "desire a society that is transparently intelligible—where nothing works behind the backs of its members, and where the causes of our actions are the considerations we have recognized and affirmed as reasons for action."[21] Such arguments, however, restrict the term "transparency" to those basic institutions that serve as conditions for democratic individuality. For individuality is diverse, ongoing, and opaque—in many ways dark and strange, for instance, in the changing play of the unconscious (underworld) and daylight consciousness in a person's awareness of death over a lifetime. Individuality is a matter of being more than elucidation.[22]

On the foregoing argument, the complex political and institutional differences between Aristotelians, liberals, and radicals turn on empirical controversies in biological and social theory—whether there are natural slaves, whether capitalist inequalities are consistent with equal liberty—and not on clashes of underlying moral and political theoretical premises. Such theories exhibit what Hegel calls in the *Phenomenology* a bacchanal or, less vividly, a conversation driven by the unfolding of individuality.[23]

Yet today many scholars question the possibility of such a conversation and adopt an intuitive metaethical and social theoretical relativism: the claim that we can give no reasonable arguments for one moral alternative as opposed to another; instead, we must supposedly reduce claims about freedom, justice, and individuality to the standards of the powerful or of particular classes, or to "our" considered intuitions.

Diverse cultural trends—a new relationship of humans to the natural environment captured in Nietzsche's insight that "God is dead" or Weber's "disenchantment of the world," the horrors of ethnocentrism, historicist versions of Marxism, a largely Weberian social science, empiricist value-freedom, many versions of postmodernism, and the like—underpin widespread conventionalist intuitions. Even Leo Strauss suggests that he cannot answer historicism.[24] More obviously, Fukuyama's celebration of freedom—"the remarkable consensus around liberal democracy"—and his critique of radicalism—that no "large state" invokes Marxism with conviction—rest on Thrasymachean worship of power. A Nietzschean distaste for the "last men" coupled with an ahistorical admiration for ancient Greece at the expense of a modernity that includes the emancipation of slaves, serfs, and women and a transformed vision of individuality marks off implausible, often—ironically—relativist versions of Straussianism from liberalism.

Yet metaethical conventionalism also undermines democratic theory. For example, on the one hand, John Rawls insists that "very great ethical values," such as rights of conscience, speech, and political association, cannot be compromised. He decries conceptions of justice which are "political in the wrong way," tailored to serve particular interests. On the other hand, Rawls's sophisticated constructivism—his metaethical appeals to a starting point in our "relatively purified intuitions," ones we affirm on reflection—takes back in moral epistemology the claims he defends with reasons in ethical judgment or political theory.[25] Given the clarity of some central moral verdicts and the self-refutingness of relativism, however, the burden of proof lies with conventionalists.

The foregoing argument about democratic individuality suggests an additional cause for the prevalence of academic relativism. Many conventionalists see complex political arguments as self-contained, motivated by "incommensurable," underlying ethical premises; they often elaborate their own conceptions without attention to central objections from critics. But if radicalism stems from the same underlying moral claims as liberalism and draws attention to politically uncomfortable facts, then the widespread adoption of relativism may—inadvertently—discourage fair rejoinders.

Oligarchy and Democratic Internationalism

This section offers a fourth core thesis of political theory, an Aristotelian-liberal-Marxian claim about democratic internationalism, and sketches institutional proposals to check the persisting antidemocratic character of American foreign policy.

Praising an international consensus on parliaments and markets, Fukuyama celebrates the role of ideas in history and dismisses power-state realism. But during the Cold War—from Guatemala and Iran to Chile, El Salvador, and South Africa, to name only a few cases—American policy belied transadministration presidential pronouncements about human rights and democracy; instead it sustained repressive oligarchies, often military dictatorships, by massive military and police aid and training as well as by covert intervention, against popular threats.[26] Even in the Clinton era, while the U.S. government sometimes seeks to limit abuses of human rights, it tolerates fledgling democracies only where ordinary citizens do not challenge the liberty-corrupting income and work hierarchies generated by the market; it maintains the repressive military-aid pipeline unabated. Great-power realism or refined radical theories of imperialism explain such antidemocratic policies more easily than does Fukuyama's vision of the straightforward effectiveness of ideas.

During the Cold War, a predominant realist paradigm in international-relations theory envisioned competing national interests as independent of domestic-regime structures; it made the study of democracy in foreign policy an anomaly. But if we grant that premise for the sake of argument, we may then ask what effect such rivalry is likely to have on democracy at home. Given repeated invocations of foreign enemies as a justification for domestic repression, the likely response is: crippling.[27] Today's neorealists such as Stephan Krasner and Samuel P. Huntington have implausibly tended to operationalize a notion of a national interest or common good as whatever strengthens state institutions. But a clearly stated *liberal* version of realism about American foreign policy, one that conceives the common good of a regime as at least the preservation of the lives of citizens, and perhaps of equal basic liberties, tends toward radicalism.

For, from the Monroe Doctrine to the Cold War, American officials have justified antidemocratic domestic policies as a means to combat "outside agitators." Since the Russian Revolution, charges of subversion by a supposedly monolithic international communist movement and the alleged impermeability of totalitarianism to change have served as part of a quasi-realist rationalization for domestic as well as foreign repression.[28] In *The Price of Empire,* former senator William Fulbright underlines some limitations of *patterned* interventionism for the freedom of ordinary Americans:

> It is easy to say—and often is said—that we cannot have tolerable relations with new revolutionary regimes. The problem is that our anticommunist paranoia has made it impossible to find out. We do not know whether Mao's declared interest in a relationship with the Americans in the 1940s or Ho Chi Minh's were sincere. And the reason we don't know is that we never tried to find out. Those who reported it was a possibility were hounded out of the foreign service because of our suspicion and fear of communism. The legacy of that era brings to mind Ivan the Terrible's practice of murdering the bearer of bad news. We are more civilized than that; we have been content simply to ruin people's careers.

Fulbright connects the militarization of the American economy with a decline in living standards; he links the interests of citizens at home with furthering democracy abroad.[29]

The peaceful evolution of parliamentary regimes in eastern Europe, Nicaragua, and the Soviet Union has removed the standard rationale for American intervention. But in the Reagan-Bush and even the Clinton eras, violent intervention has increased. One might imagine satirically that, with the end of the Cold War, Fulbright's internationalism would no longer be an isolated voice; unlike Fukuyama's, Fulbright's argument might give claims about a role for democratic ideas in international politics some moral or political cutting edge. But given the economic and political oligarchy of the United States, a radical might suggest, the publicity accorded Fukuyama's views in contrast to the silence accorded more pointed public-policy arguments, like Fulbright's or Kevin Phillips's, is not surprising.

In this context, a liberal might offer a Hegelian reformulation of democratic internationalism: the struggle for human rights and democracy has unfolded historically under unfavorable circumstances and made a long-term impact mainly through movements *from below.* In other words, citizens of one country often have common interests with citizens of others against the policies of "their own" oligarchic regime, even when that regime has a parliamentary form. This view undermines realist statism—the claim that state policies, by and large, adequately represent the interests of citizens. Such a liberal might invoke Thucydides and cite Aristotle's warning to Athenians about the threat to free institutions of seeking conquests abroad: "A polis should not be considered happy nor a legislator praised, when its citizens are trained for victory in war and the subjugation of neighboring regimes. Such a policy . . . implies that any citizen who can do so, should make it his object to capture the government of his own city."[30] In an American setting, one might recall the climate of suspicion about leftist and moderate critics, the role of centralized police forces—the CIA and FBI—in intimidation and the limiting of "respectable" political alternatives, and threats to the Constitution such as Watergate and the Iran-Contra affair.

A liberal might also invoke Kant's contrast of citizens who might resist war, sanctioned by novel republican institutions, to idle monarchs who waste subjects' lives in a mere "pleasure party" of war:

> If the consent of the citizens is required in order to decide that war should be declared . . . nothing is more natural than that they would be very cautious in commencing such a poor game, decreeing for themselves all the calamities of war. Among the latter would be having to fight, having to pay the cost of war from their own resources, having painfully to repair the devastation war leaves behind, and, to fill up the measure of evils, load themselves with a heavy national debt that would embitter peace itself and that can never be liquidated on account of constant wars in the future.[31]

Following Kant, Michael Doyle has emphasized how rarely parliamentary democracies have attacked one another; he also points to a commonality of their institutions and legitimacies which makes it harder for belligerent leaders to justify to citizens the horrors of war. As Doyle notes, this "pacific union" does not extend to unlike regimes.[32] Yet even this sophisticated liberalism from above does not explain U.S. covert interventions against parliamentary regimes—for instance, against Jacobo Arbenz in Guatemala, Cheddi Jagan in Guiana, Juan Bosch in the Dominican Republic, and Salvador Allende in Chile—its funding of French colonialism in Indochina and its overturning of the elections mandated by the Geneva

Accords, its murderous pattern of military and police aid elsewhere. For as a radical might suggest, Kant did not foresee that the political atmosphere of commercial oligarchy might resemble that of monarchy, making citizen resistance to French colonialism in Algeria or to U.S. aggression in Vietnam a hazardous, protracted project. Even in parliamentary regimes, political and economic elites remain, in an important Kantian sense, *proprietors* of the state.

Thus, a liberal view must stress the role of citizen resistance or democratic internationalism from below. As I argue in *Democratic Individuality,* referendums about the initiation of wars which would follow some period of public debate would hinder expansionary policies. Such referendums could occur whenever time allows, most obviously in cases of intervention against lesser powers like Vietnam, Iraq, Haiti, or Nicaragua. Public funding of issue-oriented committees to conduct debate could replace today's dominance by an oligarchic media. In fact, given the advantages of the powerful, a decent regime might expect—and not discourage—civil disobedience. Yet a radical might point out that, without changes in background conditions, changes undercutting the subtle influence of oligarchy in elections, social institutions, and the military, even the foregoing institutional reforms might not guarantee fair consideration of the concerns of ordinary citizens. A worked-out, liberal version of democratic internationalism from below tends toward radicalism.[33]

A critic might, however, try to undercut democratic internationalism by suggesting that citizens are—as contemporary patriotism in the United States sometimes shows—bellicose.[34] Paraphrasing Aristotle, this critic might wonder what distinguishes such peoples from "a herd of beasts." Yet a radical (or liberal) might respond: first, if true, the claim undercuts liberalism as well as radicalism, showing that modern democracy is predatory. But, then, Thucydides' and Aristotle's warnings about the likely authoritarian fate of such regimes is warranted. Second, internationalist movements have often been quite strong—for instance, the socialist parties before World War I or the communist-led resistance to Nazism. That these movements did not accomplish mammoth aims—that is, stopping world wars—shows neither their insignificance nor lack of potential. Further, during the American Civil War, English workers checked their government's intervention on the side of slaveholders; the German November Revolution canceled the expansionary Treaty of Brest-Litovsk.[35] Third, given the prevalence of the "ruling ideas" or oligarchic hegemony, a radical expects some degree of popular imperialism. Fourth, conjoining these two points, radicals insist that democratic organization from below is needed to sustain internationalism. That need is heightened by the fact that no two wars have the same dynamic (consider the United States in Vietnam and Iraq). As a German imperialist opponent of social democratic internationalism, Max Weber also stressed the importance of political organization: "Experience shows that the pacifist interests of petty bourgeois and proletarian strata very often and very easily fail. This is . . . because of the easier accessibility of all unorganized 'masses' to emotional influences."[36] Fifth, given the existence of predatory nationalism among ordinary people, a radical thesis needs a psychological account of chauvinism toward "outsiders."[37] Because internationalist movements have been widespread, however, these psychological dynamics need not be decisive.

In addition, radicals can learn a more *political* emphasis from Aristotelian and Kantian views. For Marxians have often overemphasized the influence of particular firms—say, of oil companies in the Middle East—or of even broader economic and strategic interests—for instance, in their structural accounts of oligarchy. But an internationalist view suggests that the elites of prevailing parties, as well as capitalists, have a *political* stake in the currency of antiradical and, today, antipatriotic stereotyping. As E. L. Doctorow puts it pointedly, "This poisonous thing I'm trying to describe is (a) characteristic way of dealing with criticism. It used to be enough to brand a critic as a radical or a leftist to make people turn away. Now we need only to call him a liberal. Soon 'moderate' will be the M word, 'conservative' will be the C word, and only fascists will be in the mainstream."[38] "Lani-ing"—the suppression of congressional and media discussion of Professor Guinier's proposals for reforms to check majority-rule-sanctioned patterns of racism—continues this trend. Such ideologies license banal but often effective sexist and militarist voting appeals that contrast "weak" with "real" men and stigmatize reasoned proposals for a common good. They divert attention from domestic decline, victimizing most people as well as individual candidates (they even sometimes, as in John F. Kennedy's, George Bush's, and Richard Nixon's campaigns, make a self-defeating caricature of the victor). Yet such ideologies serve a collective or "bipartisan" elite interest, one that sets a bar for admission to or survival in mainstream politics. Thus political and ideological concerns play a central role, alongside economic ones, in explaining the transadministration pattern of American antidemocratic intervention. Contra Fukuyama, a democratic foreign policy and sufficiently democratic institutions remain to be established.

Discipline, Eugenics, and the Making of Strangers

On a radical view, a hierarchical domestic-status order, sustained by racism, is linked to status hierarchy internationally. Such hierarchies are a locus not just of predatory interventions abroad but of internal dissension. Within parliamentary regimes, this interconnection suggests that many decent institutional reforms, facilitating countervailing democratic movements, are unlikely to deliver on the promises of liberalism.

This section invokes this interconnection to counter the liberal claim that democratic education is a sufficient vehicle to erode class and status stratification.[39] It modifies arguments of Foucault and of critical theory about instrumental rationality to explore the sociological role of IQ testing and emphasizes the interplay of renewed eugenics with increasingly oppressive hierarchy.

Radical theory has long stressed an interaction between the ruling ideas—"hegemony" in Antonio Gramsci's phrase—and practice. Marx claimed that divisions among the oppressed—in England, for instance, between citizen workers and Irish immigrants—sustained an oppressive elite. He regarded this cleavage, rooted in colonial rule in Ireland, as "the secret of the impotence of the English working class despite its [high level of craft union] organization."[40] Further, he suggested that "press, pulpit and comic paper" spawned bigotry toward the Irish.

Yet Marxians often advance functional claims at a high level of abstraction. The sometimes considerable plausibility of such approximations rests more on general facts about society than on investigations of a particular nexus of power. For example, in an oligarchy one might expect to hear, as Kevin Phillips reports, that in the Reagan-Bush years the top 1 percent of income receivers increased its share while all others held constant or lost. Radicals might have expected this occurrence because they have sometimes envisioned a highly conscious ruling class—at least in times of class conflict—or they have suggested an overarching structure of capitalist interests to which they then attribute the prevalence of racism. Given fair statement of contending theories, this radical starting point is suggestive.

Such radical claims have two features: an insistence that an elite benefits from current practices, and a sociological and (implied) psychological view about why some ordinary people adopt the ideas of their oppressors. The latter claim about psychology may suggest that the rulers get their way easily. But serious, against-the-grain, radical argument seeks to identify subversive, democratic possibilities. Thus radicals must explain and ultimately counter practices initiated or sustained by diverse individuals whose motivations are hardly to serve a ruling class.

In this context, some have found recent European arguments, notably those of Heidegger, Foucault, and critical theory, attractive. Foucault, for instance, studies the microstructure of systems of "power/knowledge." He sees such domineering systems not merely as negative and external—as one might see the way clinics use "reason" to exclude "madness"—but as the local, diverse, internal, shaping of, say, a sexual "economy of pleasure." He subtly extends a Marxian theory of alienation and Heidegger's critique of technology as stored-up, ceaseless, use-possessed willing into the psyche. Speaking of regimes of "truth," of the way truth is held within or creates a context of power, he seeks to recover the bases of current practices in Nietzschean genealogies of particular disciplines, for instance, the history of psychology and human biology.[41] Thus the torture of Damiens stemmed from ritual propitiation of the cosmos; today's silent sky is hidden by the inspector's gaze.

Foucault's depiction of the division of workers against criminals—and the stigmatization of the latter—begins from a straightforwardly Marxian insight into class struggle.[42] Further, his account of the mechanization of prisons, clinics, and education by means of a hierarchy of measuring, "normalizing" surveillance—and the acceptance of the norms of this hierarchy by participants—extends Marx's analysis of the factory into other domains; it fleshes out Weber's insights into the standing army and bureaucracies as forms of "rational" domination which remove the means of "production" from control of subordinates. In contrast to sophisticated Marxian theories, however, Foucault's lacks interplay; he does not ask how diverse forms of power might intersect, and sometimes forgets important loci of domination.

Foucault's notion of discipline highlights the destructive predominance of instrumental "reason," also emphasized by Heideggerian, Weberian, and critical theory. For Weber saw in modern domination the substitution of calculability—formal rationality—for substantive rationality. For Weber, the former is a regime of "specialists without spirit, sensualists without heart." Georg Lukács, in his critique of domination, merged Marx's notion of commodity fetishism with Weber's formal rationality to build a theory of reification; he saw the submission of the oppressed as arising from forms of interaction in which relations among humans appear as relations of exchange. Critical theorists generally contrast Hegelian reason (*Vernunft*)—seen, for example, by Jürgen Habermas as "communicative rationality"—with instrumental understanding (*Verstand*). In Habermas's conception of democracy as uncoerced conversation, critical theory is more self-consciously liberal than Foucault's.

Nonetheless, Foucault affirms the democracy of the post–May 1968 prison reform movement: "And when the prisoners began to speak, they possessed an individual theory of prisons, the penal system and justice. It is the form of discourse which ultimately matters, a discourse against power, a counter-discourse of prisoners and those we call delinquent—and not a theory *about* delinquency."[43]

For want of a worked-out, consistent moral theory, however, Foucault often offers overly generalized accounts of discipline. A theory of democratic individuality needs a more specific, differentiated vision. This section sketches such an argument about the history of IQ testing, democratic education, and today's elite revival of biological racism.

In the early twentieth century, the French psychologist Alfred Binet invented mental testing to help children with unusual educational problems. But American psychologists translated "Intelligence Quotient" (IQ) into a general instrument to predict performance in school *and* to rank individuals in an alleged hierarchy of talent. Given the class stratification of educational institutions, testing became, in Lukács's idiom, a vehicle to veil oppressive social relationships as numerical properties of individuals (reification). In Weber's idiom, it became an instrument of formal rationality, furnishing educators and employers a purported precise measure of the individual as means, with a general mental power (in Charles Spearman's jargon, "g"). In Foucault's idiom, testing became a paradigm of surveillance.

In response to the Russian Revolution, the American elite stigmatized eastern and southern European "Bolshevism." IQ examinations given in English to immigrants served to legitimize antidemocratic prejudices. Thus Ellis Island testers found that 83 percent of the Jews, 80 percent of the Hungarians, 79 percent of the Italians, and 87 percent of the Russians were "feebleminded." In addition, on World War I army tests, whites on average outscored blacks, though blacks from the North generally outscored whites from the South. Yet psychologists saw these tests as ferreting out biological potential. Their pseudoscience *made* immigrants and other citizens into lesser humans. It contributed to the widespread passage of state miscegenation and sterilization laws and of the 1924 Immigration Act, which sought to preserve "the pure Nordic stock" of the United States. During the Weimar Republic and the Nazi era, American laws provided Germany with a eugenic model to be surpassed.[44]

In retrospect, we can see that this testing need provoke no debate between those who propose genetic causes and those who propose environmental causes of alleged "group deficiencies," for the tests, framed on elite English speakers, did not mainly detect intelligence. So-called environmental explanations merely rephrased, in a pseudoscientific idiom, social standing. In the 1970s and 1980s, Richard Herrnstein has revived the correlation of IQ with status.[45] But a critic might suspect that, even today, methodological errors build this basic correlation into the testing rather than that the tests, as Herrnstein hopes, reveal the "meritocracy" of contemporary social structure.[46]

To block this liberal and radical objection from the outset, some psychologists have invoked implausible, quasi-empiricist methodological doctrines. First, they have promulgated Edwin Boring's operationalist dictum that "intelligence is whatever IQ tests test." Testers do not offer a theory of intelligence, but can supposedly measure it. In Herrnstein's cautious formulation: "When we consider whether tests measure intelligence, we can only mean whether the scores correlate with what people generally understand by the word . . . if there is any sort of correlation, then as a practical matter, *the tests measure intelligence to some extent, however obliquely.*"[47]

Yet some public-policy arguments, often by the same psychologists, maintain that low intelligence may be "hard-wired" into individuals and groups. Failure is "their own fault"; social programs should be eliminated. This psychology licenses a reactionary political translation of weak, esoteric, biological determinism into strong exoteric racism.[48]

Second, invoking the doctrine of value freedom, behaviorists implausibly maintain that their anesthetized, putatively scientific meaning of intelligence could serve any public policy. But operationalist renaming does not remove the evaluative stigma attached to lack of success in school.

Third, another empiricist doctrine—methodological individualism—seemingly also sustains IQ testing.[49] Thus, ignoring the structural inequalities built into the tests, some behaviorists have suggested that testing simply aggregates individual characteristics. For instance, Arthur Jensen's 1969 article worries about "dysgenic trends" in American cities;[50] yet Herrnstein insists, "More than 90% of that article dealt not with race but with individual differences in school performances and test scores." Similarly, Charles Murray and Herrnstein have named their forthcoming manuscript: "Individual Differences and Public Policy"; Murray avers that "the discussion of racial differences would play only a small role in a book that would take a much broader look at the way individual characteristics . . . affect success and failure."[51] Faced with such examples, a sophisticated proponent of methodological individualism might note: because IQ tests interpret social relations of discrimination *as* properties of individuals, they don't identify the right properties. Possible methodological justifications do not sanction error.

Educational testing does help to identify those with learning disabilities and unusual aptitudes.[52] Psychologists could, however, achieve these goals with a special-abilities test that did not purport to rank the population according to an alleged uniform measure of individual mental power. But testing has become an industry, and it reproduces an inegalitarian social structure. In this context, intellectual racism has been startingly entrenched, surviving even the leading case of modern scientific fraud. From the 1950s to the 1970s, Sir Cyril Burt's studies of identical and nonidentical twins reared apart provided the underpinning for biological determinism. But an outsider to this subfield, Princeton psychologist Leon Kamin, reviewed a series of Burt's articles written over fifteen years and saw that he had insisted on impossibly exact correlations over varying sample sizes (always .771); he apparently invented collaborators as well as data.[53]

A history of genocide, fraud, and stupidity has proved insufficient, however, to undermine academic and public policy fashion. On 17 March 1991, Richard Schweder's lead book review in the Sunday *New York Times* insisted: "The real news in 1991 is that with social biology back, the study of the biology of race, culture and social class is not far behind. It is led by scholars who believe that whether the subject is lactose intolerance, mathematical reasoning or shyness, the possibility of genetically determined group differences is still a proper topic of scientific inquiry, *just as it was in the 1890s*."[54]

Now, a radical might suspect that the declining competitiveness of major industries, increasingly high qualifications for good jobs (college grads earn roughly two-thirds more per year than high school grads), augmented stratification, the feminization of poverty, homelessness, the poison of fear, racism, and gang warfare in American cities, and the fact that one of every six children goes to bed hungry every night needs legitimation. A dovetailing of social circumstance, ideological climate, and methodological doctrine might help us to understand how prominent officials and researchers could yearn for "the 1890s."

Today's revived argument for public policy rests on a new set of twin studies at the University of Minnesota.[55] These studies beg the questions already raised about whether IQ measures intelligence.

In addition, critics may scrutinize the other technical doctrines underpinning studies that compare the psychological traits of twins from the same and from different eggs, raised in separate family and social environments, from birth. Such studies offer statistical analyses of the "heritability" of particular traits. Psychological and public-policy literature often suggests that this abstruse technical term involves a causal, not merely a correlational, claim and that researchers can usefully link heritability with racial and class differences on IQ tests.

One might object, first—as Richard Lewontin, a leading population geneticist, has stressed—that heritability refers to the interplay of genetic and environmental variation *in a given set of environments.* Thus experimenters can grow corn from the same seed on a mountain and in a valley. In each environment, the height of the corn will be entirely heritable; yet the cause of variation—truncated on the mountain, tall in the valley—is entirely environmental. A technical showing that intelligence—not IQ—was heritable would say nothing interesting about the possibility of changing environments to produce more democratic results.[56]

Second, claims about heritability are relevant for those rare properties of individuals caused by a single gene. Thus Wilson's disease, a result of copper deficiency, is entirely heritable (caused by a single gene), fatal in early adulthood if untreated, and totally—environmentally—curable by penacillamine. Even in these cases, genetic fatalism is fatuous. But for any major multigenic, multidimensional trait such as intelligence, no comparably simple source of genetic variation exists.

Third, unlike behaviorist psychology, population genetics and anthropology have long excised the biological term "race." As Lewontin puts it:

> The Kikuyu of East Africa differ from the Japanese in gene frequencies but they also differ from their neighbors, the Masai. . . . The social and historical definitions of race that put the two East African tribes in the same "race" but put the Japanese in a different "race" were biologically arbitrary. . . . [Further] it turns out that 75% of the different kinds of proteins are identical in all individuals tested. . . . None of the genes [that determine the other 25%] perfectly discriminates one "racial" group from another. . . . it turns out that the Masai and

> Kikiyu are as different biologically (as subgroups) as either is from the Japanese.[57]

Kamin has shown that twin studies have other difficulties, specifying, for very small numbers, that the environments are significantly different and that competing explanatory hypotheses have been excluded.[58] Further, even if the Minnesota researchers had resolved these problems, the doubts that IQ measures intelligence, coupled with the meaning of technical claims about heritability, would remove any interest from twin studies as studies of intelligence and for public policy.

A liberal critic of my argument might suggest that the current impact of biological determinism on governmental policy is not likely to be substantial. My argument, however, merely requires that IQ testing, mistakenly construed as assessment of "objective mental capacity" and however explained, significantly shapes the educational chances of individuals. Further, biological claims do seem especially influential. Thus, in *Crime and Human Nature* as well as in Justice Department–sponsored conferences with police chiefs, Herrnstein and James Q. Wilson have been possessed by the ghost of Lombroso. They have suggested that likely criminals can be identified by body type and that biologically based deficiencies in "intelligence" may cause crime by blacks. After reviewing particular studies, they advance the following, central argument: "There is not enough systematic evidence to evaluate their claims [those of four genetic theories of black crime] carefully," and yet, "It is tempting—and probably true—to say that each theory is probably correct."[59] One might pointedly rephrase their logic: I slander you four ways; you show each to be slander; nonetheless the slander is "probably correct" because there are four.[60]

In Foucault's idiom, the disciplinary discourse of IQ testing reinforces oligarchy and checks movement toward classlessness. Liberals have long hoped that public education would erode the hierarchical influence of other social institutions. They have sometimes seen reforms—such as those that ensure greater student participation in assemblies and class discussions, more interaction of teachers and parents, and busing—as fostering democracy and individuality. Now, however, with cutbacks in such programs and the decline in antiracist movements from below, liberal affirmative-action programs are under attack; despite a lack of racial integration, such practices are met with furious charges of "reverse discrimination." The making of strangers, in the midst of citizens, continues. From Germany and Bosnia to the United States, racist movements have targeted "undesirables" and immigrants. Challenging Fukuyama's end-of-history thesis, a radical might suggest that only deeper background changes in the distribution of income, housing patterns, hierarchical social and political institutions, as well as reforms of educational substance and style, can foster democracy.

Democratic Individuality versus Contractarianism

A contractarian version of democratic theory such as Rawls's—one that starts from the most abstract, impersonal features of the human capacity for moral personality—seems initially plausible; but worked-out conceptions of democratic individuality seem more controversial. The latter conjoin such factual claims as those about American expansionism and eugenics in the last section with the core moral principles of liberalism to suggest that major historical and institutional transformations remain likely. This radical feature of theories of democratic indviduality challenges the end-of-history thesis. Further, as this section argues, we need a richer theory of individuality to provide sociological and psychological stability to the institutional claims of modern *political* theory.

Claims about individuality contrast diverse, self-possessed pursuits of a good life with hierarchical individualisms. Mere facsimiles of individuality, the latter stress external, competitive success, measured by money or social standing. On a liberal view, pursuit of money or status—short of creating oligarchy—need not distort one's individuality. Nonetheless, liberal theories may focus on a distinction between a good life and what temporarily seems such a life: liberal conceptions can attend to the emptiness and corruption that arise from mere status- and money-seeking. They thus modify an Aristotelian eudaemonism, which focuses on intrinsically good relationships and activities—ones conducted for internal reasons—and the particular, changing configurations of such goods created by an individual over a life. For instance, Aristotle's conception of friendship concentrates simply on the ethical character of one's friend; Montaigne's insight that a friendship is of just these two people—"because it was he, because it was I"—is an advance, as is Mill's of friendship between women and men. Still, we can interpret modern conceptions of individuality, say Mill's or Whitman's, as variants of eudaemonism.[61]

This section recasts Charles Taylor's argument that Rawls's conception of moral character is misguidedly abstract; it then examines two issues, the relationship of unequal income to equal liberty and the threat of modernism to cultural (national) diversity. These issues suggest that democratic theory requires a more robust conception of individuality than Rawls provides.

In *Sources of the Self,* Taylor proposes three axes of a moral view: a notion of mutual regard among persons, a theory of a good life for individuals, and a notion of dignity. As he notes, modern rights-oriented views tend to constrain moral and democratic theory along the first axis. Combined with certain reductionist arguments about science, he suggests, such views delete the richness of conceptions of the good; they strip individuals to isolated bearers of rights.[62]

But contractarian views need not be atomistic. As I noted above, Rawls's conception of democratic autonomy emphasizes the interconnection of—the *mutual regard* between—diverse individuals who sanction or create institutions. In a Rousseauian vein, Rawls suggests, we may conceive such individuals, ideally, as members of a sovereign assembly, deliberating on the best structure and institutions for their society. Where such societies (rarely) realize significant features of equal freedom for all, these individuals achieve Hegelian self-consciousness. Contrary to common misimpressions, mutual recognition, free public reason, self-aware insight into a free regime are the goods praised in Aristotelian theories as political community and deliberation.

In this context, as Kymlicka has stressed, Rawls's slogan about the priority of the right over the good misguidedly contrasts contractarian and eudaemonist moral theories.[63] For Rawls's notion of an *overlapping consensus* on political autonomy reinterprets Taylor's first two axes on the right and the good and has obvious implications for his third claim about dignity. Further, Rawls's moral psychology, sketched in part three of *A Theory of Justice,* is neo-Aristotelian. Thus, Taylor's critique of Rawls's purported atomism also fails to distinguish Rawlsian contractarianism and eudaemonism. Yet one might reformulate Taylor's objection: from a moral and institutional standpoint, rights-oriented views prescind too easily from the varied comprehensive conceptions of the good which mutual regard protects. For the latter may have further overlapping elements—for instance, those invoked in an Aristotelian emphasis on internal reasons for diverse relationships and activities over a lifetime—that can be specified in ways important to institutional design.

More important, this reformulated criticism bears on the stability, as Rawls calls it, of just structures. Given initial agreement on mutual regard, Rawls maintains that we can introduce complex social theoretical and psychological claims into the argument to realize core principles of justice as need be. That suggestion would work better, however, if the political implications of democratic argument were clear and not—as they seem—dramatic. Further, Rawls fails to pursue the central controversies in social theory which arise within his argument, notably his claim that, given divisions of rich and poor, measures to secure the "fair value of equal liberty" have never "been entertained."[64]

For Rawls, promotion of equal liberty has priority over cooperative but inegalitarian economic claims, such as the difference principle (that acceptable economic inequalities must benefit the least advantaged). That priority rules out those inequalities justified by the difference principle, inequalities that give the advantaged special influence on basic political issues such as war or education. How much egalitarianism the equal-liberty principle requires can be specified only through empirical debate on just how much economic inequality generates oligarchy.

But political scientists who are sympathetic to economic redistribution have said little on this question. Robert Dahl, for instance, has abandoned a pluralist account of contemporary American democracy for an oligarchic one and has urged workers' self-management as an economic arrangement more suitable to democracy. Such a system may be superior to Rawls's own proposal, just by itself, for fair public funding of elections. Yet as Yugoslav socialism demonstrates, worker self-management can coexist with high unemployment and an ethnic dissension spurred by racism that has subsequently led to genocide. At the least, erosion of racism is a central, additional political issue.[65] Focused consideration of contending theories would be needed to specify conditions under which either introduction of worker-managed firms or equal public funding in elections would suffice to prevent oligarchy.

An explanation for this startling theoretical and empirical failure to investigate the public impact of economic inequality, a radical might suspect, is political; the American regime is far from democracy. Only dramatic changes—the advocacy of which is outside the subtle, hierarchical constraints of academic "respectability"—could realize it. A reasonable hunch is that only something near economic equality is consistent with equal liberty.

Thus an *autonomy-driven argument* for egalitarianism has very strong implications. Yet a critic might respond that it unreasonably disregards the hierarchies of income and status which fuel economic dynamism. Such egalitarianism would then be institutionally unstable. But a radical might stress an additional *individuality-based argument* for (near) economic equality, which I summarize in two main claims.

First, neoclassical economics has mistakenly seen individuals as bundles of preferences. That view can lend itself to a vision that most individuals are hungry, needing vast amounts of goods and money to be—if they can be—filled up. But following Heinz Kohut's theory of the self, David Levine has argued that most people do not need, say, an infinite supply of yachts to realize their individuality. Instead, they require quite specific items pertaining to their vocations, particular visions of friendship, changing conceptions of a good life, and the like. This conception of *need,* tied to individuality, contrasts with preference theory.[66] Further, individuality based on mutual regard conflicts with illusory self-seeking in status hierarchies. Thus an economic system that provides adequate wealth to sustain individuality, might be as—or more—innovative than capitalist systems.[67] Moreover, a policy that supports equal incomes (Levine, Gilbert, Richard Brandt) and equal resources (Ronald Dworkin) and fosters core individual capabilities and functionings (Amantya Sen, Martha Nussbaum) would make a flourishing of diversity possible. All of these egalitarian arguments are driven by concern for individuality, not by some strong notion of social "likeness."

Second, as Friedrich Hayek has emphasized, markets respond flexibly to the changing desires of individuals as central planning does not; only individuals have relevant knowledge about their own needs.[68] A liberal might reformulate Hayek's neoclassical preference theory to stress that individuals often shift patterns of consumption because of changing conceptions of a good life (for instance, a woman who has raised children returns to school to prepare for a new career). A liberal epistemological argument justifies a market in *individuality-related consumer goods.* It does not, however, sanction a modern capitalist labor market because hierarchical firms, however efficient, damage the dignity and initiative of most individuals. Further, Hayek's preference-based version suggests that entrepreneurs know the ephemeral advantages of time and place. But even that claim does not justify a capitalist labor market. For on the face of it, General Motors workers on the line in Santiago or Johannesburg know more about such "transiencies" than do executives in Detroit. We could better realize these epistemological features in an individuality-related market in consumer goods based on equal incomes.

An additional test of Rawlsian autonomy versus democratic individuality is seen in the fact that cultural diversity is threatened by modernization as well as by spectacular instances of racism and genocide. How might one justify special action by democratic regimes to preserve the cultures of oppressed minorities?

As Kymlicka has suggested, Rawls fails to consider the good of a person's cultural membership in plural communities. Among indigenous peoples, Kymlicka maintains, the diminishing of (nonharmful) repertoires of cultural roles, under severe coercion from without, undermines the core liberal good of self-respect for individuals, and thus of mutual regard in society as a whole. Further, a eudaemonist might add, members of majority cultures can often learn from the practices of minorities (consider Native American practices of grieving). Thus liberal concern with the pursuit of a good life by each person sanctions the preservation of minority cultures so long as they do not abridge the basic liberties of their members. As Kymlicka avers, a liberal theory may justify legislation to restrict outsider use of the free market—for instance, to check immigration into particular territories or rights to purchase property. Such a theory defends the capacity of individuals within the culture to accept or reject cultural membership (Kymlicka notes that freedom to *accept* is what is threatened externally).[69] Often, however, particular cultural leaderships try to bar intermarriage to preserve group identity. Because liberties of the person are basic and outweigh property rights, a liberal view justifies no restrictions on conscience and affection. While indicting genocide and ethnocide as well as lesser forms of oppression, rich theories of individuality can accommodate cultural diversity.

In Rawls's idiom, however, cultural community—more accurately, the existence of plural communities—could itself become a primary good, along with self-respect, liberty, opportunity, and some (cooperative) share of social wealth. Though Kymlicka articulates a theory of individuality, his argument also highlights resources in Rawlsian notions of democratic autonomy. In fact, a Rawlsian might suggest, a claim about democratic autonomy, combined with factual and social theoretical claims about the threat of cultural extinction, seems to do most of the theoretical and institutional work. Yet, a eudaemonist might respond, Kymlicka's richer picture of varied cultural possibilities in fostering self-respect and individuality moves away from Rawls's austere initial account of capacity for moral personality. A theory of individuality, invoking worked-out psychological arguments about self-respect and the good of cultural membership, shows what a defense of democratic autonomy institutionally requires. Only a robust theory of democratic individuality makes thin theories of the good plausible.

10 Feminism and the Crisis of Contemporary Culture

JEAN BETHKE ELSHTAIN

The end of history came and went pretty quickly. It is difficult to recapture the self-certainty and the euphoria, conceptual and political, which greeted the collapse of the Soviet empire in 1989. Surely, we were told, history had ended in the sense that the future of liberal regimes was assured. But history does not bend to our wishes or to our theories, at least not in the ways we fondly hope or optimistically project. The resurgence of militant and deadly forms of ethnocultural nationalism, most evident in the Balkans; the lurchings and wrenchings attendant on the move to a market-based democracy, evident in all the successor regimes in central and eastern Europe; the importation of not only what is best about us but what is most dubious—all speak to a complexity that cannot be willed away.

What has this to do with feminism? There are the obvious things—the fears, aspirations, hopes, and animosities variously encoded under the generic word "feminist." There is the determination of many Western feminists to export their version of the sex or gender revolution. This, in turn, leads to tension with those on the receiving end of such ideas. The early 1990s, for example, have seen an often-acerbic debate in the pages of the *Prague Post*, an English-language newspaper published by young North American emigrés in Prague, over feminism. One young Czech woman, rather wearily, intervened after the issue had been raging for several weeks to argue that Czech women would find their own way to gender equality, or to some version of transformed male-female relations. They did not need to be told what *their* society should look like in this regard.

These and other moments, so quickly frozen like an insect in amber, suggest that Walter Benjamin was right to represent the angel of history as a tragic figure. Benjamin, in his *Illuminations*, describes the position of the angel of history in these mordant words:

> His face is turned towards the past. Where we perceive a chain of events, he sees one single catastrophe which keeps piling wreckage upon wreckage and hurls it in front of his feet. The angel would like to stay, awaken the dead, and make whole what has been smashed but a storm is blowing from Paradise; it has got caught in his wings with such violence that the angel can no longer close them. This storm irresistibly propels him into the future to which his back is turned while the pile of debris before him grows skyward. This storm is what we call progress.[1]

The storm of progress has left nothing untouched, including our understanding of gender. "Gender" refers to the social construction of identities on the basis of biological difference. Gender is a grammatical category, but feminists use it to characterize social activities, relations, and identities. As an analytic tool, gender is deployed to distinguish between sexuality or biology, on the one hand, and that which is understood as the imposition on a sexual being of a particular identity from the outside, as it were. Gender has to do with that species of imposition. All feminist analyses, in one way or another, to one degree or another, hold that gender is not given as a natural category but is socially and politically defined.

But the agreement among feminists ends there. The world of feminism is as divided and marked by moral conflict as is contemporary society itself. This conflict has deep historical roots and is reflected not only in institutions, practices, laws, and norms from which the women's movement is not exempt, but in conflicts the women's movement reflects, deepens, and extends. I hope to accomplish two things in this essay: first, to put on display the diversities and complexities of feminist rhetorics and theories, in the plural, and second, to argue that an individualistic, rights-as-entitlements North American feminism distorts our understanding if it becomes the standpoint from which all activities undertaken by and in behalf of women is understood. Although "rights talk" seems at first glance to embody rather than to undermine the basic tenets of liberalism, the story is rather more complex.

A bit more of the historic backdrop may be helpful here. Feminism emerged in the West as an offshoot of liberalism and "The Declaration of the Rights of Man." The language of rights served as a potent weapon against traditional obligations, particularly those of family, duty, or any social status declared natural on the basis of ascriptive characteristics.[2] To be as free as, and equal to, men became a central aim of feminist reform. The political strategy that followed from this argument was one of inclusion: women, as well as men, are rational beings; it followed that women, as well as men, are bearers of inalienable rights; it followed further that qua woman there was no valid ground for discrimination against women. Leading nineteenth-century proponents of women's suffrage in Britain and the United States claimed that denying a group of persons basic rights on the grounds of difference cannot be justified unless it can be shown that the difference is relevant to the distinction being made. Whatever differences may exist between the sexes, none, in this view, justifies legal inequality and denial of the rights and privileges of citizenship.

Few early feminists pushed liberal universalism to its most radical conclusion by arguing that there are no justifiable bases for exclusion of adult human beings from legal equality and citizenship. Demands for the inclusion of women often did not extend to all women. Some women and men would be excluded by criteria of literacy, property ownership, disability, or, in the United States, race. At times feminist discourse turned liberal egalitarianism on its head by arguing for women's civic equality on grounds of difference: one finds the case for greater female political participation argued in terms of women's moral supremacy or characteristic forms of virtue. Elizabeth Cady Stanton, the great nineteenth-century suffragist and rhetorician, did both at various points in her long and vibrant career. These appeals spoke to and from women's social location as mothers, using motherhood as a claim to citizenship and public identity. From the vantage point of rights-based feminism, an emphasis on motherhood was a trap, but the historic discourse that evoked images of maternal virtue was one feminist response to a complex, rapidly changing political culture. That political culture in the Western democracies was committed to liberalism, but included, as well, civic republican themes of social solidarity and identity.

Feminists also turned variously to socialism, in its utopian and "scientific" aspects, and to romanticism. Finding in notions of class oppression an analogue to women's social position via-à-vis men, socialist feminists promoted notions of sex-class struggle and revolt. Feminists indebted to romanticism embraced a robust notion of a passionate, feeling self breaking the encrustations of social custom. Pressing the notion that women suffered as much from repression or internalized notions of their own incapacities as from oppression or systematically imposed rules and customs that guaranteed sex inequality, feminist romantics stressed women's "especial genius" (in the words of the American transcendentalist Margaret Fuller) and hoped to see a social transformation that would free women's difference and allow it to flourish.

The diverse history of feminism forms the basis for current feminist discourse and debate. Sexuality and sexual identity have become highly charged arenas of political redefinition. A minority of feminists urge women to separate entirely from male-dominated society. Some want full integration into that society, hence its transformation toward a version of equality they claim as the fulfillment of the liberal project. Others insist that the feminist agenda will not be completed until "women's values," correctly understood, triumph. There are feminists who embrace a strong notion of women's difference and others who reject any such idea as itself sexist.

Any attempt to explicate the defining features of contemporary feminism in its major theoretical and political constructions would be a book unto itself. Suffice it to say that all feminisms share an explicit political urge: to reform or to remake the world in line with a deeply held conviction that women have been the victims of faulty and exploitative social institutions. Each feminist perspective emerges in a variety of forms or modes of discourse, but the perspective that has come to dominate in North America is that of rights-based feminism. The particular way in which rights circulate in feminist argument, however, pits feminists in ideological combat with those who do not share their particular version of rights absolutism. Even those endorsing alternative perspectives—radical feminist separatism, Marxist feminism, and ecofeminism—make use of and celebrate the notion of rights. Reproductive "freedom" and "rights," for example, are deemed to have the status of givens, "fundamental rights" guaranteed by the Constitution under the protection of privacy and the Fourteenth Amendment, on a par with freedom of speech and assembly.

Does "rights talk" represent the triumph of liberal democracy or an ideologically charged alternative to it? To evaluate this intentionally provocative question, it helps to focus, briefly, on feminist political rhetoric and strategy. This discussion should illumine the ways in which feminism either can be absorbed within, or by, the free-market liberal surround—that world that is said to have triumphed by those who proclaim an end to history—or must exist in tension within or even in open hostility toward a liberal, constitutional order. On my reading of the situation over the past several decades, there are two dominant feminist narratives that represent ideological worlds hostile to liberal tenets, even when the language of rights is deployed. A third feminist story is compatible with a version of liberalism as long as principles of rights are chastened by other important values and, additionally, as long as liberalism does not present itself in triumphalist end-of-history terms.

First, there is the narrative of *sex neutrality.* This form of feminist political rhetoric begins with the assumption that real or presumed sex differences are imposed on generic human material from birth. The contemporary political vision of sex equality which flows from the presumption of sex neutrality is one in which equality requires some form of homogeneity, with men and women becoming interchangeable social actors playing out identical *roles.* Second, there is the narrative of *sex polarity.* This narrative starts with the presumption that the sexes are radically divided and that they must and should remain so. If this separatism is given an ontological base, the sexes are construed as a "separate species": the world is viewed in potently dualist terms: and politically separatist strategies follow. Third, there is *sex complementarity.* This narrative is less prominently featured in feminist political rhetoric than in women's studies scholarship, particularly feminist literary criticism, cultural anthropology, and social history. Complementarities can be agonistic and conflicted, but complementarity neither presumes nor requires, as the other positions seem to do, a terribly abstract vision of male and female actors which ignores the body altogether, on the one hand, or constrains women within pregiven ontological forms having a biological base, on the other. As well, complementarity narratives are more respectful of the importance of sustaining some sort of distinction between public and private speech, identity, context, imperatives, and values—a possibility central to liberalism which the other two narratives tend to repudiate or to disdain.

The sex-neutrality story, in its prototypical form, begins thus: In the beginning man made oppression. Oppression requires an object, a subject to subjugate, and she was there. The narrative requires a pregiven female "self" that is then denied self-status by pregiven males driven by a collective intention to tyrannize. Thus women became the first oppressed class. All subsequent oppression—that of class, race, the Third World—is modeled on this original fall. Woman's oppression alone is pancultural and universal, coterminous with history itself.[3] Women are variously constituted through this discourse as a "sex-class," a "sex-caste," or a permanent "Fourth World" that antedates "Third World oppression." Indeed, those working within this framework claim that the fact that women are everywhere denied self-determination is "self-evident."

The only way for women to get out of this situation is through a thoroughgoing social, cultural, and political revolution that leaves nothing as it was before. For women are caught in the snare of a systemic *sex-gender system*. Generic humans, "the biological raw material," go into the system, and gendered "social products" come out.[4] The system is operative in all societies, for all known societies, past and present, consigned women to one sphere and men to another on the basis of genitalia. The dominant male is the only maker of history and layer down of the Law (of the Father), a transcendent being-for-himself who occupies the productive sphere of history making, the superordinate arena of social existence.

Needless to say, a liberal polity can scarcely accommodate *this* vision. For one of the central features of the sex-neutrality vision is that, in a future ideal society, there would no longer be a private sphere (often called the realm of reproduction) as we know it. Either reproduction will have been thoroughly socialized (in the sense of being turned into the work of sex-rearing experts devoted to sex neutrality and the androgynous project), although women may continue to give birth, or birth itself—the entire reproductive process—may be revolutionized so that men will give birth, or one woman may inseminate another, or perhaps no human being will reproduce another human being at all—that task having been given over to a benign crew of cybernetic engineers in the zanier versions of this project.

The implicit theory of human nature imbedded in uncompromising sex neutrality narratives is familiar to all students of Western political philosophy: *tabula rasa.* We are raw materials that become social products. After the feminist revolution, "going in" as generic humans and no longer assigned more or less arbitrarily (genitalia alone are seen as the variable here) to a gender category, we will come out stamped with the imprint of sex neutrality and infused with a combination of "the positive capacities" of each gender "but without the destructive extremes" gendered identity now requires.[5]

What the sex neutralists promise is what those in possession of a totalizing ideology have always promised: transcendence from a current dismal state of affairs and entry into an androgynous promised land. Ultimately, patriarchal culture having been deconstructed, human beings will no longer be reared in ways that guarantee a psychology of sex oppression, and hence they will no longer need to coerce or to manipulate others. This is the way the story ends; indeed, this is how it must end (and history with it, but not until then), given the motor of teleological necessity which drives it. The political self-descriptions of sex neutralists range from liberal to Marxist and socialist. Despite many differences on questions of strategy and categories of analysis (does gender trump class, for example, or coexist with it?), the commitment of feminists of various strands to a sex-neutrality posture—and hence to the view that the world as we know it is hopelessly distorted because we make distinctions on the basis of gender and these distinctions are always and everywhere invidious, and can and must be put right—is powerfully evident as one unpacks presumptions and the strategies to which they give rise.

A contender for an all-encompassing narrative yielding a call to arms is the sex-polarity position. This version of feminist rhetoric and politics divides the sexes into something akin to a separate species. There is a mythic, archetypal quality to the sex-polarity narrative which helps to give it its compelling power. In common with the sex-neutrality narrative, sex polarists tell a tale of the historic subjugation of the female, though she is located more as history's universal victim than as its prototypical oppressed class. This subjugation, in some versions, represents the male defeat of an age of matriarchy: all of "patriarchal history," therefore, is stained with the taint of its origins. The narrative presumes powerful universals. The key is patriarchy—a category deployed to describe and to explain history and every culture known to or within it.

The remorselessness of male victimization of the female taps the deeply rooted Western narrative form of goodness enchained. Thus the rhetoric of radical feminist separatism on the matter of destructive versus positive forms of sexual expression has at its disposal powerful symbols of despoilation of the innocent victim; the vicious triumphalism of the evil perpetrator. An unmediated conduit is presupposed between the "patriarchal, repressive" family and the heterosexual male's "normal" violence—up to and including militarism, wars, nuclear technology, despoilation of nature, advertising, pornography: all are construed as the predictable, inevitable outgrowths of unchained masculinism.[6]

Here is a flavor of this rhetorical strategy and the politics that (necessarily) flows from it, drawn from an anthology on feminism and nonviolence. "Women must understand that the female self is the enemy under fire from the patriarchy. . . . Women are the first victims of the patriarchy state of war." Or: "Under Patriarchy men are entitled to everything. It follows that Patriarchy is inherently violent because it thrives on captured prey." In light of this, a proposed solution: "To secure a world of female values and female freedom we must, I believe, add one more element to the structure of the future: the ratio of men to women must be radically reduced so that men approximate only ten percent of the total population." Given the "overwhelming association of men with violence, why the reduction to ten percent only? Why have any men at all? I take that question quite seriously."[7] *That* particular question can be "taken seriously" only within the framework of an unbridgeable divide between female victims and male brutes.

Suffice it to say, this sex-polarity narrative yields separatist strategies scarcely compatible with liberal understanding of shifting coalitions and public identities not reducible to some pregiven identity (ur-female or ur-male). There is no notion of a citizen in either the sex-neutrality or the sex-polarity narratives. As well, there is little room for ambiguity in these dogmatic positions. Those certain of hard-and-fast truths and the politically correct actions they inspire rightly see theories and rhetorics of complexity, contradiction, irony, and paradox—theories and rhetorics more at home in liberalism than in totalistic ideologies—as corrosive of ideological commitment. To live in a world beyond compromise is to jettison the liberal project, and the spokeswomen for the sex-neutralist and sex-polarist positions recognize that more-open narrative possibilities are thorns in their sides for they complicate the political as well as the discursive universe.

The sex-complementarity position is more difficult to summarize succinctly. But the point of this feminist approach is to put men and women in the same narrative but in a supple way at odds with the static oppositions featured in the closed narratives of neutrality and polarity. Sex complementarity offers no privileged standpoint, presuming instead that all points of view are partial and incomplete and that hermeneutical dilemmas cannot be evaded. Though knowledge and understanding may, in some interesting ways, be embodied—and this embodiment might help to explain why men and women, at least some of the time and to culturally specific ends and purposes, experience the world in different ways—no embodied being, male or female, has access to the whole or to anything like the totality.

Not being hobbled in advance by the conceptual chains of gender as prison, the critic is open to intimations and possibilities of gender as prism. Much of the best women's-studies work is done from inside a set of complementarity presumptions, that is to say, from the understanding that the world does not divide simply into gendered categories and, moreover, that while gender may be vital to some ends and purposes it is not all-determinative in the construction of human identity and human politics, especially of liberal politics, which presumes variability and limits. Curiously enough, the embrace of paradox and variety by feminist thinkers currently often goes hand-in-hand with what can only be called a rights-based absolutism and triumphalism indebted to liberal discourse but wary of liberalism's commitment to a variety of goods, individual and social. If feminists more and more discover "difference," individual and cultural, in their scholarly work and their analytic assessments, the world of feminist politics has, if anything, rigidified in ways that embody the triumph of sex-polarist and sex-neutralist presumptions but couched in the name and in the language of rights.

Here is how it works: Affirming the primacy of rights, feminists indebted to liberal discourse have tended to deny the same, or any status at all, to any principle of belonging or obligation. Closely linked to the primacy of rights is the central importance liberalism attaches to freedom, understood as freedom to choose one's own mode of life, to constitute and choose values for oneself. But in making freedom of choice an absolute—a perspective Charle Taylor calls ultraliberalism—one winds up exalting choice as the defining human capacity. This perspective carries with it the demand that if we are to rise to the level of self-consciousness and autonomy, we must entirely eschew older notions of a self that is bounded by variations on traditional constraints. If choice is the trump card in each and every debate, any tension between individual right and social obligation can be ignored. One simply gives everything over to the individualist pole in advance. Thus, at present, those feminists indebted to rights-based liberalism offer an ethic that combines a strong quest for control over one's body, over social circumstance, over the socialization of children so that they are not imprinted with a strong gender code (all desiderata flowing from sex-neutralist presumptions) with an equally robust commitment to the notion of individual freedom, presumably for all persons although this is often none too clear.

The broad, historicizing sweep of this perspective gathers all differences of culture, past and present, into a single bin by presuming that a system of controls and reinforcements can consistently produce conventional results. By resocializing away from sexed identities, we can erase men and women, eliminate any biological need for sex to be associated with procreation, eradicate all sex-based role differentiation, and, at last, transcend gender. This is very much the sex-neutralist revolutionary project.

But the absolute-rights stance rests uneasily on the heads of its wearers, for lurking in the shadows is the phantasm of difference.

Unsurprisingly, the tension between calling for an end to gender-based distinctions even as gender-based solutions are sought in the name of equality, and on the premise of the sameness of women and men, pitches contemporary feminists into one quandary after another. For example, in 1981, the National Organization for Women, which has from its inception championed the perspective that women have the right to do or be anything that men have done or been, filed a legal brief as part of a challenge to the all-male military draft. Beginning with the claim that compulsory universal military service is central to the concept of citizenship in a democracy, NOW insisted that if women are to gain first-class citizenship they, too, must have a right to fight. Laws excluding women from draft registration and combat duty perpetuate archaic notions of women's capabilities based on unacceptable assumptions of sex difference; moreover, "devastating long term psychological and political repercussions" are visited on women because of their exclusion from the military of their country.[8] No doubt this position is not a particularly happy one for many liberal feminists, but it is consistent with the assumptions with which rights-based feminism is entangled.

The Gulf War of 1991 brought the absolutist arguments of rights-based feminism to the fore in a flurry of excited comments concerning the historic turnabout in the matter of whether women are or should be war fighters. On the one hand, rights-based feminists were enthusiastic about women's right to fight; on the other hand, these same spokeswomen often repaired to the utopian presumption of Enlightenment fundamentalism by condemning wars as irrational, atavistic throwbacks to a barbaric, preenlightened era. War, the story goes, will be rendered obsolete in the light of rising interdependence of nations and the spread of uniform liberal laws throughout the globe. The end of history beckons but not quite yet: the matter of gender equality, as an absolute norm, must be instantiated first.

Though pretty much undermined by events, this trust in the teleology of progress continues to simmer just beneath the surface of such argumentation, requiring that civic loyalty to one's own country should take a back seat to some sort of international identity or connection at the same time that fighting for one's country becomes one in a long litany of enlightenments. What is also in play here, though it is rarely brought to the forefront in liberal feminist argumentation, is the hope that if women ran things—states, armies, and so on—those things would be differently (read more amicably and more peaceably) run. Linking rights-based feminist liberalism to grand utopian hopes departs from the "underlaboring" of historic liberalism, of course, but it happens frequently enough given the presumptions—of either neutralist or polarist or a combination of the two—with which the activist or polemicist begins.

Let me offer a second and more sustained example of the tensions at work within contemporary liberal feminism. It is by now commonplace that modern, technological society faces new and daunting challenges, among them a panoply of real or potentially realizable techniques for manipulating, redirecting, controlling, and altering human reproduction which some have called the new eugenics: in-vitro fertilization, AID (Artificial Insemination by Donor), embryo flushing, surrogate embryo transfer, surrogate motherhood, sex preselection. What was once science fiction is now social fact. As one explores this issue from rights-based feminism, one discovers that there are ways in which an explicit stance—say, opposition to surrogacy—is undermined by a tacit commitment to a framework embedded in presumptions that erode such opposition. Contemporary feminist discourse is dedicated to the notion of reproductive freedom. But few feminists thinkers, until recently, paid much attention to newer technologies for controlling human reproduction other than to issue manifestos in behalf of a one-hundred-percent-safe and effective contraception and in behalf of abortion on demand. The voices from within the feminist camp which questioned arguments for abortion cast exclusively in the language of absolute freedom of choice or rights did not prevail in the debates. But those voices now seem prescient in the context of the runaway developments of the past decade.

For rights-based feminists, the new eugenics seems to present few serious problems. The only possible opposition to the new eugenics which can emerge from within a perspective that associates rights with the possibility of *total* control over oneself and one's social life takes the form of warning that masculinists and antifeminists are controlling the means of control. An ongoing political struggle is required to ensure that enemies of feminism do not succeed in this effort. But such caveats are compromised by the fact that those uttering them share, rather than oppose, the assumptions of their masculinist foes: that nature must be overcome: that where human beings find the will to indulge acts of overcoming they must find a way; that only the fearful and the backward will cavil at these inexorable developments—a cluster of presumptions which rejects the claims of "traditional" family authority only in order to place far too much faith in the authority of modern science.

Some rights-based arguments go so far as to envisage forms of biological engineering which would totally overcome biological constraints by permitting women to inseminate one another, men to lactate, and so on. The standard of evaluation in such fanciful and grotesque scenarios is control—what abets it is good, what mutes it is bad. Thus the way is paved for legitimating invasive techniques in and upon human bodies as a form of biosocial engineering.

Seeing in women's links to biology, especially birth and nurturance, only the vestiges of our animal origins and patriarchal control, anything that breaks those links is endorsed. To be sure, there are feminists who proclaim reproductive freedom but ponder the nature of many choices the new technology throws up. Is amniocentesis really a free choice or is it all too often a coercive procedure with only one correct outcome: to abort if the fetus is "defective"? What about the right to have one's own child promoted by the new technologies? Is this yet another imposition of male-dominated society upon women who see themselves as failures if they cannot get pregnant or is it a route to the brave new world of control?

Liberal feminists face a series of dilemmas, then, when they are confronted with transformations in human reproduction. This quandary crystalized several years ago with the infamous "Baby M" case, in which Mary Beth Whitehead had agreed to bear a child for another woman, and changed her mind after the birth of the child. Here was a situation in which biological motherhood and social parenting were severed as liberal feminists had long claimed they should be. Here was a case in which everyone had freely agreed to a contract, and liberal feminism emphasizes contractarian perspectives. Yet many liberal feminists, including Betty Friedan, saw in the initial denial of any claim by Whitehead as natural mother to her child "an utter denial of the personhood of women, the complete dehumanization of women. It is an important human rights case, to put it at the level of contract law is to dehumanize women and the human bond between mother and child."[9] Friedan here implies, though she does not spell out, an ethical limitation to freedom of choice and contract.

My point for now is that what Mary Ann Glendon calls rights talk has become an impoverished way of talking about politics and political life. Missing is the language of responsibility. Missing are defining features of our sociality. We find, instead, an illusion of control featuring a freestanding, juridical, rights-bearing subject as the defining standard for political and social life. Absolute rights talk, including the feminist variety, has turned into what Fred Siegel calls a judicialized politics. This is a politics that bypasses public debate and consent, writes Siegel, producing winner-take-all outcomes in which the losers are likely to feel embittered. That bitterness and resentment, whose symbolic residues are the stuff of thirty-second political-attack ads, now help drive American politics.[10]

The burden of my argument at this juncture is not to dismiss the language of rights but to recuperate rights as embodying a moral perspective of limits and immunities by contrast to absolute entitlements and demands. This task of recuperation will not and cannot be undertaken by any group driven by *ressentiment* at the human condition itself. I have in mind here those sex neutralists and sex polarists for whom the very existence of distinctive gendered identities is either a blight to be fought and overcome or the occasion for the triumph of one group of gendered beings over another. As we sit uncomfortably poised on the edge of the next century, what it comes down to would seem to be this: if there is any feminism that is defensible, it is a feminism at home with uncertainty and the need for civility, committed to the preservation of tensions between public and private life, hence a feminism with the capacity for living with conflict without end.

We live in an era in which we are not well served by the old political categories as we witness the political realities of a half-century crumple and give way. The drama of democracy, of conflict and compromise, turns on our capacity for making distinctions and offering judgments. It turns on our recognition that the rules of conduct which flow out of private relationships—loyalty, intimacy, fidelity—are not altogether transferrable to public relationships, in which different criteria, including the capacity for provisional alliances, are required. The political identity I have in mind is relational and interdependent, but responsible and self-determining as well. This, then, is a complex moral universe, a world of justice and mercy, autonomy and caring, particular ties and universal aspirations. I see no reason why feminism cannot be at home within such a universe and a central part of it. But I am forced to admit that this feminist possibility seems ongoingly swamped by the absolutist seductions of ideology, even when the coin of the realm is rights.

11 The End of Leninism and History as Comic Frame

RICHARD RORTY

At the beginning of his *New Reflections on the Revolution of Our Time,* Ernesto Laclau says, "The cycle of events which opened with the Russian Revolution has definitively closed . . . as a force of irradiation in the collective imaginary of the international left. . . . The corpse of Leninism, stripped of all the trappings of power, now reveals its pathetic and deplorable reality."[1] I agree with Laclau, and I hope that the intellectuals will use the death of Leninism as an occasion to rid themselves of the idea that they know, or ought to know, something about deep, underlying, forces—forces that determine the fates of human communities.

We intellectuals have been making claims to such knowledge ever since we set up shop. Once, we claimed to know that justice could not reign until kings became philosophers or philosophers kings; we claimed to know this on the basis of a searching inspection of the human soul. More recently, we have claimed to know that it will not reign until capitalism is overthrown and culture decommodified; we claimed to know this on the basis of a grasp of the shape and movement of History. I would hope that we have reached a time at which we can finally get rid of the conviction common to Plato and Marx, the conviction that there just *must* be large theoretical ways of finding out how to end injustice, as opposed to small experimental ways.

A shortened, revised, version of this paper appeared as "The Intellectuals at the End of Socialism," *Yale Review* 80 (April 1992), 1–16.

Alan Ryan has suggested that the best we can hope for now is "a kind of welfare-capitalism-with-a-human-face, not easy to distinguish from a 'socialism' with a big role for private capital and individual entrepreneurs."[2] Agreeing with Ryan as I do, I think the time has come to drop the terms "capitalism" and "socialism" from the political vocabulary of the left. It would be a good idea to stop talking about "the anticapitalist struggle" and to substitute something banal and untheoretical—something like "the struggle against avoidable human misery." More generally, I hope that we can banalize the entire vocabulary of leftist political deliberation. I suggest that we start talking about greed and selfishness rather than about bourgeois ideology, about starvation wages and lay-offs rather than about the commodification of labor, and about differential per-pupil expenditure on schools and differential access to health care rather than about the division of society into classes.

As one reason for such banalization, I cite Laclau's thesis that "the transformation of thought—from Nietzsche to Heidegger, from pragmatism to Wittgenstein—has decisively undermined philosophical essentialism" and that this transformation enables us to "reformulate the materialist position in a much more radical way than was possible for Marx."[3] I think that the best way to be more radically materialist than Marx is to strip leftist political deliberation of Hegelian romance. We should stop using "History" as the name of an object around which to weave our fantasies of diminished misery. We should concede Francis Fukuyama's point (in his celebrated essay "The End of History?") that, if you still long for total revolution, for the Radically Other on a world-historical scale, the events of 1989 show that you are out of luck. Fukuyama suggests, and I agree, that no more romantic prospect stretches before the left than an attempt to create bourgeois democratic welfare states and to equalize life chances among the citizens of those states by redistributing the surplus produced by market economies.

Fukuyama, however, sees nothing but boredom ahead for us intellectuals, once we have admitted that bourgeois democratic welfare states are the best polities we can imagine. He thinks that the end of romantic politics will have the same dampening effect on our collective imaginary as the admission that contemporary Athenian institutions were the best he could imagine would have had on

Plato. As a follower of Leo Strauss and Alexandre Kojève, Fukuyama regrets this dampening. In the intellectual tradition to which he belongs, political philosophy is first philosophy. Utopian politics, the sort of politics whose paradigm is Plato's *Republic,* is the root of philosophical thought.

On a Straussian view, the hope of creating a society whose hero is Socrates, rather than Achilles or Themistocles, lies behind what Heidegger calls Western metaphysics. So to damp down political romance is to impoverish our intellectual life, and perhaps make it impossible. Straussians tend to agree with Heideggerians that the end of metaphysics means the beginning of a nihilistic wasteland, a wasteland in which bourgeois freedoms and bourgeois happiness may become universal, but in which there will be no appreciative readers of Plato. They tend to agree with Kojève that if we give up on "the Platonic-Hegelian *ideal* of the Wise Man," if we "deny that the supreme value is contained in Self-Consciousness," then we "take away the meaning of all human discourse whatsoever."[4]

Heartily disagreeing with Kojève as I do, I would urge that the Plato-Hegel-Marx-Heidegger brand of romance, the romance of world history, is something that intellectual life and leftist politics would now be much better off without—that this romance is a ladder that we should now throw away. I distrust the way in which Kojève let his imagination be dominated by the Master-Slave section of Hegel's *Phenomenology*—and in particular by the passage that suggests that full moral seriousness, and perhaps full intellectual awareness, is possible only for those engaged in a life-and-death struggle. Kojève's use of that passage brings together Hegel's account of history as the story of increasing self-consciousness with the more bloodthirsty side of Marxism, the specifically Leninist side. Kojève, Strauss, Adorno, Nietzsche, and Heidegger are linked to Lenin and Mao by an urge to extirpate: either to abolish the bourgeoisie as a class or, at least, to root out bourgeois culture, the culture that Nietzsche and Heidegger thought would turn Europe into a wasteland. That culture—the culture of Nietzsche's "last men"—is the contemporary counterpart of the culture that put Socrates to death: both are cultures for which self-consciousness is *not* the supreme virtue, and for which the Platonic-Hegelian ideal of the Wise Man is not all that important.

Thanks to Marxism, the term "bourgeois culture" has become a way of lumping together anything and everything intellectuals despise. Calling that lump by that name was a way of linking the intellectual's romance of self-creation with the oppressed worker's desire to expropriate the expropriators. Such linkages help us intellectuals to associate ourselves with the ideals of democracy and human solidarity. These linkages let us have the best of both worlds: we have been able to combine the traditional disdain of the wise for the many with the belief that the present, degenerate, bourgeois many will be replaced with a new sort of many—the emancipated working class.

But now that we leftist intellectuals can no longer be Leninists, we have to face up to some questions that Leninism helped us evade: Are we more interested in alleviating misery or in creating a world fit for Socrates, and thus for ourselves? What is behind the sense of regret we feel when we are forced to conclude that bourgeois democratic welfare states are the best we can hope for? Is it sadness at the thought that the poor will never get all the way out from under the rich, that the solidarity of a cooperative commonwealth will never be attained? Or is it, instead, sadness at the thought that we, the people who value self-consciousness, may be irrelevant to the fate of humanity, that Plato, Marx, and we ourselves may be just parasitical eccentrics, living off the surplus value of a society to which we had nothing in particular to contribute? Was our thirst for world-historical romance, and for deep theories about deep causes of social change, caused by our concern for human suffering? Or was it at least in part a thirst for an important role for ourselves to play?

So far I have been suggesting that what Fukuyama, like Nietzsche and Kojève before him, is worried about is not the end of history, but the end of the philosophy, and thus the romance, of history. What bothers him is our diminished ability to use History as an object around which we intellectuals can wrap our fantasies. This ability has, indeed, been diminished. To quote Laclau again: "If 'the end of history' is understood as the end of a conceptually graspable object encompassing the whole of the real in its diachronic spatiality, we are clearly at the end of 'history.' "[5] But if that is what we mean, then it would be better to say that what is over is our conviction that there is some object—the human soul, the will of God, the evolutionary process, History, or Language, for example—a better conceptual grasp of which will increase our chances of doing the right thing.

Laclau's attempt to be more radically materialist than Marx leads him to say that the loss of that conviction leaves us at "the beginning of history, at the point where historicity finally achieves full recognition."[6] I agree, but I think that to recognize historicity fully would mean sticking to small experimental ways of relieving misery and overcoming injustice. It would mean keeping the distinction between real leftist politics—that is, initiatives for the reduction of human misery—and cultural politics firmly in mind. It would mean being content to be concrete and banal when talking real politics, no matter how abstract, hyperbolic, transgressive, and playful we become when we turn, in a mood of relaxation, to cultural politics.

There are a lot of fantasies that can stand on their own, without being twined around some large conceptually graspable object. These are the homely, familiar fantasies shared by the educated and the uneducated, by us middle-class intellectuals in American and European universities, and by people living in shantytowns outside of Lima. They are concrete fantasies about a future in which everybody can get work in which they take some satisfaction and for which they are decently paid, and in which they are safe from violence and from humiliation. We intellectuals have, since Plato, supplemented these small concrete, local, banal fantasies with a larger, blurrier, and more sophisticated set of fantasies. Between the times of Plato and Hegel, these were fantasies that tied in the small concrete fantasies with a story about human beings' relation to something ahistorical—something like God, or Human Nature, or the Scientifically-Knowable Nature of Reality. After Hegel, and especially after Lenin, we switched to a story about human beings' relation to History. History, reified into something that has a shape and a movement, took the place of an atemporal power. But we still explain why the small fantasies have not been realized by claiming that their fulfillment depends on attaining a closer relation to something larger and more powerful than ourselves. We say, for instance, that our efforts have so far failed because the "right historical moment" has not yet come.

Our belief in such explanations has let us intellectuals feel that we can be useful to nonintellectuals by telling them how they can get what they want, what it would take to make some of the small fantasies we all share come true. Such explanations let us feel that our special gifts are good for more than giving ourselves sophisticated private pleasures—that these gifts have social utility, permit us to function as an avant-garde in a universal human struggle. Since Hegel, we have been able to think of ourselves as internalizing the Incarnate Logos, of becoming one with God's increasing self-consciousness, his realization of himself in the history of the human race. With Hegel, "World History" became the name of the inspiring blur produced by fudging the differences between the immaterial and the material, the atemporal and the temporal, the divine and the human. The Marxist-Leninist version of this blur called history helped us both overcome our fear of elitism and gratify our blood lust by letting us picture ourselves as swept up by the aroused masses—borne along toward the final slaughter bench of history, the altar where the bourgeoisie will be redemptively sacrificed.

As I see it, Hegel's turn away from fantasies of individual salvation through contact with a blurry other world and toward fantasies of the blurry end of a historical sequence was a good thing. That was because it adumbrated a sort of protopragmatism. It helped us stop talking about the way things were always meant to be—God's Will, Nature's Way—and begin talking about the way things never had been but might, with our help, become. With Hegel, the intellectuals began to switch over from fantasies of contacting eternity to fantasies of constructing a better future. Hegel helped us start substituting hope for knowledge.

This substitution was, of course, by no means complete in Hegel. Hegel still tried to break culture up into parts labeled "Philosophy," "Art," "Natural Science," and the like, and he tried to give priority to Philosophy. In particular, he insisted that there was something called the "System" or "Absolute Knowledge"—something so big and so finely structured as to eliminate any residual blurs. This insistence that there might be a completed object of knowledge provoked justified ridicule from, among others, Kierkegaard, Marx, and Dewey. Nobody since their time, with the possible exception of Kojève, has taken seriously the idea that there was something called "Philosophy" which had reached its completion with Hegel. Rather, we have treated Hegel as a reductio ad absurdum of the idea of Absolute Knowledge, and so have dropped the Platonic-Hegelian ideal of the Wise Man. We have become content to say what Hegel himself said once, and Marx and Dewey said pretty consistently: that philosophy is, at most, its time held in thought.

Marx went on to do what Hegel only rarely did. He tried to hold his time in thought by calculating just how it might be improved for the benefit of future generations. He took Hegel's historicism and protopragmatism more seriously than Hegel himself had managed to take them, because he blurred the distinction between understanding the world and knowing how to change it. His suggestion was that it could be changed for the better by replacing capitalism with communism, and by replacing bourgeois culture with the new forms of cultural life which would arise naturally from the emancipation of the working class. This Marxian suggestion has been the principal legacy of Hegel's work to the social imagination of the last two centuries. Switching from the World-Spirit to the working class made it possible to save Hegelian hope, as well as the Hegelian narrative of History as the expansion of freedom, from the Hegelian "System."

This Marxian suggestion now has to be dropped. The events of 1989 have convinced those who were still trying to hold on to Marxism that we need a way of holding our time in thought, and a plan for making the future better than the present, which drops reference to capitalism, bourgeois ways of life, bourgeois ideology, or the working class. We must give up on the Marxist blur, as Marx and Dewey gave up on the Hegelian blur. We can no longer use the term "capitalism" to mean both "a market economy" and "the source of all contemporary injustice." We can no longer tolerate the ambiguity between capitalism as a way of financing industrial production and capitalism as The Great Bad Thing that accounts for most contemporary human misery. Nor can we use the term "bourgeois ideology" to mean both "beliefs suited for societies centered around market economies" and "everything in our language and habits of thought which, if replaced, would make human happiness and freedom more easily realizable." Nor can we use the term "working class" to mean both "those who get least money and least security out of market economies" and "the people who embody the true nature of human beings."

These ambiguities will no longer seem tolerable if one agrees, as I do, with Jürgen Habermas about the lesson of 1989: "The revolutionary changes that are culminating under our eyes at the present time contain one unequivocal lesson: complex societies cannot reproduce themselves if they do not leave intact the logic of self-regulation of a market economy."[7] The leftist use of the terms "capitalism," "bourgeois ideology," and "working class" depends on the implicit claim that we can do better than a market economy, that we know of a viable alternative available to complex, technologically oriented societies. But at the moment, at least, we know of no such option. Whatever program the left may develop for the twenty-first century, it is not going to include nationalization of the means of production or the abolition of private property. Nor is it likely to include the detechnologization of the world, simply because nobody can think of a way to counter the effects of bad old technological-bureaucratic initiatives except the development of new and better technological-bureaucratic initiatives.

I agree with Habermas when he goes on to say that "the non-communist left has no reason to be depressed" and that there is no reason to abandon hope for "the emancipation of human beings from willed immaturity [*selbstverschuldeter Unmündigkeit*] and from degrading conditions of existence."[8] But I have no clear sense of what mechanisms might realize that hope. For example, when Alan Ryan says that "it is impossible to believe that we should give up on the hope that broad-brush planning reduces waste and at any rate diminishes the irrationalities of production and distribution,"[9] I should very much like to agree with him. But I feel no assurance. I no longer think that I have much grasp of what options remain open to economic planners, or of what can and cannot be safely turned over to the state. I detest the complacent satisfaction that admirers of Ronald Reagan and Margaret Thatcher are now taking in the downfall of Marxism, and I am terrified by the tendency, among intellectuals in recently liberated central European countries, to assume that free markets solve all social problems. But these reactions are not enough to give me any clear sense of how state power *should* be related to economic decisions. I do not think that

I am alone in this, and I refer to my own perplexity merely as an instance of what seems to me widespread bewilderment among leftist intellectuals. We have no reason to be depressed, but we also have little sense of how to make ourselves useful.

Because "capitalism" can no longer function as the name of the source of human misery, or "the working class" as the name of a redemptive power, we need to find new names for these things. But unless some new metanarrative eventually replaces the Marxist one, we shall have to characterize the source of human misery in such untheoretical and banal ways as "greed," "selfishness," and "hatred." We shall have no name for a redemptive power save "good luck." Speaking with the vulgar in this way makes it hard for us intellectuals to continue believing that our special gifts suit us for positions in the avant-garde of the struggle against injustice. For there seems to be nothing in particular that we know that everybody else doesn't also know. The old large blurry fantasies are gone, and we are left with only the small concrete ones—the ones we used to associate with "petty-bourgeois reformism" and "bourgeois liberalism."

This sense that we can no longer function as an avant-garde is, I think, what lies behind the widespread feeling, even among leftists who have no use for Strauss and Kojève, that Fukuyama was onto something. What he latched onto was the loss of "History" as a term that we intellectuals could use in our self-descriptions, could use to reassure ourselves that we have a social function, that what we do is relevant to human solidarity. By inventing "History" as the name of an object that could be conceptually grasped, Hegel and Marx made it possible to keep both the romance of the Christian story about the Incarnate Logos, and the Christian sense of solidarity against injustice, even after we lost religious faith. But now we have either to spin some new metanarrative that does not mention capitalism, yet has the same dramatic power and urgency as the Marxist narrative, or else to give up the idea that we intellectuals are better at holding our time in thought than our fellow citizens. Because I have no idea how to do the former, I suggest we do the latter.

I RETURN TO Laclau's sentence about how Lenin and the Bolshevik Revolution have, for a long time, irradiated "the collective imaginary of the international left." No political movement can survive for long without such irradiation, irradiation by concrete events and heroic individuals. If there had been no Lenin and no Bolshevik Revolution, if we had had to settle simply for Marx's revision of Hegel's blurry story about the Incarnate Logos, our collective imaginary would have long since ceased to glow. So now we have to ask ourselves: What events might replace the Bolshevik Revolution, and what figure might replace Lenin, in the imaginations of the generation born around 1980, the people who will be leftist university students in the year 2000? What might irradiate the collective imaginary of leftists who take for granted that state ownership of the means of production is no longer an option?

One plausible answer to this question is: the sequence of events in Czechoslovakia in the last months of 1989, and the figure of Vaclav Havel. I have no idea how that revolution is going to proceed, or any good guesses about whether the moral and political consensus that swept Havel to power will endure. But neither, I take it, does Havel. One of the most surprising and refreshing things about Havel is that he cheerfully admits that he doesn't. Havel seems prepared to go all the way in substituting groundless hope for theoretical insight. As he says in the interviews collected as *Disturbing the Peace*, "Hope is not prognostication." Throughout those interviews, he emphasizes his lack of interest in underlying forces, historical trends, and large, conceptually graspable objects. The following passage, describing the events of 1967–69, is typical:

> Who would have believed—at a time when the Novotny regime was corroding away because the entire nation was behaving like Schweiks that half a year later that same society would display a genuine civic-mindedness, and that a year later this recently apathetic, skeptical and demoralized society would stand up with such courage and intelligence to a foreign power! And who would have suspected that, after scarcely a year had gone by, this same society would, as swiftly as the wind blows, lapse back into a state of demoralization far deeper than its original one! After all these experiences, one must be very careful about coming to any conclusions about the way we are, or what can be expected from us.[10]

"Us" here means "us Czechs and Slovaks," but what Havel is saying works just as well if we take it to mean "us human beings."[11]

Lenin would not have agreed with Havel that "we have to be careful about coming to any conclusions about the way we are, or what can be expected of us." Scientific socialism, Lenin thought, gave us the tools to formulate, and demonstrate the truth of, just such prognostications. Lenin would have expected Marxist theory at least to retrodict, if not predict, the varying behaviors of the Czechs and Slovaks at various historical moments. But the end of Leninism will, with luck, rid us of the hope for anything like scientific socialism, and for any similar source of theoretically based prognostication. It will, I hope, leave us with only what Martin Jay calls "fin-de-siècle socialists." These are people who think, as Jay puts it, that "there is sufficient work to be done without being haunted by the need to measure what modest successes might be granted to us against the daunting model of a normatively totalized, fully redeemed, social order."[12]

Havel is, in Jay's sense, a fin-de-siècle thinker, but he is not a fin-de-siècle socialist. The revolution over which he is presiding has had no better ideas than to give back the expropriated properties and to sell off the nationalized factories to whatever private entrepreneurs will buy them. The choice between Dubcek and Havel for president became clear when people in Prague found themselves saying "Dubcek is a great man, of course, but he is, well—what can one say?—he is, after all . . . a *communist*." One reason that all of us in the international left are going to have to weed terms like "capitalism," "bourgeois culture" (and, alas, even "socialism")[13] out of our vocabulary is that our friends in central and eastern Europe will look at us incredulously if we continue to employ them. The more Czechs, Poles, and Hungarians we talk to, the more of our old habits we are going to have give up. For example, we shall have to stop regretting the Cold War, stop excusing the Stalinism of people like Jean-Paul Sartre, and start realizing that to a Czech the phrase "the romance of American Communism" sounds as odd as "the romance of the German-American Bund" sounds to a Jew.

Part of the reason the next century looks so blank and formless to us is that we intellectuals have grown accustomed to thinking in world-historical, eschatological terms. We have become impatient with anything smaller, discontent with patchwork solutions and temporary stopgaps. No sooner do we think that we have an idea about what might help the ghetto children in the United States than we realize that our idea has no relevance to the children in Uganda. Then we feel guilty for not having a theory that will cover children everywhere. No sooner do we have a suggestion about how to minimize pollution in Los Angeles than we realize it is irrelevant to Calcutta, and then we feel ashamed of having been ethnocentric. Part of our inheritance from Hegel and Lenin is that we feel guilty about having no planetary project under which to subsume our local hopes, no global leftist strategy. That, I think, is one reason why we leftists in the American academy now spend more of our time on postmodernist philosophy and on what we like to think of as "transgressive" and "subversive" cultural studies, than on deliberating about what might reenergize the Democratic party or about how to refund Head Start programs.[14] Lately we have been concentrating on cultural politics and trying to persuade ourselves that cultural, and especially academic, politics are continuous with real politics. We have been trying to believe that upsetting our students' parents will sooner or later help upset unjust institutions. As long as we can believe that, we can still feel that the gifts that got us our cushy jobs in universities are being used on behalf of human solidarity. We can escape, at least for a while, the suspicion that we are just using those gifts for our private pleasures, in aid of private projects of self-creation.

But these maneuvers are, I suspect, only ways of postponing the questions we shall be asked by students whose collective imaginary has been irradiated by Havel rather than by Lenin. These are questions about what exactly we would do if we suddenly achieved real political power: what sort of utopia we would try to create, and how we would set about it. I hope that we can learn to reply to such questions by saying that, at the moment, we have no clear idea what a redeemed social order would look like, that we can sketch no ground plan for the egalitarian cooperative commonwealth whose spires we glimpse in our dreams. Still, we *can* offer a long list of laws, international agreements, border rectifications, judicial decisions, and the like, which we should try to have promulgated.

To be satisfied with making such a reply, we shall have to get over our fear of being called bourgeois reformers or opportunistic pragmatists or technocratic social engineers—our fear of becoming mere liberals as opposed to radicals.[15] We shall have to get over the hope for a successor to Marxist theory, a general theory of oppression which will provide a fulcrum that lets us topple racial, economic, and gender injustice simultaneously. We shall have to drop the ideology idea, the idea Havel mocks when he says that a mark of the good communist is that he "subscribes to an ideology and believes that anyone who doesn't subscribe to it must therefore subscribe to another ideology, because he can't imagine anyone's not subscribing to an ideology."[16] This will mean giving up the claim that philosophical or literary sophistication is important because it prepares us for the crucial, socially indispensable role that history has allotted to us—the role of "critic of ideology."

Finally, to come back to the topic with which I began, dropping the ideology idea will mean dropping History as a temporalized substitute for God or nature, as a large blurry object around which to weave our concrete local fantasies. Instead, we might come to see the record of the past as Kenneth Burke suggests we see it: as a collection of anecdotes which help us construct what he calls a comic frame.[17] Instead of looking for a world-historical trend that would help us prognosticate, we could echo Burke's remark that "the future is really disclosed by finding out what people can sing about."[18] We can supplement this remark by adding, with Havel, that in any given year you will probably not be able to guess which songs will be on people's lips in twelve months' time.

In his 1936 book, *Attitudes toward History*, Burke says, under the entry "Opportunism": "Every situation in history is unique, requires its own particular gauging or sizing-up of the factors that shall be considered pivotal in the situation. The 'scientists' of history have brought us unintentionally to the realization that the gauging of the 'right historical moment' is a matter of *taste*" (p. 308). In the section "Comic Correctives" he says: "The comic frame, in making a man the student of himself, makes it possible for him to 'transcend' occasions when he has been tricked or cheated, since he can readily put such discouragements into his 'assets' column, under the heading of 'experience.' . . . In sum, the comic frame should enable people to be observers of themselves, while acting" (p. 171). Burke says that he prefers comic to tragic frames, even though what he calls contemporary exasperations (by which I take him to mean the world of the 1930's) "make us prefer the tragic (sometimes melodramatic) names of 'villain' and 'hero' to the comic names of 'tricked' and 'intelligent' " (pp. 4–5). I take his point to be that we should view history's slaughter bench through the eyes of the prudent calculator of the consequences of future actions rather than with those of the moralist. We should see the horrors of our century not as clues to something deep in ourselves or as hints of our ultimate destiny, but as instructive lessons.

One application of Burke's suggestion to our more-recent exasperations would be to see what Laclau calls "the cycle of events which opened with the Russian Revolution" as one in which we leftists, often with the best of intentions, tricked ourselves, fooled ourselves, outsmarted ourselves, yet gained a lot of useful experience. That attitude would help us avoid either congratulating ourselves on our courageous radicalism or accepting the Reagan-Thatcher view that we were cruel villains or idiotic dupes. Accepting Burke's suggestion that we view recent history as a within a comic frame rather than within an epic or a tragic one would mean making the best we could out of the deaths of millions by viewing the circumstances of those deaths as instructive in the avoidance of future deaths. It would mean using our acquaintance with the various butchers who have presided over the slaughter benches of history—people like Hadrian and Attila, Napoleon and Stalin, Hitler and Mao—to avoid imitating them.

Burke develops his rather idiosyncratic, and probably misleading, sense of the term "comedy"—a sense that does not have much to do with laughter—in the following passage: "Comedy requires the maximum of forensic complexity. In the tragic plot the *deus ex machina* is always lurking. . . . Comedy deals with *man in society,* tragedy with the *cosmic man*. . . . Comedy is essentially *humane,* leading in periods of comparative stability to the comedy of manners, the dramatization of quirks and foibles. But it is not necessarily confined to drama. The best of Bentham, Marx, and Veblen is high comedy" (p. 42). Seen from a Burkean angle, Hegel-style philosophy of history is a device for getting by with a bare minimum of forensic complexity. It is a continuation of metaphysics by other means—a continuing attempt to put humanity in a cosmic context even after the cosmos had been found to be largely irrelevant to our hopes. It is a way of short-circuiting political argument by labeling any new work of art, or philosophical movement, or political suggestion, "progressive" or "reactionary." The people whom Burke calls "the 'scientists' of history" suggested that all one had to do was enter the new item as the value of a variable in a set of equations, calculate the result, and thereby discover whether the new suggestion would accelerate or retard the movement of the big blurry object on which their theory had given us a firm conceptual grasp.

If we could drop the pursuit of this pseudoscience and stop using "History" as the name of a large blurry object about which large theories are required, we could read Bentham, Marx, Veblen—and, nowadays, Foucault—as people who help us understand how we tricked ourselves in the past, rather than as people who tell us the right thing to do in the future. They could be read as exhibiting the unexpected and painful consequences of our ancestors' attempts to do the right thing, rather than as explaining the inadequacy of our ancestor's concepts to the great big object they and we are trying to grasp. Reading them in that way might help us stop attempting to find a successor to capitalism or bourgeois ideology as the name of The Great Bad Thing. We might then stop trying to find a successor to the working class—for example, "difference" or "otherness"—as a name for the latest Incarnation of the Logos. Reading this historical record in Burke's way might help us avoid what Stanley Fish calls "anti-foundationalist theory hope"[19]—the idea that a materialism and a sense of historicity more radical than Marx's will somehow provide a brand-new, still bigger albeit still blurrier, object—an object called, perhaps, "Language" or "Discourse"—around which to weave our fantasies.[20]

Burke strikes me, in short, as having the sort of attitude toward history which Havel might like. I see him as a sort of anti-Marx, a counterpart to Havel's anti-Lenin. For Burke thinks of history as a collection of cautionary tales rather than as a coherent dramatic narrative. If we adopt Burke's conception of history, we might become less fond of apocalyptic talk of crisis and endings, less inclined to eschatology. For we should no longer imagine a great big Incarnate Logos called Humanity whose career is to be interpreted either as heroic struggle or as tragic decline. Instead, we should think of lots of different past human communities, each of which has willed us one or more cautionary anecdotes. Some of these anecdotes may serve the turn of one or more of the different human communities of the present day, depending on their different needs and options.

To think of history in this way would be to stop trying to pick out world-historical turning points or figures, stop trying to find historical events that somehow encapsulate and reveal the whole sweep of "History" by laying out the whole range of possibilities open to "Humanity." It would be to apply to social criticism what Burke said of literary criticism: "Works vary in their range and comprehensiveness. One man's character is but another man's mood. We are simply suggesting that, when you lump the lot, discounting each poetic category according to its nature, they seem to add up nearest to comedy. Which might be a roundabout way of saying: whatever poetry may be, criticism had best be comic."[21]

A few years ago, Havel and the other signers of Charta 77 supplied us with a new example of social poetry, of the poetry of social hope. That example makes clear that such hope can exist, and can sometimes even be fulfilled, without backup from a philosophy of history, and without being placed in the context of an epic or tragedy whose hero is Humanity. Burke's way of thinking about social criticism—as comparison and contrast between such social poems, comparison and contrast that eschews the attempt to be long-range and cosmic and is content to be short-range and prudential—is something we might recommend to students whose imaginations have been irradiated by that example.

12 The Age of Limits

CHRISTOPHER LASCH

The collapse of communism as a serious competitor to liberal capitalism has generated euphoria among liberals of the right and center, qualified only by the reflection that the "end of history," in Francis Fukuyama's celebrated phrase, will be a "very sad time" for those who value "daring, courage, imagination, and idealism." The "unabashed victory of economic and political liberalism," as Fukuyama sees it, means the universal rule of law, the globalization of the "classless society" that has already been achieved in the United States, the "receding of the class issue," a steady expansion of the supply of consumer goods, a "universal homogenous state," and a "post-historical consciousness" in which "ideological struggle . . . will be replaced by economic calculation, the endless solving of technical problems, environmental concerns, and the satisfaction of sophisticated consumer demands."[1]

Fukuyama's article recalls earlier predictions of the end of ideology by liberals; but it is curiously reminiscent, as well, of Herbert Marcuse's one-dimensional man and the Frankfurt School's horrifying vision of a totally administered society without contradictions and therefore completely resistant to change. Because Fukuyama, like Marcuse and his friends, takes his inspiration from Hegel, it is not surprising that their different versions of the end of history have so much in common. For that matter, the convergence of technological optimism with cultural despair, of the worship of

Professor Lasch revised this essay before his death but his final text did not include notes. The editors have added notes but in a few cases have been unable to identify a page reference.

progress with nostalgia, has been a persistent current in modern thought ever since the Enlightenment. The triumph of reason looks like the promised land of harmony and freedom until we remind ourselves that people have learned to value freedom only in the course of competition and conflict. With that realization, Max Weber's "iron cage" of rationality looks like a more accurate description of the future. Fukuyama, after dwelling at length on the beauties of liberalism and the feebleness of the forces now opposed to it, unexpectedly leaves us with the prospect of "centuries of boredom." The new order, he says, calls up the "most ambivalent feelings"—on the one hand, the satisfaction of knowing that liberalism no longer faces an ideological challenge of any importance and, on the other hand, a "powerful nostalgia for a time when history existed."[2]

But the liberal order is far from secure in fact. In the hour of its seeming triumph, its fragility is exposed more clearly than ever before, nowhere more clearly than in the United States. Having defeated its totalitarian adversaries, liberalism is crumbling from within. The absence of an external threat makes it more difficult than before to ignore this decay. The Gulf War provided a momentary distraction, but it ended all too quickly; and although we can look forward to further distractions of this kind, it will be impossible, in the long run, to avoid the day of reckoning. Already the signs of impending breakdown are unmistakable. Drugs, crime, and gang wars are making our cities uninhabitable. Our school system is in collapse. Our parties are unable to enlist the masses of potential voters into the political process. The global circulation of commodities, information, and populations, far from making everyone affluent (as theorists of modernization used to predict so confidently), has widened the gap between rich and poor nations and generated a huge migration to the West and to the United States in particular, where the newcomers swell the vast army of the homeless, unemployed, illiterate, drug-ridden, derelict, and effectively disfranchised. Their presence strains existing resources to the breaking point. Medical and educational facilities, law-enforcement agencies, and the available supply of goods—not to mention the supply of racial good will, never abundant to begin with—all appear inadequate to the enormous task of assimilating what is essentially a surplus population.

Even the children of privilege are no longer assimilated into the culture of liberalism. One survey after another shows that college students no longer command even a rudimentary knowledge of Western history, literature, or philosophy. A kind of deculturation has clearly been going on for some time, a process of unlearning without historical precedent (which explains why we don't have a better word to describe it). What E. D. Hirsch calls cultural illiteracy is probably a more serious danger than the more obviously ideological attacks on liberal culture. The right repudiates "secular humanism," while the left denounces any attempt to uphold a core of common values as cultural imperialism and demands equal time for minorities. The modernization of the world, as it was conceived when liberals were running the show, implied the creation not only of a global market but of a global culture in which liberal values—individual freedom, open inquiry, religious tolerance, human dignity—would be universally respected. We have a global culture all right, but it is the culture of Hollywood, rock and roll, and Madison Avenue—not a liberal culture but a culture of hedonism, cruelty, contempt, and cynicism.

So much for the symptoms of liberal decline—which should elicit just as much ambivalence, incidentally, as its supposed ascendancy and the resulting "end of history." I turn now to the causes of this decline. It is pointless to speculate about what is to be done—whether we should seek to rescue liberalism, to replace it with something else, or resign ourselves to the decline not just of liberalism but of our national experiment as a whole—until we get a better understanding of exactly what is happening to our political traditions and why. If liberalism retains the capacity for growth and development along new lines, it would be foolish to desert our dominant tradition. If, on the other hand, it has reached the outer limits of its growth, we should probably turn to submerged traditions in American life, which have been overshadowed but never altogether extinguished by the reigning political creed.

To speak of any kind of limits at all is another way of speaking about the plight of liberalism, a political tradition predicted on unlimited economic expansion. In its most persuasive form, liberalism rests on a chastened belief in progress, one which does not presuppose any naive illusions about the perfectibility of human nature but assumes merely that a steady growth of consumer demand—a revolution of rising expectations—will sustain economic expansion indefinitely. Liberalism has identified itself with policies designed to assure full employment and thus to expand the capacity to consume. The promise of universal abundance has contained egalitarian implications without which it would have carried very little moral authority. Those implications, to be sure, were open to conflicting interpretations. Some people argued that it was enough to increase the general pool of goods and services, in the expectation that everyone's standard of living would rise as a result. Others demanded more radical measures designed not merely to increase the total wealth but to distribute it more equitably. But no one who believed in progress conceived of a limit on productive capacity as a whole. No one envisioned a return to a more frugal existence; such views fell outside the progressive consensus.

The belated discovery that the earth's ecology will no longer sustain an indefinite expansion of productive forces deals the final blow to the belief in progress. A more equitable distribution of wealth, it is now clear, requires at the same time a reduction in the standard of living enjoyed by the rich nations and the privileged classes. The attempt to extend Western standards of living to the rest of the world, on the other hand, would lead very quickly to the exhaustion of nonrenewable resources, the irreversible pollution of the earth's atmosphere, drastic changes in its climate, and the destruction of the ecological system on which human life depends. "Let us imagine," Rudolf Bahro writes, "what it would mean if the raw material and energy consumption of our society were extended to the 4.5 billion people living today, or to the 10–15 billion there will probably be tomorrow. It is readily apparent that the planet can only support such volumes of production . . . for a short time to come."[3] Let us imagine further an India in which every family owned a pair of cars and every house came with air-conditioning, stereo sets, VCRs, and a kitchen fully equipped with the latest appliances.

The growing importance of environmental issues provides the most dramatic but by no means the only indication that we have entered a new age of limits—limits not only to economic development but more generally to human control over nature and society.

It is a commonplace observation that technological innovations have unforeseeable consequences that often render them self-defeating, compounding the very problems they were meant to solve. The widespread use of antibiotics leads to the proliferation of bacteria resistant to antibiotics. Medical technologies that prolong life create still another class of dependent, superfluous persons whose numbers overwhelm the facilities for taking care of them. Automobiles, supposedly a fast, cheap, and efficient means of transportation, merely disguise the cost of getting from one place to another. By taking account of the time required to maintain and pay for these machines, to drive and park them, and to earn the money to buy gas, insurance, and repairs, Ivan Illich once calculated that the average driver achieved an average speed of only 4.7 miles an hour—not much faster than walking.[4] David Ehrenfeld, after citing many other examples of self-defeating technologies in his *Arrogance of Humanism,* argues that it is no longer possible to avoid the conclusion that our inability to make long-range predictions with any accuracy, to control the innumerable complexities that enter into such calculations, and to allow for unanticipated effects caused by our own procedures of diagnosis and measurement impose severe limits on our capacity for control.[5] In a recent book, Ehrenfeld continues his analysis of our "misplaced faith in control" by showing how overmanagement, in the private as well as the public sector, makes society increasingly unmanageable. The sheer volume of paperwork absorbs energies that might be used more constructively. Obsessive record keeping makes it more and more difficult to distinguish useful from useless information or to locate appropriate information when it is needed. Obsessive supervision undermines the judgment and competence and self-confidence of those under supervision and creates a need for still more supervision. The cost of maintaining elaborate structures of management drains resources away from more productive investments. The administered society, it appears, is inherently unstable. There are limits beyond which it cannot operate without collapsing under its own weight—limits we are rapidly approaching.[6]

In its classic version, liberalism reduces the functions of government to a bare minimum. Diplomacy, war, police protection, and education pretty much exhaust the responsibilities of the state, as it was conceived by liberals in the eighteenth and nineteenth centuries. This drastic simplification of government was an important source of liberalism's appeal, together with its promotion of religious tolerance and free speech. Yet the liberal state has now evolved into a leviathan, and even the misnamed private sector is dominated by huge bureaucracies exercising quasi-governmental powers and closely linked to the public bureaucracy, notwithstanding their impatience with regulation. What explains this curious line of historical development, as a result of which liberalism has come to be associated with a social order that would have seemed completely repellant to the founders of liberalism? Is it simply that liberals have betrayed their own heritage, as right-wing critics argue when they try to recall liberalism to its free-market origins? Or is there something in the very nature of liberalism—some inner contradiction, as we used to say—which gives rise to the need for elaborate structures of management, supervision, and control?

Through all the permutations and transformations of liberal ideology, two of its central features have persisted over the years—its commitment to progress and its belief that a liberal state could dispense with civic virtue. The commitment to progress alone generated many of the difficulties that now threaten to bury the liberal state, because progress meant large-scale production and the centralization of economic and political power. The belief in progress also contributed to the illusion that a society blessed with material abundance could dispense with the active participation of ordinary citizens in government—which brings us to the second point, the heart of the matter. In the aftermath of the American Revolution, liberals began to argue, in opposition to the older view that "public virtue is the only foundation of republics," in the words of John Adams, that a proper system of constitutional checks and balances would "make it advantageous even for bad men to act for the public good," as James Wilson put it. According to John Taylor, "an avaricious society can form a government able to defend itself against the avarice of its members" by enlisting "the interest of vice . . . on the side of virtue." Virtue lay in the "principles of government," Taylor argued, not in the "evanescent qualities of individuals." The institutions and "principles of a society may be virtuous, though the individuals composing it are vicious."[7]

The trouble with this agreeable paradox of a virtuous society based on vicious individuals is that liberals didn't really mean it. They took for granted a good deal more in the way of private virtue than they were willing to acknowledge. Even today, liberals who adhere to this minimal view of citizenship smuggle a certain amount of citizenship between the cracks of their free-market ideology. Milton Friedman himself admits that a liberal society requires a "minimum degree of literacy and knowledge" along with a "widespread acceptance of some common set of values."[8] It is not clear that our society can meet even these minimal conditions, as things stand today; but it has always been clear, in any case, that a liberal society needs more virtue than Friedman allows for. A system that relies so heavily on the concept of rights presupposes individuals who respect the rights of others, if only because they expect others to respect their own rights in return. The market itself, the central institution of a liberal society, presupposes, at the very least, sharp-eyed, calculating, and clear-headed individuals—paragons of rational choice. It presupposes not just self-interest but enlightened self-interest. It was for this reason that nineteenth-century liberals attached so much importance to the family. The obligation to support a wife and children, in their view, would discipline possessive individualism and transform the potential gambler, speculator, dandy, or confidence man into a conscientious provider. Having abandoned the old republican ideal of citizenship along with the republican indictment of luxury, liberals lacked any grounds on which to appeal to individuals to subordinate private interest to the public good. But at least they could appeal to the higher selfishness of marriage and parenthood. They could ask, if not for the suspension of self-interest, for its elevation and refinement. Rising expectations would lead men and women to invest their ambitions in their offspring. The one appeal that could not be greeted with cynicism or indifference was the appeal summarized in the slogan of our own times, "our children: the future"—a slogan that makes its appearance only when its effectiveness can no longer be taken for granted. Without this appeal to the immediate future, the belief in progress could never have served as a unifying social myth, one that kept alive a lingering sense of social obligation and gave self-improvement, carefully distinguished from self-indulgence, the force of a moral imperative.

Thomas Hopkins Gallaudet, a prominent educator and humanitarian (a pioneer in education for the deaf, among other things) expressed a view widely shared by liberals when he wrote, in 1837, that the "good order and welfare of society" had to rest on "that indescribable parental attachment to offspring which secures to the child every particular, constant, and fond attention which its peculiar condition demands." Neither "legislative enactments" nor prisons nor a large police force could guarantee social order. Even the school, on which liberals characteristically put so much of the burden of social control and improvement, could not succeed unless it saw itself as "co-operating with the [family and] . . . greatly aiding its operations."[9] Now that the family's educational role has been so greatly diminished, with the result that the schools expend most of their efforts in teaching things that should have been learned at home, we can appreciate the wisdom of these nineteenth-century platitudes about the dependence of the school on the family. Educators in the twentieth century have tried to assure us that well-managed schools can replace the family, in effect. John Dewey's version of this new consensus was more modest than most. Because modern industry had "practically eliminated household and neighborhood occupations," he argued, the school would have to "supply that factor of training formerly taken care of in the home"—training, that is, in the "physical realities of life."[10] Abraham Flexner and Frank Bachman went much further. "Social, political and industrial changes," they wrote in 1918, "have forced upon the school responsibilities formerly laid upon the home. Once the school had mainly to teach the elements of knowledge, now it is charged with the physical, mental, and social training of the child as well."[11] In our own day, it is charged, in addition to all that, with the still-more-sweeping task of instilling a sense of racial and ethnic pride in disfranchised minorities, at the expense of the basic education that is really needed. Yet it is more and more widely acknowledged, even by educators, that the schools can't teach anything at all unless the importance of learning is upheld in the home. Without a substructure of strong families to build on, the school system will continue to deteriorate.

The history of education provides an especially striking illustration of a general principle, namely that the replacement of informal types of associations by formal systems of socialization and control weakens social trust, undermines the willingness both to assume responsibility for oneself and to hold others accountable for their actions, destroys respect for authority, and thus turns out to be self-defeating. The informal associations that have been allowed to wither away (except when they have been deliberately and systematically destroyed by ill-conceived adventures in social engineering) include not only the family but the neighborhood, which serves, much more effectively than the school, as an intermediary between the family and the larger world. Jane Jacobs speaks of the "normal, casual manpower for child rearing" which is wasted when city planners and other well-meaning reformers seek to get children off the streets into parks, playgrounds, and schools where they can be professionally supervised.[12] The whole thrust of liberal policy, ever since the first crusades against child labor, has been to transfer the care of children from informal settings to institutions designed specifically for that purpose. Today this trend continues in the movement for day care, often justified on the grounds not merely that working mothers need it but that day-care centers can take advantage of the latest innovations in pedagogy and child psychology. This policy of segregating children in age-graded institutions under professional supervision has been a massive failure, for reasons suggested by Jacobs in *The Death and Life of Great American Cities*—an attack on city planning which applies to social engineering in general, right across the board. "The myth that playgrounds and grass and hired guards or supervisors are innately wholesome for children and that city streets, filled with ordinary people, are innately evil for children, boils down to a deep contempt for ordinary people." In their contempt, planners lose sight of the way in which city streets, if they are working the way they should, teach children a lesson that cannot be taught by educators or professional caretakers—that "people must take a modicum of public responsibility for each other even if they have no ties to each other." When the corner grocer or the locksmith scolds a child for running into the street, the child learns something that can't be learned simply from lecturing. What the child learns is that adults unrelated to one another except by the accident of propinquity uphold certain standards and assume responsibility for the neighborhood. With good reason, Jacobs calls this the "first fundamental of successful city life"—one that "people hired to look after children cannot teach because the essence of this responsibility is that you do it without being hired."[13]

A neighborhood encourages "casual public trust," according to Jacobs.[14] In its absence, the city has to rely on formal agencies of law enforcement. In Los Angeles, a city that has turned its back on the street, we see this pattern in its most highly developed form—the "militarization of city life," as Mike Davis calls it in his *City of Quartz*. A vastly expanded police force, equipped with the technology and increasingly with the mentality of a police state, still finds itself unable to assure safety and order and has to be supplemented by an army of private policemen. According to Davis, the private sector specializes in labor-intensive law enforcement, the public sector in aerial surveillance, paramilitary operations, wiretapping, and the maintenance of its elaborate criminal files. "Fortress L.A.," as Davis calls it, is becoming a city of "enclosed communities," heavily guarded compounds prepared to repel intruders at the slightest hint of trouble.[15]

Los Angeles, the triumph of counterurbanization, embodies the triumph of liberalism, together with its collapse. It is literally the end of the road, simultaneously the last refuge of the liberal dream and the nightmare that was always implicit in the dream. Liberalism promised progress, abundance, and above all privacy. The freedom to live as you please, think and worship as you please—this privatization of the good life was liberalism's greatest appeal. Having set definite limits to the powers of the state, at the same time relieving individuals of most of their civic obligations, liberals assumed that they had cleared away the outstanding obstacles to the pursuit of happiness. What they allowed themselves to forget was that public order is not just a function of the state, which can safely be entrusted with the responsibility for education and law enforcement while citizens go about their private affairs. A society in working order has to be largely self-policing and to a considerable extent self-schooling as well. City streets, as Jacobs reminds us, keep the peace and instruct the young in the principles of civic life. Neighborhoods recreate many features of the village life that is celebrated in American folklore, even as Americans reject the promiscuous sociability of the village in favor of "life-style enclaves," as Robert Bellah calls them, in which they can associate exclusively with those who share their own tastes and outlook.[16] Neighborhoods provide the informal substructure of social order, in the absence of which the everyday maintenance of life has to be turned over to professional bureaucrats. In Los Angeles, a city deliberately designed to maximize privacy, we see how this hyperextension of the organizational sector is the necessary consequence of the retreat from the neighborhood. But Los Angeles is exceptional only in its single-minded dedication to a deeply antisocial version of the American dream and in the scale of the social problems that result. The same pattern can be seen in every other American city, where the police, the educational bureaucracy, and the health and welfare bureaucracies fight a losing battle against crime, disease, and ignorance.

I shall explore one more illustration of the principle that the atrophy of informal controls leads irresistibly to the expansion of bureaucratic controls. I refer to the growing demand for the censorship of pornography, obscenity, and other forms of unacceptable speech, not to mention the outcry against flag burning. Here is another instance in which liberalism seems to be reaching its limits—in this case, the limits of more-or-less-unconditional guarantees of free speech. It is suggestive that the strongest case for censorship today does not come from professional patriots and right-wing advocates of ideological conformity—that is, from the kind of people who never grasped the importance of free speech in the first place. It comes instead from the kind of people who formerly upheld the First Amendment against its critics, from people on the left, especially from feminists who take the position that pornography exploits women and ought to be subject to some kind of public regulation. It is not necessary to accept their contention that pornography represents an invasion of women's civil rights (a contention that stretches the concept of civil rights out of all resemblance to its original meaning) in order to see the justice of their opposition to pornography. But pornography is not just a women's issue, and the best argument against it is not simply that it demeans women, corrupts children, or injures some other class of victims but that it "offers us an unacceptable mirror of ourselves as people," in the words of Elizabeth Fox-Genovese. Like obscene speech, it corrupts our public culture. The pervasiveness of obscene images and speech, not just in the media but in everyday conversation, reminds us that morality is a public matter, not just a matter of private taste (except when someone can claim to be injured) and that what makes it public is the need for common standards, not just the possibility that pornography or obscenity will impinge on the rights of women or demean them in some other way. As Fox-Genovese observes, "A society unwilling or unable to trust to its own instinct in laying down a standard of decency does not deserve to survive and probably will not survive."[17]

Every culture has to narrow the range of choices in some way, however arbitrary such limitations may seem. To be sure, it also has to see to it that its controls do not reach too far into people's private lives. Still, if it allows every impulse for public expression—if it boldly declares that "it is forbidden to forbid," in the revolutionary slogan of 1968—then it not only invites anarchy but abolishes the distinctions on which even the category of truth finally depends. When every expression is equally permissible, nothing is true. The heart of any culture, as Philip Rieff rightly insists, lies in its "interdictions." Culture is a set of moral demands, of "deeply graven interdicts, etched in superior and trustworthy characters." This is why Rieff can describe the United States today as a "cultureless society." It is a society in which nothing is sacred and nothing, therefore, can be effectively forbidden. An anthropologist might say that a cultureless society is a contradiction in terms, but Rieff objects to the way in which liberal social scientists have reduced the concept of a culture to a "way of life." In his view, culture is a way of life backed up by the will to condemn and punish those who defy its commandments. A way of life is not enough. A people's way of life has to be embedded in "sacred order," that is, in a conception of the universe, ultimately a religious conception, that tells us "what is not to be done."[18]

If Rieff and Fox-Genovese are correct in their belief that culture rests on a willingness to uphold public standards and to enforce them, then the "remissive" culture of liberalism cannot be expected to survive indefinitely. In the past, liberals could afford a broad definition of free speech only because they could take for granted the existence of informal sanctions against its misuse. The First Amendment was not designed to protect obscene or pornographic speech, which eighteenth-century conventions relegated to strictly private circulation. Here as elsewhere, liberalism presupposed a morality inherited from the preenlightened past. The persistence of that morality, supported by families, the churches, and a code of common decency so widely accepted that it hardly needed to be articulated, concealed contradictions in liberalism which are beginning to surface now that a certain reticence and propriety can no longer be taken for granted. The danger is that a belated recognition of the importance of common standards will lead to a demand for organized repression which will endanger hard-won rights of free speech. We see this not only in the movements for censorship of pornography or (at the opposite end of the political spectrum) in the officially sanctioned pressure for an amendment against flag burning but in the ill-advised measures adopted by universities against "verbal harassment" and more generally in the attempt to enforce a stifling standard of politically correct speech.

The search to find organized controls for situations in which informal controls no longer seem to operate promises to existinguish the very privacy liberals have always set such store by. It also loads the organizational sector, as we have seen, with burdens it cannot support. The crisis of public funding is only one indication, although it is also the clearest indication, of the intrinsic weakness of organizations that can no longer count on informal, everyday mechanisms of social trust and control. The taxpayers' revolt, although itself informed by an ideology of privatism resistant to any kind of civic appeals, also grows out of a well-founded suspicion that tax money merely sustains bureaucratic self-aggrandizement. The state is obviously overburdened, and nobody has much confidence in its ability to solve the problems that need to be solved. Of course a disenchantment with the welfare state does not in itself imply a commitment to some other kind of solutions. It may well signify nothing more than indifference, cynicism, or resignation. Although almost everybody now believes that something has gone radically wrong with our country, no one has any clear ideas about how to fix it. The increasingly harsh, intemperate quality of public debate no doubt reflects this shortage of ideas and the frustration to which it gives rise.

As formal organizations break down, people will have to improvise ways of meeting their immediate needs: patrolling their own neighborhoods, withdrawing their children from public schools in order to educate them at home. The default of the state will thus contribute in its own right to the restoration of informal mechanisms of self-help. But it is hard to see how the foundations of civic life can be restored unless this work becomes an overriding goal of public policy. We have heard a good deal of talk about the repair of our material infrastructure, but our cultural infrastructure, as we might call it, needs attention too, and more than just the rhetorical attention of politicians who praise "family values" while pursuing economic policies that undermine them. It is naive or cynical to lead the public to think that dismantling the welfare state is enough to ensure a revival of informal cooperation—"a thousand points of light." People who have lost the habit of self-help, who live in cities and suburbs where shopping malls have replaced neighborhoods, and who prefer the company of close friends (or simply the company of television) to the informal sociability of the street, the coffee shop, and the tavern are not likely to reinvent communities just because the state has proved such an unsatisfactory substitute. They still need help from the state, in the form of policies designed to strengthen the family, say, and to enable families to exert more control over professionals when they have to depend on them or at least to give them more freedom in the choice of professionals. A voucher system for schools is the type of reform which answers this need, and the same principle might be applied to other professional services a well.

Such reforms will not, in themselves, be enough to restore the structures of informal self-government in an overorganized society. But even these modest beginnings require far more energy and vision than our leaders have shown in recent years. The belief that liberal societies have achieved a state of almost perfect equilibrium—that "liberal outcomes are stable once reached," in the words of one of Fukuyama's admirers, Stephen Sestanovich[19]—adds one more reason to the list of reasons that appear to justify a policy of drift. The "end of history" contributes to the disinclination to undertake fundamental changes. The stability of liberal states is an illusion, however, and the sooner we recognize it as such, the sooner we can hope to summon up the "daring, courage, imagination, and idealism"—qualities prematurely consigned by Fukuyama to the dustbin of history—that will enable us to address the unsolved problems that will otherwise overwhelm us.

NOTES

1. On the Possibility of Writing a Universal History (Francis Fukuyama)

1. See Plato, *Republic* 8.543c–69c, and Aristotle, *Politics* 5.1301a–16b.

2. For overviews of past attempts to write universal histories, see J. B. Bury, *The Idea of Progress* (New York: Macmillan, 1932); Robert Nisbet, *Social Change and History* (London: Oxford University Press, 1969); and William Galston, *Kant and the Problem of History* (Chicago: University of Chicago Press, 1975).

3. That is to say, the appeal of Islam, while undoubtedly great in countries that were culturally Islamic to begin with, is almost nonexistent beyond those borders. Moreover, the very strength of Islam is in a sense a measure of the cultural threat that Islamic societies faced from Western ideas in the nineteenth and early twentieth centuries.

4. See Francis Fukuyama, "Liberal Democracy as a Global Phenomenon," *Political Science and Politics* 24 (December 1991), 659–64.

5. The exact count of the number of democracies in the world at any given time depends, of course, on the definition of democracy one uses. These numbers are drawn from Michael Doyle, "Kant, Liberal Legacies, and Foreign Affairs," *Philosophy and Public Affairs* 12 (Summer 1983), 205–35.

6. See Thomas S. Kuhn, *The Structure of Scientific Revolutions,* 2d ed. (Chicago: University of Chicago Press, 1970), particularly pp. 95–110, 139–43, and 170–73.

7. See Samuel Huntington, *Political Order in Changing Societies* (New Haven: Yale University Press, 1967), pp. 154–56. This point is also made in Walt Rostow, *The Stages of Economic Growth* (Cambridge: Cambridge University Press, 1960), pp. 26–27, 56.

8. Seymour Martin Lipset, "Some Social Requisites of Democracy: Economic Development and Political Legitimacy," *American Political Science Review* 53 (1959), 69–105.

9. See Talcott Parson's "Evolutionary Universals in Society," *American Sociological Review* 29 (1964), 339–57.

10. For evidence of the relatively poorer economic performance of democratic Third World countries, see Samuel P. Huntington and Jorge I. Dominguez, "Political Development," in *Handbook of Political Science,* vol. 3, ed. Fred Greenstein and Nelson Polsby (Reading, Mass.: Addison-Wesley, 1975), p. 61.

11. There is, of course, a legitimate question as to whether Kojève's interpretation of Hegel is really Hegel as he understood himself or whether it contains an admixture of ideas that are properly termed "Kojèvian." Kojève does take certain elements of Hegel's

teaching, such as the struggle for recognition and the end of history, and make them the centerpiece of that teaching in a way that Hegel himself did not do. Although uncovering the original Hegel is an important task, for the purposes of the present argument I am interested not in Hegel per se but in Hegel-as-interpreted-by-Kojève or perhaps in a new, synthetic philosopher named Hegel-Kojève. In subsequent references to Hegel, I actually refer to Hegel-Kojève.

12. Many people, particularly in the empiricist tradition, will immediately object that Hegel (and, for that matter, Kojève) was not a liberal, that he was a corporatist or an apologist for the Prussian monarchy, and so forth. I do not have the space here to defend Hegel from these charges, except to note that universal recognition *is* in fact a very useful way to interpret the reality of contemporary liberal societies.

2. *Hegel on History, Self-Determination, and the Absolute (Terry Pinkard)*

1. An excellent recent account in this vein is Allen Wood's *Hegel's Ethical Thought* (Cambridge: Cambridge University Press, 1990).

2. G. E. Mueller in his "The Hegel Legend of 'Thesis-Antithesis-Synthesis,' " *Journal of the History of Ideas* 19 (1958), 411–14, managed to track down the odd historical influence of Herr Chalybäus. The matter is also discussed by Wood in his *Hegel's Ethical Thought*, pp. 3–4.

3. I am here indebted to Robert Pippin's *Modernism as a Philosophical Problem: On the Dissatisfactions of European High Culture* (Oxford: Basil Blackwell, 1991) for many of these points about the structure of modernity. Pippin traces the role of the principle of autonomy in modernity in a profound and original way from Kant to Heidegger. I have found Pippin's treatment of the basic themes in modernity to be indispensable for an understanding of the overall project of German idealism.

4. The classical statement of the nonmetaphysical interpretation is Klaus Hartmann's "Hegel: A Non-Metaphysical View," in *Hegel: A Collection of Critical Essays*, ed. Alasdair MacIntyre (Garden City, N.Y.: Doubleday, 1972), pp. 101–24. More recent divergent views include Robert Pippin's important work *Hegel's Idealism: The Satisfactions of Self-Consciousness* (Cambridge: Cambridge University Press, 1988). Another version of the nonmetaphysical view is also to be found in Terry Pinkard, *Hegel's Dialectic: The Explanation of Possibility* (Philadelphia: Temple University Press, 1987).

5. See Richard Rorty, *Contingency, Irony, Solidarity* (Cambridge: Cambridge University Press, 1989), for a recent statement of his views about conversations.

6. In the *Enzyklopädie*, Hegel says: "In these surroundings, thought is free and withdrawn into itself, free from all stuff, purely by itself. This pure being-with-itself belongs to free thought, to that thought disembarking into the open sea, where nothing is below us and nothing is above us, and we stand in solitude with ourselves alone." *Werke in zwanzig Bänden*, ed. Eva Moldenhauer and Karl Markus Michel (Frankfurt a.M.: Suhrkamp Verlag, 1969), *Enzyklopädie der philosophischen Wissenschaften*, vol. 8, §31, *Anmerkung* (my trans.; hereafter cited as *Werke*).

7. "If Hegel had written the whole of his logic and then said, in the preface, that it was merely an experiment in thought in which he had even begged the question in many places, then he would certainly have been the greatest thinker who had ever lived. As it is he is merely comic." Remark 497 in Kierkegaard's *Journals*, trans., sel., and with an introd. by Alexander Dru (New York: Harper and Row, 1959).

8. To put it like this is anachronistic. Hegel wrote the *Phenomenology* several years before he wrote the *Logic*. In his stay in Jena (1801–7), he drafted a system of logic and metaphysics and then put it aside (despite the fact that he was in desperate straits and badly needed a book in order to land an academic position for himself). He then turned to writing a new work, which became the *Phenomenology*. The *Phenomenology* appeared in 1807, and the first volume of the *Logic* appeared in 1812.

9. In the language used by Hegel in the *Phenomenology*, those authoritative standards are always called the "essence" of a "formation of consciousness."

10. This account of the *Phenomenology of Spirit* is based on a much longer and more detailed treatment of the book and the way Hegel tries to complete it in his later Berlin 'system' in my *Hegel's "Phenomenology": The Sociality of Reason* (Cambridge: Cambridge University Press, 1994).

11. Thomas Nagel, *The View from Nowhere* (Oxford: Oxford University Press, 1986).

12. In his lectures on the philosophy of history, Hegel notes, "This makes the Greek character into *beautiful individuality*, which is brought forth from spirit when it restructures the natural into an expression of itself. . . . It is not free self-determining spirituality but naturalness cultivated into spirituality—spiritual individuality." *Werke*, 12:293.

13. The Cavalier poet John Lovelace captures the aristocratic ethic nicely in his explanation to Lucasta about why he must go to battle: "True; a new Mistresse now I chase / The first Foe in the Field; And with a stronger Faith embrace / A Sword, a Horse, a Shield. / Yet this Inconstancy is such, / As you too shall adore; I could not love thee, Deare, so much / Lov'd I not honour more."

14. It is not noted by Hegel, but it is nonetheless significant that women were able to fulfill the requirements of the character ideal of the *philosophe*; the character ideal of the gentleman obviously did not offer such possibilities to women.

15. See Ernst Cassirer's discussion of Kant's comparison of Rousseau to Newton in his *The Philosophy of the Enlightenment*, trans. Fritz C. A. Koelin and James P. Pettegrove (Princeton: Princeton University Press, 1951), pp. 153–60.

16. One of Hegel's closer students, Karl Ludwig Michelet, claimed that Hegel said the following of the *Phenomenology*: "He went in for calling this piece, which appeared in 1807, his voyage of discovery, because here the speculative method, which for him particularly suited the history of philosophy, traveled through and took possession of the whole range of human knowledge." Cited in Günther Nicolin, *Hegel in Berichten seiner Zeitgenossen* (Hamburg: Felix Meiner Verlag, 1970), #107, p. 76.

17. Hegel also has a long section on the philosophy of nature in the *Encyclopedia*, something that develops the much shorter treatment of science in the *Phenomenology* in the section "Observing Reason." Hegel's treatment of natural science can only be sketched here. (I have dealt in more detail with the *Phenomenology*'s treatment of natural science in *Hegel's "Phenomenology."*) Hegel's philosophy of nature is double-edged. On the one hand, he wants to provide a set of reflections on how the basic conceptions arrived at by the scientific community cohere with the rest of our conceptions, in particular with the conception of ourselves as free, self-determining individuals. In doing so, Hegel wishes to locate the practice of modern science within the larger context of constructing an account of what it means for us to take the 'principle' of freedom as authoritative for ourselves. On the other hand, Hegel wishes to show how the development of notions of causality and functional teleology which are appropriate for the study of nature are supplanted by more historical conceptions that are appropriate for the study of 'spirit.' This point is explicitly made by Hegel in the *Phenomenology of Spirit*, see *Hegel's "Phenomenology of Spirit,"* trans. A. V. Miller (Oxford: Oxford University Press, 1977), ¶295, pp. 178–79; *Phänomenologie des Geistes*, ed. Johannes Hoffmeister (Hamburg: Felix Meiner Verlag, 1952), p. 220.

18. Robert Pippin suggested this formulation to me. In his "Idealism and Agency in Kant and Hegel," *Journal of Philosophy* 88 (1991), 532–41, Pippin also compares Hegel's conception of both agency and freedom with Kant's conception of them, pointing out that "Hegel's account of the differing conceptual schemes necessary in understanding *Natur* and *Geist* sees these schemes as continuous. Kant, famously, sees them as discontinuous" (p. 535).

19. See Hegel, *Aesthetics: Lectures on Fine Art,* trans. T. M. Knox (Oxford: Oxford University Press, 1975), 1:54–55; *Werke,* 13:80–82. He notes, "These are oppositions which have not been invented at all by the subtlety of reflection or the pedantry of philosophy; in numerous forms they have always preoccupied and troubled human consciousness, even if it is modern cultivation [*Bildung*] that has first worked them out most sharply and driven them up the peak of harshest contradiction. Spiritual culture [*Bildung*], the modern understanding, produces this opposition in man which makes him an amphibious animal, because he now has to live in two worlds which contradict one another. The result is that now consciousness wanders about in this contradiction, and, driven from one side to the other, cannot find satisfaction for itself in one or the other. . . . But for modern culture and its understanding this discordance in life and consciousness involves the demand that such a contradiction be resolved. . . . If general culture [*allgemeine Bildung*] has run into such a contradiction, it becomes the task of philosophy to sublate the oppositions, i.e. to show that neither the one alternative in its abstraction, nor the other in the like one-sidedness, possesses truth, but that they are both self-dissolving; that truth lies only in the reconciliation and mediation of both, and that this mediation is no mere demand, but what is in and for itself accomplished and is ever self-accomplishing."

20. See Michael Walzer, *Spheres of Justice: A Defense of Pluralism and Equality* (New York: Basic Books, 1983).

21. Even though Hegel quite (in)famously argues that arranged marriages have a certain rationality to them, he saw that nonetheless the modern principle of freedom in social life required there to be an element of completely free choice in modern marriages and that this choice had to rest on an emotional bond between the partners (hence the use of the term 'companionate family,' to describe Hegel's position, even though Hegel did not use the term himself). But even so, Hegel clearly endorsed a patriarchal family structure, and some of his comments on women read like a feminist's nightmare. Nonetheless, it is also clear from his marginalia to the *Philosophy of Right* that he struggled to make his views of family life coherent with his general insistence on the principle of freedom as the norm of modern life. One finds, for example, the following entries for §167: "Free undivided love—the honor of personality—the man according to his individuality—the woman to be *respected as equal to himself* [*sich gleich achten*] and placed—not higher—as in chivalry as it were having its religion in the woman. . . . Equality, self-sameness [*Dieselbigkeit*] of rights and of duties—The man should not count for more than the woman." *Werke,* 7:321. Hegel also holds polygamy to be equivalent to the slavery of women, and he also notes that in his view Asian women are slaves because they are not permitted to direct the affairs of the house. (For Hegel, only the modern *Hausfrau* is therefore a truly free woman because she is sovereign over her own sphere.) Hegel's specific views on women and the family are not, shall we say, the kinds of things to which many reflective individuals nowadays subscribe, and, for this reason, it is altogether too easy to dismiss his views out of hand without looking more carefully at his arguments for them. Hegel, for example, comes close to arguing for the social nature of what we now call gender roles. Wood offers an interesting reconstruction of Hegel's views on the family in terms of the way in which Hegel's own principles go against some of what he says and draws out the ways in which Hegel's thoughts interestingly enough coincide

with certain lines of modern feminist thought. See Wood, *Hegel's Ethical Thought,* pp. 244–46. I also treat Hegel's conception of the family in more detail in *Hegel's "Phenomenology."*

22. Hegel's views on children's roles are expressed in the following passages: "What the person ought to be he does not possess from instinct; rather he must first acquire it for himself. On this is founded the child's right to become educated. People under patriarchal [*väterlichen*] governments are in the same position as children: they are fed from central stores and are not regarded as independent and as adults [*Majorenne*]. The services which may be demanded from children should therefore have education as their sole end and be related to that." *Philosophy of Right,* §174, Addition. Hegel also says, somewhat poignantly, "It is to be noted that on the whole children love their parents less than the parents love their children, for the children are facing their independence and are growing stronger and are thus leaving their parents behind, whereas the parents have in the children the impartial objectivity [*objektive Gegenständlichkeit*] of their bond." *Philosophy of Right,* §175, Addition.

23. Although Hegel argues for a monarchical state, there is some debate about just what form of monarchy he envisioned. The published text of the *Philosophy of Right* is not entirely clear on the matter, and it can, not wholly implausibly, be read as endorsing some form of absolute monarchy. His lectures on the subject matter of the *Philosophy of Right,* however, make it clear that he has constitutional monarchy in mind. The monarch, he says in his lectures, only dots the *i*'s of the legislation that the civil servants draft. (See §280, Addition. Hegel's editors for the posthumous edition of his works incorporated notes from the lectures into the paragraphs of the *Philosophy of Right*; moreover, since the 1970s many of these lectures in the form of detailed student notes taken from them have been published.) Hegel's considered view seems to be that monarchy is necessary because of the important symbolic role that the monarch plays in the modern state. Because the modern state is so complex and, so Hegel also argues, is essentially bureaucratic, it is not something for which loyalty or identification comes naturally. (One does not naturally identify with a faceless, rule-oriented bureaucracy.) The person of the monarch, on the other hand, gives citizens an intuitive object for their allegiance, a person with whom they can identify. For Hegel, the monarch represents the whole political community in a way that is much more accessible than the more abstract representations of the unity of the political community as offered, for example, by philosophy. Hence, the monarch must be seen to be above the divisive struggles of politics; he can be seen *only* as dotting the *i*'s, not as involving himself in any way in the more divisive areas of modern life. Hegel obviously would not think that a ceremonial presidency, such as that of the current Federal Republic of Germany, could satisfactorily fulfill this function. (An alternative way of representing the unity of the community that is also immediate and accessible is of course the ideal of ethnic or linguistic unity—in other words, nationalism—but this is not seriously considered by Hegel, and represents one way in which he misunderstood part of the dynamic of modern life.)

24. Part of Hegel's reputation for glorifying the militaristic Prussian state comes from his comments on the necessity of war and on war's "ethical significance." See *Philosophy of Right,* §324. Hegel has been taken in these passages to be expressing militaristic 'Prussian' views on war, since he seems not only to be reconciling us to war's necessity but to be glorifying its slaughters, because according to Hegel war is "the state of affairs which deals in earnest with the vanity of temporal goods and concerns" (§324, Remark). Such readings misunderstand Hegel's point, which is made fairly clearly in his remarks on war. Sometimes wars have produced good results; moreover, for a free society to remain free, it must be prepared to defend itself and to struggle for its freedom: "peoples unwilling or afraid to tolerate sovereignty at home have been subjugated from abroad,

and they have struggled for their independence with the less glory and success the less they have been able previously to organize the powers of the state in home affairs—their freedom has died from fear of dying" (§324, Remark). Mark Tunick in his *Hegel's Political Philosophy: Interpreting the Practice of Legal Punishment* (Princeton: Princeton University Press, 1992) puts Hegel's comments on war into perspective, pointing out that in his lectures Hegel advocated securing the political community's freedom through just laws and good social organization as a better alternative to war. See Tunick, pp. 88–90.

25. Hegel's views on religion are complex and controversial enough such that any short summary of them is bound to be unsatisfactory. Nonetheless, a quick sketch of how I take Hegel's arguments about religion can at least show in general how I understand those views to fit into the broader perspective for which I have argued. Hegel understands religious practice to be one of a set of historically developed practices whose function is to reflect on humanity's 'highest interests.' (The others are art and philosophy.) Indeed, only when those social practices are established whose function is to reflect on, and thereby to affirm or disaffirm, that what a given form of life takes as authoritative reasons for belief and action *really are* authoritative reasons, can there be a *teleological* historical progression at all, for only such reflection can generate that kind of self-undermining of what is authoritative for a form of life such that it then requires a resolution in a later form of life, which in turn will have its own distinctive account of itself and its own set of reflective institutions. (More generally put: using Hegel's terminology, we would say that "absolute spirit" is the presupposition of "objective spirit.") Religion is a form of such reflection on what, in Hegel's terminology, exists "in and for itself." For Hegel, this object "existing in and for itself" turns out to be reason, which is itself constituted out of the dialectical history of the communal practices of reason-giving, reflection, self-undermining attempts at reassurance and the development of new accounts. Reason itself is thus the "divine," that is, the ground of all else that we value. Because reason is the result of a complex history of the human practices of criticism of practices themselves, Hegel holds that reason grounds the idea of the sacredness of rational, self-conscious human life, and Christian religion, so he thinks, puts this into proper symbolic form with its idea of the divine and the human fusing together. Such Christian symbolism underpins the possibility of modern political community (as involving the idea that all people are inherently free, because understanding the sacredness of rational, self-conscious life means that treatment of such life as if it were of only relative importance is an offense against the divine). I discuss Hegel's views on religion in much more depth in *Hegel's "Phenomenology."*

26. In speaking of the development of the "principle of thought" as implying the idea of self-determination, Hegel says, "This formally absolute principle brings us to the *last stage in history, to our world, to our time." Philosophy of History,* trans. J. Sibree (New York: Dover, 1956), p. 442; *Werke,* 12:524.

27. Hegel, *Philosophy of History,* p. 104; *Werke,* 12:134.

28. An often-cited passage in the *Philosophy of History* shows that Hegel entertained the possibility that world history might now begin a different story than it has up until now. The passage concerns his reflections on North America: "North America will be comparable with Europe only after the immeasurable space which that country presents to its inhabitants shall have been occupied, and the members of the political body shall have begun to be pressed back on each other. . . . America is therefore the land of the future, where, in the ages that lie before us, the burden of the world's history shall reveal itself—perhaps in a contest between North and South America. It is a land of desire of all those who are weary of the historical lumber-room of old Europe. . . . *It is for America to abandon the ground on which hitherto the history of the world has developed itself* . . . and as a land of the future, it has no interest for us here, for, as regards *history,* our concern

must be with that which has been and that which is." *Philosophy of History,* pp. 86–87; *Werke,* 12:114 (my italics).

29. On Lorenz von Stein's importance for contemporary thought, see E.-W. Böckenförde, "Lorenz von Stein als Theoretiker der Bewegung von Staat und Gesellschaft zum Sozialstaat," in E.-W. Böckenförde, *Staat, Gesellschaft, Freiheit* (Frankfurt a.M.: Suhrkamp Verlag, 1976), pp. 146–84. I treat von Stein's ideas briefly in Terry Pinkard, *Democratic Liberalism and Social Union* (Philadelphia: Temple University Press, 1987), chap. 4.

30. Something like the project for this kind of revised Hegelianism is suggested by Robert Pippin in the closing arguments of his *Modernism as a Philosophical Problem.*

4. *Kant's Idea of History (Susan Shell)*

1. On Kant's treatment of history, see Patrick Riley, *Kant's Political Philosophy* (Totowa, N.J.: Rowman and Littlefield, 1983); and Bernard Yack, *The Longing for Total Revolution* (Princeton: Princeton University Press, 1986). Yack's synoptic discussion of post-Kantian thought brings much-needed attention to the influence of Kant on several waves of (silent) epigones. Other valuable works in English on Kant's treatment of history include Yirmiahu Yovel, *Kant and the Philosophy of History* (Princeton: Princeton University Press, 1980); William A. Galston, *Kant and the Problem of History* (Chicago: University of Chicago Press, 1975); George Armstrong Kelly, *Idealism, Politics, and History: Sources of Hegelian Thought* (Cambridge: Cambridge University Press, 1969); William James Booth, *Interpreting the World: Kant's Philosophy of History and Politics* (Toronto: University of Toronto Press, 1986); Richard L. Velkley, *Freedom and the End of Reason* (Chicago: University of Chicago Press, 1989); Peter D. Fenves, *A Peculiar Fate: Kant and the Problem of World-History* (Ithaca: Cornell University Press, 1991); and Emil L. Fackenheim, "Kant's Concept of History," *Kant-Studien* 48 (1957), 381–98. Alexandre Philonenko, in *La théorie kantienne de l'histoire* (Paris: Vrin, 1986), draws useful attention to the bearing of the *Nachlasse* of the 1770s on Kant's treatment of history.

2. Page references are to the Akademie edition of Kant's works (Immanuel Kant, *Gesammelte Schriften* [Berlin: Königlich Preussischen Akademie der Wissenschaften, 1902–], followed, where indicated, with a page reference to the English translation of H. B. Nisbett (Kant, *Political Writings,* 2nd enl. edn. ed. Hans Reiss [Cambridge: Cambridge University Press, 1991]). Translations presented in the text are usually my own.

3. Hannah Arendt, *Lectures on Kant's Political Philosophy,* ed. Ronald Beiner (Chicago: University of Chicago Press, 1982), p. 77. Arendt rightly emphasizes the "melancholy" implications of Kant's interest in history; her treatment of Kant suffers, however, from a tendency to depreciate the importance of his explicit constitutional doctrine (which she incorrectly attributes only to his last writings, published after 1790); her own more "aesthetic" reconstruction of Kant's politics depends in no small measure on such a depreciation. See, for example, pp. 15 and 72–74.

4. See, for example, Yovel, *Kant,* p. 155. Yovel sees an inconsistency between the "dogmatic," merely political, history of the *Idea* (in which progress is achieved "unconsciously") and the cultural history of the *Critique of Judgment,* in which the highest moral good is to be consciously realized (pp. 127–29). In fact, however, no such inconsistency exists; for Kant in the *Idea* is (as my reading will attempt to show) perfectly aware of the inevitable tension between a natural and a moral conceptualization of humanity. Far from ignoring the problem posed by the relation between nature and culture, *Idea* takes that relation as its central problem.

5. *Absicht* here can be translated as either "viewpoint" or "intention."

6. The passage appeared in the twelfth issue of the *Gothaische Gelehrte Zeitungen,* 11 February 1784. Kant's essay was published in the *Berlinische Monatsschrift* 4 (11 November 1784). Kant claims to be publishing the *Idea for a Universal History* in order to elucidate the above passage, which otherwise would have "no conceivable sense." The entire self-proclaimed context of the essay is thus a need or desire on Kant's part to correct an otherwise misleading, not to say abortive, act of intellectual propagation.

7. Kant, *Critique of Pure Reason,* A/316 = B/373. Cf. Arendt, *Lectures,* p. 15.

8. Cf. Kant, *Critique of Pure Reason,* A/570 = B/597.

9. The first part of Herder's *Ideen zur Philosophie der Geschichte der Menschheit* had opened with thinly veiled praise for his former teacher. Kant's three published reviews were (Herder felt) highly condescending; they certainly did not disguise their irritation with Herder's entire approach—one whose exuberant pursuit of "analogies" and failure to observe the boundary between nature and reason may well (as Fenves remarks, p. 181) have reminded Kant of his own youthful *Universal Natural History* (1755). That Kant titles his 1784 essay an "idea" of history, where Herder's work speaks (plurally) of "ideas," already suggests the depth of their differences—where Herder glories in the sheer variety of natural and cultural forms, Kant insists on a single unifying thread as the only alternative to chaos. Interestingly enough, it is Kant, not Herder, who insists on the existence of different human "races," a fact that must be weighed in the balance in any attempt to compare their respective understandings of the unity of "humanity."

10. A figure, perhaps, more in keeping with the "galactic" or milky connotations of its name.

11. "If one seeks the cause of the obstacles that keep man in such deep abasement, it will be found in the grossness of the matter in which his spiritual part is sunk, in the inflexibility of the fibers and sluggishness and immobility of the sap that should obey its stirrings. The nerves and fluids of his brain deliver to him only gross and unclear concepts, and because he cannot, in the inwardness of his faculty of thought, counterbalance sufficiently powerful representations against the enticements of sensible experience, he is carried away by his passions, and confused and overwhelmed by the tumult of the elements that maintain his [bodily] machine." When one regards "the nature of *most* men, man seems to be created as a plant, to draw in sap and grow, to propagate his sex, and finally to grow old and die. Of all creatures, he least achieves the end of his existence, because he consumes his more excellent fitnesses for such purposes as lower creatures achieve more securely and decently with less. He would indeed be the most contemptible of all, at least in the eyes of true wisdom, if the hope of the future did not lift him up, that is, if there were not a period of full development in store for the forces shut up in him" (I 356).

12. In the *Universal Natural History,* Kant conceives of man's problem in terms of a struggle between spiritually and physically erotic forces of "attraction." The soul can philosophically "ascend" only by overcoming the physical machinery on which it also vitally depends. It is not just a case of "too soon old, too late smart," for our mental potency depends on the very animal vitality that makes stupidity so tempting, a dilemma from which only the most mentally precocious can escape. Rousseau's *Emile* provides a more democratic remedy (which by Kant's own account turned him around) from the gap that separates man's physical and spiritual maturity.

13. On this conversion, see especially Velkley, *Freedom and the End of Reason.*

14. So that, as Kant here puts it, "in the end, we do not know what sort of concept we should make of our species, so fanciful/imaginary in its pretentions [was man sich von unserer ouf ihre Vorzüge so eingebildeten Gattung für einen Begriff machen soll]."

15. See Kant, *Critique of Judgment,* trans. Werner S. Pluhar (Indianapolis: Hackett, 1987), V 307–20, pp. 174–89. Cf. Kant, *Anthropology,* trans. Mary J. Gregor (The Hague: Martinus

Nijhoff, 1974), p. 95 [VII 226]. Kant here divides the labor (later ambiguously united in the genius) of seizing on the *Absicht* or idea and cognizing its worldly realization, the latter requiring more natural favor than Kant is willing or able at this point to claim. In calling for another Kepler or Newton, Kant also indirectly suggests the insufficiency of Rousseau, whom he once called the Newton of the moral world and whom he once praised for discerning the "deeply hidden laws" that underly the ever-shifting shapes of human affairs. Beyond the physical and moral laws of Newton and Rousseau respectively, Kant seeks a third principle, which will eventuate in the *Critique of Judgment,* one that will at last permit him satisfactorily to conceive man as a *Gattung,* or species, being.

16. On the theme of consolation in the *Idea for a Universal History,* see Fenves, *A Peculiar Fate,* pp. 112–14.

17. On the biological meaning of *Spiel* (as in "play of nature") see Jacob and Wilhelm Grimm, *Deutsches Wörterbuch* (Leipzig: Verlag von S. Hirzel, 1854). Cf. Kant's own use of *Spielart,* in "On the Different Races of Mankind" (II 430), to designate a genetic trait that does not invariably repeat in the next generation. Kant distinguishes the variations that define two races (e.g., white and black skin) from varieties (or *Spielarten*) within a single race (e.g., blond and brown hair). In the former case, interbreeding produces a blending; whereas in the latter case, the characteristic of a parent may not appear in the offspring (e.g., the blond child of a blond father and brunette mother). (See also VIII 94.)

18. The "monster" at the center of the labyrinth of classical myth was itself, of course, the offspring of a mating between man and beast. The theme of the "labyrinth of nature" appears frequently in baroque thought (including that of Leibniz). Kant in his early works often recurs to the labyrinth image, along with that of Ariadne's thread, which he identifies in the *Universal Natural History* with both the mathematical infinite and the principle of "analogy." In the *Critique of Pure Reason,* by way of contrast, reason is said to provide its own "guiding thread" via the Ideas.

19. See Kant, *Groundwork of the Metaphysics of Morals,* trans. H. B. Paton (New York: Harper Row, 1964), p. 62, (IV 394). At the same time, this very harshness is presented as beneficent.

20. Cf. Kant, *Critique of Judgment,* #83, 84.

21. See here Kant's reference to culture as the domain of man's "social value" (VIII 21; 44), a phrase that recalls the threefold classification of value (*Marktpreis, Affectionpreis,* and *Würde*) in the *Groundwork.*

22. Or, alternatively, "more than human."

23. The latter "mutual resistance" results as each acknowledges in himself a tendency to want things his own way (*nach seinem Sinne richten zu wollen*) while anticipating the same tendency in others; as such, it represents a misdirected (yet in its own way just) intimation of equality.

24. Cf. the opening image of Rousseau's *Emile,* which compares man in society to a shrub "which chance has caused to be born in the middle of a path and that the passers-by soon cause to perish by bumping into it from all sides and bending it in every direction." Rousseau's call upon the would-be cultivator of souls to "erect an enclosure" around his charge is replaced, in Kant's account, by the self-regulating mechanism of a forest (albeit one whose "containment" seems to presuppose some sort of artifice). Rousseau's tutor is to give way (as Kant suggests in the *Anthropology*) to history (or Providence) as the solution to the otherwise insoluable problem of human education. The ultimate limits of that solution are suggested by the fact that where Rousseau attributes man's "crookedness" wholly to society (or "chance"), Kant insists it is inherent.

25. Cf. Ecclesiastes 1:14–15.

26. The difficulty "which the very idea of this task lays before the eyes, is this: that man is an animal who, when he lives with others of his kind, requires a master," because

"though as a rational creature he wishes a law to set limits on the freedom of all," his "animal inclination" leads him to exempt himself. The fundamental problem arising from man's dual character thus remains to be solved.

27. *Ungefähr*, which means accidental or safe (hence "approximate," i.e., close enough to avoid danger), also suggests lack of evil intention. Given that "blind accident" is for Kant synonymous with great danger, i.e., a progress annihilating fate, his argument itself inverts the word's historically accreted meaning. That the world might be governed by an *evil* intention is precluded by Kant's association of reason with an ordering intentionality, an intentionality, therefore, whose goodness goes without saying. The greatest danger is not something like Descartes's "evil genius," but a question whose unanswerability would render us unable to predict (or "speak of before [the fact]") a progressive course for man. Even this fate can be averted (without answering the question) if we assume that nature's secret "thread" is itself "tied to" wisdom, a figure whose vaguely umbilical suggestion leaves (purposefully?) obscure the character of the connection.

28. *Heilen*, to heal, can also mean to make whole.

29. The physiological metaphor of obstructed formation is both reinforced and countered by Kant's reference to "engraftment" onto a morally good *Gesinnung*. That *Gesinnung*, we may conclude, does not itself develop or grow from an amoral parent but is present from the start, a self-originating stock into which another species (animal man) is inserted, like a plant. The idea itself is unchanging. And yet the "idea in us," which is not present *to us* (i.e., consciously acknowledged) from the start, involves *Bildung*, or education. (The "in itself," as Hegel will later put it, must become "for itself.") In any case, man's hybrid status—(vegetable,) animal, and rational—remains intact.

30. There are thus two circles at issue: mankind's actual completion of its course (and with it, the realization of our specieshood), and the ideal anticipation that Kant here attempts, an anticipation that allows us somehow to conceive our species, as it were, before the fact. Kant's essay is a continuing meditation on the meaning of man's hybrid and/or engrafted status, that is to say, the paradoxical relation between freedom and nature which constitutes our humanity.

31. In an earlier note, Kant referred to man's very artificial (*künstlich*) role—as compared to what may go on on other planets—as a way of underscoring the fact that nature requires only approximation (*Annährung*) to the idea. Man is "forced" by his asociability (itself born of his love of freedom) to discipline himself and thus develop through "compelled art" the seeds of nature (VIII 22, 23n.; 46, 47n.). One could hardly find a more artful way to reconcile the dual provenance of man in freedom and nature.

32. *Durchgängig* is also a medical term meaning "permeable" or "unobstructed."

33. Kant does not, however, actually work out such a history, or even try to establish that the latter can be done. It is only the *attempt* to work out a philosophic history on whose possibility Kant here insists. All he means, or needs, to establish is the reasonableness of the attempt, as it were, of an attempt. Cf. his later essay *An Old Question Raised Again: Is the Human Race Constantly Progressing?* (pt. 2 of the *Conflict of the Faculties* [1798]). Kant here locates the definitive sign of man's historical wholeness in an accomplished fact—the sympathy of disinterested onlookers for the French Revolution.

34. *Kurzsichtig* can also be translated as "shortsighted."

35. On Kant's treatment of generation conceived as the eruption of reason out of unreason, see the exchanges with Herder and Georg Forster. Kant's first review of Herder criticized him for espousing an "idea of organic force" which opens up the possibility that all species may have emerged "out of a single primordial womb" (*einem einzigen erzeugenden Mutterschoosse*), a possibility "leading to ideas so monstrous [*ungeheur*] that reason recoils trembling from them" (VIII 54). Forster, defending Herder, here accused Kant of an "unmanly terror" (Forster, *Sämtliche Schriften, Tagebücher, Briefe*, Achter Band,

bearbeitet von Siegfried Scheibe [Berlin: Akademie-Verlag, 1974], p. 140). In his own defense, Kant replied that he was merely reacting to the "horror vacui" that causes healthy reason to recoil "when struck by an idea by which nothing can be thought." The dispute between Kant and Herder centers on the question of reason's autonomy, an autonomy that Kant's "idea" of history maintains (at least this side of infinity), but that Herder's notion of "organic force" tends to dissolve. For his part, Herder accuses Kant of an "Averroist" conflation of the "whole human species" into a single mind, a systematic distortion that Herder links both with an exaltation of human reason "to a position of supremacy independent of the senses and organs" *and* to the eagerness of certain "philosophers" to believe that a man may become all he is "entirely by his own efforts." As little, according to Herder, as a person "springs forth from himself" in his natural birth, so is he just as little a "self-birther" in the "use of his spiritual forces." See Herder, *Ideen*, book 9, I.

36. Cf. the "*Foedus Amphictyonum*" VIII 24; 47, on which Kant may be punning. A *foedus amphictyonum* is literally a league of neighbors, or "those who dwell around," and was traditionally made up of cities in close proximity which engaged in trade and other sorts of peaceful intercourse.

37. See Kant, *Contest of the Faculties* (VII 158).

38. Kant here cites, but also slightly misquotes, Hume. Thucydides takes issue on that first page with the Athenian myth of autochthony (or origination of a people from the earth). It is, according to Thucydides, precisely the sterility of Attic soil which accounts for Attica having been inhabited "from great antiquity" by the same people. Regions of richer soil, by way of contrast, experience perpetual "seditions" and "removals" of population. Thucydides notes that before the Trojan War "nothing appears to have been done by the Greeks in common" and that before the time of Hellen, son of Deucalion (himself the supposed offspring of Prometheus and Pandora), there is not even a name for Greece (Hellas). The origin of the Greeks, at least insofar as it can be "conjured out of Homer," is thus itself political, arising from the fact that Hellen of Phthiotis and his sons, being powerful, were called in to aid other cities, which consequently began to "converse" with the former. Only with the Trojan War, however, did the Greeks enter into genuine joint action—a break with the "imbecility of former times." According to Thucydides, then, the entity Greece (Hellene) succeeds its name, and is genuinely constituted only with the strength and correspondence consequent to the common military effort represented by the Trojan War. What makes the contemporary events that he records worth writing down is their unprecedented commotion, and their shattering of what that earlier war created. Although most ancient things "cannot by any means clearly be discovered," he is persuaded, on the basis of what can be construed of times prior to the Trojan War, that the commotions of the past were not very great.

The first page of Thucydides thus incorporates a number of themes crucial to Kant's own idea of history—the essential darkness of the most ancient things, the dubiousness of traditional mythic accounts, including those of Athens (which hold, among other things, that Athenians sprang from the soil like grasshoppers), the importance of political or federative origins over those that are merely national, not least because, unlike their natural counterparts, political origins are in principle knowable—in short, an almost critical methodological caution on Thucydides' part, when compared, say, with Herodotus, about whom Kant is here silent.

39. Cf. Kant's related treatment, in the *Critique of Pure Reason*, of reason's "architectonic" as the idea or "original germ" that underlies all true philosophy (A/835 = B/863; see also Yovel, *Kant*, p. 236). Kant sets out this idea as an alternative to the principle of *generatio aequivoca* (or spontaneous generation of life from the nonliving) which apparently governs earlier philosophic systems, systems that seem to be ordered, in this respect, like lowly

organisms (*Gewürme*). "It is unfortunate," Kant notes, "that only after we have spent much time in the rhapsodic [*rhapsodistisch*] collection of materials at the suggestion of an idea lying hidden in our minds, and after we have, indeed, over a long period assembled the materials in a merely technical manner, does it first become possible for us to discern the idea in a clearer light, and to devise a whole architectonically in accordance with the ends of reason." The history of philosophy as a whole organized according to an idea is the history of the emergence of the germ of reason to full consciousness. As a fuller discussion of this section would make clear, the history of human reason is repeated (and retrospectively completed) phylogenically, in Kant's own intellectual biography. Kant's final history of reason retrospectively interprets the equivocations and confusions of his own earlier philosophic rhapsodies (and in particular, the *Universal Natural History*) as birth pangs. Man's philosophic self-generation combines the spirituality Kant earlier reserved to divine creation with the "historical" character that he associates with natural propagation (in the sense that bees and beavers have an evident "natural history"). As with Hegel, moreover, human history so conceived (i.e., as the germ of reason actualized by becoming conscious of itself) is necessarily retrospective, a fact that crucially distinguishes it, in Kant's case, from the practical history of the human race (or history with a cosmopolitan, and not merely architectonic, intention), which necessarily looks toward the future. In this one respect, at least, Kant's essay on the idea of history is indistinguishable from what he dismissively calls rhapsody. Or to put matters somewhat more accurately, it treads the line between philosophy and rhapsody, a boundary he elsewhere compares to the transition between dreaming and being awake.

40. *Gedanke*, or thought, has generally in Kant's work a further connotation of emptiness, as in "mere thought." See, for example, his use of *Gedanke* in discussion of the Second Paralogism, where *Gedanke* refers to the mere thinking (as in the "I think" that accompanies all of our representations) from which dogmatists falsely infer the existence of the soul as simple substance (*Critique of Pure Reason*, A/355–A361). See also Kant's cognate use of *Gedankending* and *Gedankenswesen* in conjunction with the "Amphibole" of reason (A/292 = B/348) and with reason's "natural dialectic" (see A/673 = B/701). In the latter case, *Gedankenswesen* (which Kemp Smith translates as "thought-entities") are specifically *distinguished* from ideas. (For a thematic discussion of the problem of emptiness in Kant, see Martin Sommer, *Die Selbsterhaltung der Vernunft* [Stuttgart: Fromman-Holzbook, 1977].)

There is another meaning of *Gedanke*—as in *Gedankenstrich* (a dash or stroke that, as Keith Spalding puts it, "indicates that the writer falls silent and allows the reader to pursue his own thoughts")—which Kant may (also) have in mind when he states, by way of conclusion, that his idea of history is not intended to replace empirical inquiry (*Historie*), but is rather to be interpreted as "thought [*Gedanke*] of what a philosophic head . . . might be able to attempt from another standpoint." Kant's idea so construed is literally a dash—a speechless stroke inviting completion by another. See Spalding, *An Historical Dictionary of German Figurative Usage* (Oxford: Blackwell, 1952–).

41. According to Spalding, *Leitfaden* and *Gängelband* were in Kant's day sometimes used as synonyms. The emancipation of humanity can be described as the transformation or replacement of nature's leading strings (with their suggestion of a young child or toddler whose inability to walk on his own keeps him attached) by reason's own ideas, which Kant repeatedly likens to the (Arachne-like?) projection of a guiding thread. Cf. *Critique of Pure Reason*, B/xiii.

42. See Kant, *Jäsche Logic* (IX 25).

43. Kantian "humanity," one could say, is both canceled and preserved in the irreducible "strangeness" of its history.

44. The problem here is precisely that of moral individuation—the fact that each must act in pursuit of an end that can be attained only with the cooperation of all the others—a cooperation beyond the power of any individual to assure. The idea of history partially—but only partially—relieves this problem, by making it at least thinkable that nature here cooperates.

6. *Nietzsche and Spengler on Progress and Decline (Werner J. Dannhauser)*

1. See Johann Wolfgang von Goethe, *Faust,* pt. 1, line 250.
2. Thucydides, *History* 1.1.
3. Aristotle, *Politics* 1268B.
4. Aristotle, *Poetics* 1449A.
5. Oswald Spengler, *The Decline of the West,* vol. 1: *Form and Actuality* vol. 2: *Perspectives of World-History* (New York: Knopf, 1926–28). For background material on Spengler, I have consulted, among other books, H. Stuart Hughes, *Oswald Spengler: A Critical Estimate* (New York: Scribners, 1952; rev. ed., 1962).
6. Spengler, *Decline of the West* 1:xiv, 5–8, 104, 111, 155–57; 2:32.
7. For representative comments on Hegel, see ibid., 1:22, 367, 374; 2:78.
8. Ibid., 1:232–34; 2:28, 58, 261.
9. For representative comments on Shaw, see ibid., 1:346, 371; 2:105, 484.
10. Friedrich Nietzsche, *Thus Spoke Zarathustra,* in *The Portable Nietzsche,* ed. and trans. Walter Kaufmann (New York: Viking, 1954), pp. 128–31.
11. Nietzsche, *Twilight of the Idols,* in op. cit., pp. 546–47.
12. See especially Nietzsche, "On Self-Overcoming," in *Thus Spoke Zarathustra,* pp. 225–28.
13. Nietzsche, *Thus Spoke Zarathustra,* pp. 264–67. The best exposition of the doctrine of the eternal return, not yet available in English, is Karl Lowith, *Nietzsches Philosophie der ewigen Wiederkehr des Gleichen* (Stuttgart: Kohlhammer, 1956).
14. Nietzsche, *Thus Spoke Zarathustra,* pp. 384–87.
15. Alexis de Tocqueville, *Democracy in America,* trans. George Lawrence (Garden City, N.Y.: Anchor Books, 1969). See, for example, p. 111.
16. Blaise Pascal, *Pensées,* trans. A. J. Krailsheimer (Baltimore: Penguin Books, 1968). See, for example, p. 283.

7. *Political Conflict after the Cold War (Samuel P. Huntington)*

1. Francis Fukuyama, "The End of History?" *National Interest,* no. 16 (Summer 1989), pp. 3–18.
2. John J. Mearsheimer, "Back to the Future: Instability in Europe after the Cold War," *International Security* 15 (Summer 1990), 5–56.
3. Edward Luttwak, "From Geopolitics to Geo-economics," *National Interest,* no. 20 (Summer 1990), 17–23.
4. Daniel Bell, "Germany: The Enduring Fear," *Dissent* 37 (Autumn 1990), 466.
5. Donald L. Horowitz, "Ethnic Conflict Management for Policymakers," in *Conflict and Peacemaking in Multiethnic Societies,* ed. Joseph V. Montville (Lexington, Mass.: Lexington Books, 1990), p. 121.

6. William Wallace, *The Transformation of Western Europe* (London: Royal Institute of International Affairs–Pinter, 1990), pp. 17–18.

7. See Mamoun Fandy, "The Hawali Tapes," *New York Times*, 24 November 1990, p. 21; also Bernard Lewis, "The Roots of Muslim Rage," *Atlantic Monthly*, September 1990, 47–54.

9. *"What Then?" (Alan Gilbert)*

1. Kevin Phillips, *The Politics of Rich and Poor* (New York: Basic Books, 1988); G. W. F. Hegel, *Grundlinien der Philosophie des Rechts* (Stuttgart: Reclam, 1970), pp. 377–78.

2. Aristotle called the legislator who first constructed a political association "the greatest of beneficiaries of mankind." *Politics* 1252b16–23, 1253a30–31.

3. G. W. F. Hegel, *Die Vernunft in der Geschichte* (Hamburg: Meiner, 1955), p. 62; my translation.

4. Alan Gilbert, *Democratic Individuality* (hereafter *DI*) (Cambridge: Cambridge University Press, 1990), chaps. 1–3.

5. Francis Fukuyama, "The End of History?" *National Interest*, no. 16 (Summer 1989), 3–18, adapts a notion of "an end of history" from Hegel too easily.

6. Hegel, *Die Vernunft*, p. 62. See also Will Kymlicka, *Liberalism, Community, and Culture* (Oxford: Oxford University Press, 1991), chaps. 1–5.

7. Karl Marx and Friedrich Engels, "The Manifesto of the Communist Party," in Marx and Engels, *Selected Works* (New York: International, 1977), p. 52.

8. Karl Marx and Friedrich Engels, "Moralizing Criticism and Critical Morality," in Marx and Engels, *Collected Works* (New York: International, 1975–), 6:321–23.

9. Aristotle, *Politics* 1281b20–24; Hegel, *Grundlinien*, pp. 377–78.

10. Hegel, *Grundlinien*, p. 46.

11. Hegel downplayed the conflicts of serfdom. In the idiom of the *Communist Manifesto*, his argument prefigures "true socialism" or "red monarchy."

12. Karl Marx, *Grundrisse*, trans. Martin Nicolaus (New York: Random House, 1973), p. 463.

13. Gilbert, *DI*, chap. 8, suggests that a radical regime must adopt many features of liberal democracy, especially an independent judiciary. For radicals as well as liberals, democratization has to do with altering institutions *enough* so that, even in the absence of mass extraparliamentary protest, the state no longer acts on central issues to defend the rich or privileged. That criterion is a hard one to meet. See Richard Miller, "Democracy and Class Dictatorship," *Social Philosophy and Policy* 3, no. 2 (1984), 59–76.

14. See Allen Wood, "The Marxian Critique of Justice," *Philosophy and Public Affairs* 1 (1972), 244–82; Milton Fisk, "History and Reason in Rawls' Moral Theory," in *Reading Rawls*, ed. Normal Daniels (New York: Basic Books, 1975).

15. Immanuel Kant, *On History*, trans. Lewis White Beck, Robert E. Anchor, and Emil L. Fackenheim (Indianapolis: Bobbs-Merrill, 1963), pp. 43–44.

16. John Rawls, *A Theory of Justice* (Cambridge: Harvard University Press, 1971), pp. 542–48; Gilbert, *DI*, chap. 6.

17. See Karl Marx, *Capital*, trans. Samuel Moore and Edward Aveling (Moscow: Foreign Languages Publishing House, 1954–), 1:716, 732–36; Shlomo Avineri, ed., *Karl Marx on Colonialism and Modernization* (New York: Doubleday, 1968), pp. 137, 206.

18. Montesquieu, *De l'esprit des lois*, pp. 337–43; see Gilbert, " 'Internal Restlessness': Individuality and Community in Montesquieu," *Political Theory* 22, no. 1 (1994), 45–70.

19. Marx and Engels, "Manifesto of the Communist Party," p. 52.

20. Marx and Engels, *Writings on the Paris Commune,* ed. Hal Draper (New York: Monthly Review Press, 1971), p. 153; see also Alan Gilbert, "Radical Democracy," in *Cambridge Companion to the Philosophers: Marx,* ed. Terrell Carver (Cambridge: Cambridge University Press, 1991).

21. Kymlicka, *Liberalism, Community, and Culture,* p. 63.

22. See Alan Gilbert, "Eurydice's Music," *Pequod,* no. 37 (1994), 96–104; "When the Poem Sees into You," *Denver Quarterly* 29 (Summer 1994), 120–29. One might think of myth or poetry—say, Rilke's *Duino Elegies*—or nonreductionist psychoanalysis—James Hillman's *A Blue Fire*—or Heidegger's largely Rilkean interpretation of language as a "peal of stillness." See Martin Heidegger, *Poetry, Language, Thought* (New York: Harper, 1971), p. 207.

23. Hegel, *Phenomenology of Spirit,* trans. A. V. Miller (Oxford: Oxford University Press, 1977), p. 27.

24. Leo Strauss, *Natural Right and History* (Chicago: Chicago University Press, 1965), pp. 7–8.

25. John Rawls, "The Priority of Right and Ideas of the Good," *Philosophy and Public Affairs* 17, no. 4 (1988), 251. If we stress, as Rawls means to, informed, critical reflection, then our understanding of equal freedom may simply be an inference to the best explanation of a decent regime. A defense of *limited* moral objectivity, pertaining to the public values of equal liberty which protect individuality and diversity, may be part of what Rawls calls free public reason rather than a special—in his idiom, more comprehensive—view of the good. See Gilbert, *DI,* pp. 82–84, 221–22.

26. See John McCamant, "Intervention in Guatemala," *Comparative Politics* 17 (1984), 373–407; Noam Chomsky and Edward Hermann, *The Political Economy of Human Rights* (Boston: South End, 1975), vol. 1.

27. Alan Gilbert, "Must Global Politics Constrain Democracy? Realism, Regimes, and Democratic Internationalism," and "Power Rivalry–Motivated Democracy," *Political Theory* 20 (1992), no. 1: 8–37; no. 3: 681–89.

28. Realists have often doubted whether such policies served a national interest. See Hans J. Morgenthau, *Politics among Nations* (New York: Knopf, 1973), chap. 1.

29. J. William Fulbright, *The Price of Empire* (New York: Basic Books, 1989), pp. 171, 136–37, 142.

30. Aristotle, *Politics* 1333b29–33.

31. Kant, *On History,* p. 144.

32. Michael W. Doyle, "Kant, Liberal Legacies, and Foreign Affairs," *Philosophy and Public Affairs* 12 (Summer/Fall 1983), 205–35, 323–53.

33. See Alan Gilbert, "Marx on Internationalism and War," *Philosophy and Public Affairs* 17 (1978), 346–69; Alan Gilbert, "Must Global Politics Constrain Democracy?" *Political Theory* 20 (1992), I: 8–37.

34. See Hannah Arendt, *The Origins of Totalitarianism* (New York: Harcourt Brace, 1973).

35. See Gilbert, *DI,* chaps. 7, 11.

36. Max Weber, *Economy and Society* (New York: Bedminster, 1963), 2:92. Gilbert, *DI,* chap. 10.

37. See Susan Griffin, *A Chorus of Stones* (New York: Vintage, 1992). A variety of psychoanalytic views suggests that, given patriarchal family dynamics, the banishing of a child's own feelings to the unconscious in order to be "good" and the consequent emergence of self-hatred and denial fuel projections of hostile images onto outsiders.

38. See E. L. Doctorow, Commencement Address, Brandeis University, 1989; Gilbert, *DI,* chap. 12; Gilbert, "Must Global Politics Constrain Democracy?"

39. See Fukuyama, "The End of History?"

40. Marx to Meyer and Vogt, in Marx and Engels, *Selected Correspondence* (Moscow: Progress Publishing, 1955), pp. 230–32. For a contemporary econometric version of this view, see Michael Reich, *Racial Inequalities*, (Princeton: Princeton University Press, 1981).

41. Against his self-refuting epistemological relativism, however, Foucault sometimes suggests that a (transproblematic) truth can be captured in a more democratic empowering regime: "The essential political problem for the intellectual is not to criticize the ideological contents supposedly linked to science . . . but of ascertaining the possibility of constituting a new politics of truth. . . . It's not a matter of emancipating truth from every system of power (which would be a chimera, for truth is already power), but of detaching the power of truth from the forms of hegemony, social, economic, and cultural, within which it operates at the present time." Michel Foucault, *Power/Knowledge* (Sussex: Harvester, 1986), p. 133.

42. Michel Foucault, *Discipline and Punish* (New York: Pantheon, 1977), p. 175; Foucault, *Power/Knowledge* p. 53.

43. Michel Foucault, *Language, Countermemory, Practice* (Ithaca: Cornell University Press, 1977), p. 209.

44. See Stephen Jay Gould, *The Mismeasure of Man* (New York: Norton, 1981), p. 166; Stephen L. Chorover, *From Genesis to Genocide* (Cambridge, Mass.: MIT, 1975), pp. 98–101.

45. Richard Herrnstein, "IQ," *Atlantic*, 1981; Herrnstein, *IQ in the Meritocracy* (Boston: Little, Brown, 1974); Herrnstein, "In Defense of Intelligence Tests," *Commentary*, February 1980.

46. Note that testing does not treat cultural groups uniformly. Thus immigrant groups that traditionally emphasize education and are not central targets in particular historical periods sometimes, by and large, do well. See Fukuyama, "The End of History?"

47. Herrnstein, "In Defense of Intelligence Tests," p. 44. N. J. Block and Gerald Dworkin, "IQ, Heritability, and Inequality," in *The IQ Controversy*, ed. Block and Dworkin (New York: Pantheon, 1974).

48. Herrnstein, "In Defense of Intelligence Tests," illustrates this translation. On the one hand, he defends stereotypes based on test responses: "culturally specific items typically show smaller differences between blacks and whites than items that seem to be relatively free of cultural information ["geometrical-inference items"]" (p. 50); on the other hand, he notes, "Do not assume that group differences in test scores are genetic, even if individual scores are to a degree. In particular, the differential treatment of blacks and whites in society makes it impossible to draw *firm conclusions* about the origins of the average difference beteeen the races in intelligence-test scores" (pp. 50–51). Yet he is unable to resist *infirm* hypotheses: "Given the overlapping distributions of scores, and assuming for the sake of argument a color-blind society, blacks and whites should be found on every rung of the social ladder, *although not necessarily in the same proportions*" (p. 49).

49. See Alan Garfinkel, *Forms of Explanation* (New Haven: Yale University Press 1981).

50. Arthur Jensen, "How Much Can We Boost IQ and Scholastic Achievement?" *Harvard Educational Review* 39 (Winter 1969), 1–123.

51. Herrnstein, "In Defense of Intelligence Tests," pp. 40–41; Charles Murray as cited in *New York Times*, 30 November 1990.

52. Herrnstein, "In Defense of Intelligence Tests"; Gould, *The Mismeasure of Man*, p. 308.

53. In a review of Francis Hearnshaw's reluctantly devastating official biography of Burt, N. J. MacKintosh raises the appropriate issue: "the crucial evidence that [Burt's] data on IQ are scientifically unacceptable does not depend on any examination of Burt's diaries or correspondence. It is to be found in the data themselves. The evidence was there . . . in 1961. It was, indeed, clear to anyone with eyes to see in 1958. But it was not seen until 1972, when Kamin first pointed to Burt's totally inadequate reporting of his

data, and to the impossible consistencies in his correlation coefficients. Until then, the data were cited, with respect bordering on reverence, as the most telling proof of the heritability of IQ. It is a sorry comment on the wider scientific community that 'numbers . . . simply not worthy of our current scientific attention' should have entered nearly every psychology textbook." Cited in Richard Lewontin, Leon Kamin, and Steven Rose, *Not in Our Genes* (New York: Pantheon Books, 1984), pp. 105–6.

54. Richard Schweder, "Dangerous Thoughts" (review of Carl N. Degler, *In Search of Human Nature*), *New York Times*, 17 March 1991.

55. Thomas Bouchard, Jr., David T. Lykken, Matthew McGue, Nancy L. Segal, and Auke Tellegen, "Sources of Human Psychological Differences: The Minnesota Study of Twins Reared Apart," *Science*, 12 October 1990, 223–28.

56. Richard Lewontin, "The Analysis of Variance and the Analysis of Causes," in Block and Dworkin, *IQ Controversy*; Lewontin, Kamin, and Rose, *Not in Our Genes*. Bouchard et al., "Sources," p. 223, obliquely refer to this point: "This evidence for the strong heritability of most psychological traits, *sensibly construed*, does not detract from the value or importance of parenting, education, and other propaedeutic interventions."

57. Lewontin, Kamin, and Rose, *Not in Our Genes*, pp. 121–22.

58. Leon Kamin, *The Science and Politics of IQ* (New York: Wiley, 1974).

59. James Q. Wilson and Richard Herrnstein, *Crime and Human Nature* (New York: Simon & Schuster, 1985).

60. In "Biology and Crime," p. 3, delivered to the National Institute of Justice, 1988, Herrnstein avers, "The bits of evidence may be individually disputed, but taken together, the case for some genetic involvement in criminal behavior cannot be plausibly rejected." In a 1989 *Atlantic* article "IQ and Falling Birth Rates" (vol. 283, no. 5, 72–79), Herrnstein mourns that high IQ women produce too few children, and calls for eugenic statism: "We should be conscious of how public policy interacts . . . with the differential in the fertility rates of women of different intelligences. . . . Nothing is more private than the decision to bear children, yet *society* has a vital interest in the aggregate effects of these decisions."

61. See Gilbert, *DI*, chap. 7.

62. Charles Taylor, *Sources of the Self* (Cambridge, Mass.: Harvard University Press, 1990), pp. 15, 82–84, 88–89, 17, 26.

63. Kymlicka, *Liberalism, Community, and Culture*, chap. 1.

64. Rawls, *A Theory of Justice*, p. 226; Alan Gilbert, "Equality and Social Theory in Rawls' *A Theory of Justice*," *Occasional Review* 7 (1978), 95–117.

65. See Gilbert, *DI*, chap. 11.

66. David P. Levine, *Needs, Rights, and the Market* (Boulder, Colo.: Rienner, 1988).

67. See G. A. Cohen, "Reconsidering Historical Materialism," in *Marxism Today, Nomos* ed. J. Roland Pennock (New York: New York University Press, 1984).

68. Friedrich Hayek, "The Use of Knowledge in Society," *American Economic Review* 35 (1945), 519–30.

69. Kymlicka, *Liberalism, Community, and Culture*, pp. 195–99.

10. *Feminism and the Crisis of Contemporary Culture (Jean Bethke Elshtain)*

1. Walter Benjamin, *Illuminations* (London: Fontana, 1973), p. 259.

2. Portions of my discussion of competing modes of feminism are drawn from my "Ethics in the Women's Movement," *Annals of American Academy of Political and Social Science*, May 1991, 126–39.

3. Note that the categories I here deploy are not new to my work. I first set forth a discussion of feminism with various rhetorical strategies (also theoretical positions) in mind in "Feminist Political Rhetoric and Women's Studies," in *The Rhetoric of the Human Sciences,* ed. J. Nelson, A. Megill, and D. McCloskey (Madison: University of Wisconsin Press, 1987), pp. 319–40. I have folded paragraphs from that piece into this one for my laying out of the three prototypical strategies.

4. The quoted material is from Gayle Rubin's feminist classic "The Traffic in Women: Notes on a 'Political Economy' of Sex," in *Toward an Anthropology of Women,* ed. Rayna R. Reiter (New York: Monthly Review Press, 1975), p. 165, and Nancy Chodorow, *The Reproduction of Mothering* (Berkeley: University of California Press, 1978), p. 9.

5. See, for example, Ann Ferguson, "Androgyny as an Ideal for Human Development," in *Feminism and Philosophy,* ed. M. Vetterling-Braggin, F. Elliston, and J. English (Totowa, N.J.: Littlefield, Adam, 1977), pp. 62–63. The androgyny literature is enormous at this date and challenged by an equally enormous mountain of "difference" argumentation.

6. For one of the liveliest examples of the genre by one of its best-known spokeswomen, see Mary Daly, *Pure Lust* (Boston: Beacon Press, 1984).

7. From the following essays: Barbara Zanotti, "Patriarchy: A State of War," pp. 16–19; Donna Warnock, "Patriarchy Is a Killer," pp. 20–29; Sally Miller Gearhart, "The Future—If There Is One—Is Female" pp. 266–84, in *Reweaving the Web of Life,* ed. P. McAllister (Philadelphia: New Society Publishers, 1982).

8. The brief is available from the NOW Legal Defense and Education Fund, 132 West 42d St., New York, N.Y. 10036.

9. Cited in James Barron, "Views on Surrogacy Harden after Baby M Ruling," *New York Times,* 2 April 1987.

10. Fred Siegel, "The Politics of Rights," unpub. ms., 1989, p. 2.

11. The End of Leninism (Richard Rorty)

1. Ernesto Laclau, *New Reflections on the Revolution of Our Time* (London, Verso, 1990), p. ix.

2. Alan Ryan, "Socialism for the Nineties," *Dissent* (Fall 1990), 442.

3. Laclau, *New Reflections,* p. 112.

4. Alexandre Kojève, *Introduction to the Reading of Hegel: Lectures on "The Phenomenology of Spirit,"* trans. J. H. Nichols, Jr. (Ithaca: Cornell University Press, 1969), p. 91.

5. Laclau, *New Reflections* p. 83. Italics added.

6. Ibid., p. 84.

7. Jürgen Habermas, *Die nachholende Revolution* (Frankfurt: Suhrkamp, 1990), pp. 196–97. My translation.

8. Ibid., p. 203.

9. Ryan, "Socialism for the Nineties," p. 442.

10. Václav Havel, *Disturbing the Peace* (New York: Knopf, 1990), p. 109.

11. We can put Havel's refusal to prognosticate in an American context by asking, Who would have guessed that the white middle class, which acknowledged the justice of Harry S. Truman's desegregation of the military, the Supreme Court's reversal of the separate-but-equal doctrine, and Martin Luther King's freedom marches—the white middle class that turned King into a schoolbook hero—would now decide that it is more important to cut taxes than to protect ghetto children by building safe havens for them? Who can know whether, a decade further down the road, that same middle class may

not become disgusted with its own greed and throw out the rascals who have been pandering to its selfishness?

12. Martin Jay, *Fin-de-Siècle Socialism and Other Essays* (London: Routledge, 1988), p. 13. The line I am taking in this essay owes a lot to Jay's discussion of "totalization" in this book and in his *Marxism and Totality* (Berkeley: University of California Press, 1984).

13. Toward the end of his "Thinking about Socialism" (written in 1985) Irving Howe asks, "Suppose, indeed, we were to conclude that the socialist label creates more trouble than it's worth; we would then have to cast about for a new vocabulary, something not to be won through fiat. How much would actually change if our words were to change? . . . The substance of our problems would remain, the weight of this century's burdens still press upon us. We should still regard capitalist society as an unjust society, still find intolerable its inequities, still be repelled by its ethic of greed, and still be trying to sketch the outlines of a better society." Howe, *Selected Writings, 1950–1990* (New York: Harcourt Brace Jovanovich, 1990), p. 489.

I agree with what Howe says here, but would add that now, after 1989, it has become clear that the label *does* create more trouble than it is worth. The quarter of the world which has worn that label the longest never wants to hear the word again. Why should it have to?

14. Much of what goes on under the heading "cultural studies" in American universities seems to me well described in the words Kenneth Burke (whom I discuss below) used to describe Emilio Marinetti and Futurism: "To any who might say 'This modern world is disease,' it could answer 'But what a *perfect* example of disease!' Its affinity with the antics of our recent 'hard-boiled' school is apparent. We may also note (unruly thought!) the *sentimental* aspect of both. Futurism, so cast, could provide the most rudimentary kind of solace. Were the streets noisy? It could counter by advocating an uncritical cult of noise. Might there be stench? It would discuss the 'beauties' of stench. *Apparently* active, it was in essence the most passive of frames, an elaborate method for feeling *assertive* by a resolve to drift with the current." Burke, *Attitudes toward History* (rpt. ed.; Los Altos, Calif.: Hermes, 1959), p. 33. What Burke says here about the "hard-boiled" school and about Futurism seems to me to apply quite well to, for example, Fredric Jameson's *Postmodernism: or, The Cultural Logic of Late Capitalism* (Durham, N.C.: Duke University Press, 1991).

15. Two friends who have criticized my attempt to be a faithful follower of John Dewey while remaining a nonradical liberal—Richard Bernstein and Thomas McCarthy—have quoted against me the passage in *Liberalism and Social Action* (*The Later Works of John Dewey*, vol. 11, [Carbondale: Southern Illinois University Press], 1987, p. 45) in which Dewey says that "liberalism must become radical, meaning by 'radical' perception of the necessity of thoroughgoing changes in the set-up of institutions and corresponding activity to bring the changes to pass. . . . 'reforms' that deal now with this abuse and now with that without having a social goal based upon an inclusive plan, differ entirely from effort at re-forming, in its literal sense, the institutional scheme of things. . . . If radicalism be defined as perception of need for radical change, then today any liberalism which is not also radicalism is irrelevant and doomed."

I intepret this passage as presupposing Dewey's claim, a few pages earlier, that "the system that goes by the name of capitalism is a systematic manifestation of desires and purposes built up in an age of ever-threatening want and now carried over into a time of ever increasing potential plenty." This claim seems to me wrong—both in its suggestion that we know how to replace capitalism with something better, and about ever-increasing plenty. I think that Dewey was occasionally tempted, especially in the 1930s, to assume that we already had in mind some better alternatives to market economies and private property. I wish that assumption had been true, but I do not think it was. After 1989, I see even less reason to think that the left has "an inclusive plan" for "thoroughgoing changes in the set-up of institutions." I devoutly wish we did, but until I can peruse such a plan I shall continue to view Bernstein's and McCarthy's descriptions of themselves as radicals as amiable exercises in nostalgia.

16. Havel, *Disturbing the Peace,* p. 80.

17. Burke, characteristically, never quite defines this phrase. At p. 237 of *Attitudes toward History,* he says, "In this book . . . we have said much about the 'comic frame'. We have advocated, under the name of 'comedy', a procedure that might just as well have been advocated under the name of 'humanism'. Presumably we selected 'comedy' because, for one reason or another, the word 'sounded better' to us. And when the author selects one word rather than another because it 'sounds better' to him, his choice is guided by 'overtones' that may not apply to his auditor at all." I take it that Burke does not think that the historical record is *funny* and that his use of "comic" has the overtone of "rueful" rather than of "amusing."

18. Ibid., p. 335.

19. Stanley Fish, *Doing What Comes Naturally* (Durham, N.C.: Duke University Press, 1989), pp. 322–23.

20. Frank Lentricchia, in his *Criticism and Social Change* (Chicago: University of Chicago Press, 1983), has set Burke over against Paul de Man and criticized de Man's attempt to make "Language" the name of a new object of the sort I describe. I agree with the gist of what Lentricchia says about the relative value of Burke's and de Man's work, and have made some similar points in my "Deconstruction" (forthcoming in volume 8 of *The Cambridge History of Literary Criticism*) as well as in "Paul de Man and the American Cultural Left" (in my *Essays on Heidegger and Others* (Cambridge: Cambridge University Press, 1991). In particular, I agree with Lentricchia that "one of the great things about Burke is that he knew the truths of de Man early" (p. 51), a claim confirmed by Burke's Nietzschean remarks about concepts as dead metaphors. Burke, *Attitudes,* pp. 12, 229.

21. Burke, *Attitudes toward History,* p. 107. This passage chimes with Dewey's claim that there is no such thing as radical evil, evil which is evil all the way down. Evil, Dewey said, is always a rejected good—the good of some previous situation. I suspect that adopting this Deweyan attitude toward evil is necessary if we are to throw away the ladder of world-historical romance. My view contrasts with, for example, Cornel West's. West, though an admirer of Dewey, sees Royce's insistence on the radicality of evil as essential to the "left romanticism" that he, Dewey and Royce share. I should argue that all the left needs is romance on a homely, local, noncosmic, non-world-historical scale.

12. *The Age of Limits (Christopher Lasch)*

1. Francis Fukuyama, "The End of History?" *National Interest,* no. 16 (Summer 1989), 5, 9, 18.

2. Ibid., p. 18.

3. Rudolf Bahro, "What Are We Taking On? Thoughts on the Elements of a New Politics," in *Socialism and Survival* (London: Heretic Books, 1982), p. 103.

4. Ivan Illich, *Energy and Equity* (New York: Harper & Row, 1974), pp. 18–19.

5. David Ehrenfeld, *The Arrogance of Humanism* (New York: Oxford University Press, 1978), pp. 125–27.

6. David Ehrenfeld, *Beginning Again: People and Nature in the New Millennium* (New York: Oxford University Press, 1993), pp. 49–64.

7. The three quotations are taken from Gordon Wood, *The Creation of the American Republic, 1776–1787* (Chapel Hill: University of North Carolina Press, 1969), pp. 570, 591–92, 611–12.

8. Milton Friedman, *Capitalism and Freedom* (Chicago: University of Chicago Press, 1962), p. 86.

9. See Thomas Hopkins Gallaudet, "Family and School Discipline," *American Annals of Education* (1837).

10. John Dewey, *The School and Society*, in *John Dewey: The Middle Works, 1889–1924*, ed. Jo Ann Boydston (Carbondale: Southern Illinois University Press, 1976), vol. 1, pp. 8–9.

11. See Abraham Flexner and Frank Bachman, *Public Education in Delaware* (New York: General Education Board, 1918).

12. Jane Jacobs, *The Death and Life of Great American Cities* (New York: Random House, 1961), p. 82.

13. Ibid., pp. 82 and 83.

14. Ibid., p. 56.

15. Mike Davis, *City of Quartz: Excavating the Future in Los Angeles* (London and New York: Verso, 1990), pp. 223 and 246.

16. Robert Bellah et al., *Habits of the Heart: Individualism and Commitment in American Life* (Berkeley: University of California Press, 1985), pp. 71–75.

17. Elizabeth Fox-Genovese, *Feminism without Illusions: A Critique of Individualism* (Chapel Hill: University of North Carolina Press, 1991), pp. 107, 111.

18. See Philip Rieff, *The Feeling Intellect: Selected Writings*, ed. Jonathan B. Imber (Chicago: University of Chicago Press, 1990).

19. Stephen Sestanovich, "Responses to Fukuyama," *National Interest*, no. 16 (Summer 1989), 33.

NOTES ON CONTRIBUTORS

JOSEPH CROPSEY is Distinguished Service Professor of Political Science Emeritus at the University of Chicago. He is the author of *Polity and Economy: An Interpretation of the Principles of Adam Smith* (1957) and *Political Philosophy and the Issues of Politics* (1977). He is coeditor (with the late Leo Strauss) of *History of Political Philosophy* (3d ed., 1987). His most recent book is *Plato's World* (1995).

CONOR CRUISE O'BRIEN has served as a diplomat for the United Nations and the Republic of Ireland, as minister in the Irish cabinet, and as senator in the Irish Parliament. His most recent books are *God Land: Reflections on Religion and Nationalism* (1988) and *The Great Melody: A Thematic Biography and Commented Anthology of Edmund Burke* (1992). He is at work on his autobiography, *My Life and Themes*.

WERNER J. DANNHAUSER is Visiting Professor of Political Science at Michigan State University. He is the author of *Nietzsche's View of Socrates* (1974) and editor of *On Jews and Judaism in Crisis: Selected Essays by Gershom Scholem* (1976). His next book, a collection of his essays, will be titled *Nietzsche, Religion, and Evil*. Professor Dannhauser is Senior Research Fellow at the Symposium on Science, Reason, and Modern Democracy.

JEAN BETHKE ELSHTAIN is Laura Spellman Rockefeller Professor of Ethics at the University of Chicago. Her books include *Public Man, Private Woman: Women in Social and Political Thought* (1981), *Meditations on Modern Political Thought: Masculine/Feminine Themes from Luther to Arendt* (1986), *Women and War* (1987), and *Power Trips and Other Journeys: Essays in Feminism as Civic Discourse* (1990). Her most recent book is *Democracy on Trial* (1995).

FRANCIS FUKUYAMA is a resident consultant at the RAND Corporation. From 1983 to 1989 he was Senior Staff Member in the Department of Political Science at RAND and published widely on Soviet foreign policy. In the summer of 1989, while Deputy Director of Policy Planning at the State Department, he published an essay titled "The End of History?" This generated a worldwide debate on the future of liberal democracy. The argument of the essay was the germ of his first book, *The End of History and the Last Man* (1992). His second book will be on the relationship of economics and culture.

ALAN GILBERT is Professor in the Graduate School of International Studies at the University of Denver. He is the author of *Marx's Politics: Communists and Citizens* (1981) and *Democratic Individuality* (1990). He is at work on a new book, *Friendless Aliens, Friendless Citizens.*

SAMUEL P. HUNTINGTON is Eaton Professor of the Science of Government and Director of the John M. Olin Institute for Strategic Studies at Harvard University. His many books include *American Politics: The Promise of Disharmony* (1981) and *The Third Wave: Democratization in the Late Twentieth Century* (1991).

CHRISTOPHER LASCH was, until his death, Don Alonzo Watson Professor of History at the University of Rochester. He was the author of *The New Radicalism in America, 1889–1963: The Intellectual as a Social Type* (1965), *The Agony of the American Left* (1969), *Haven in a Heartless World: The Family Besieged* (1977), *The Culture of Narcissism* (1979), *The Minimal Self: Psychic Survival in Troubled Times* (1984), and *The True and Only Heaven: Progress and its Critics* (1991). Just before his death, he completed *The Revolt of the Elites* (1995).

HARVEY C. MANSFIELD is William R. Kenan, Jr. Professor of Government at Harvard University. He is the author of *Machiavelli's New Modes and Orders: A Study of the "Discourses on Livy"* (1979) and translator of Machiavelli's *Prince* (1985). His most recent books are *The Taming of the Prince: The Ambivalence of Modern Executive Power* (1989) and *America's Constitutional Soul* (1991). He is at work (with Nathan Tarcov) on a translation of Machiavelli's *Discourses.*

ARTHUR M. MELZER is Associate Professor of Political Science at Michigan State University. He is the author of *The Natural Goodness of Man: On the System of Rousseau's Thought* (1990). He is a Director of the Symposium on Science, Reason, and Modern Democracy and an editor of its first volume of essays, *Technology in the Western Political Tradition* (1993).

TERRY PINKARD is Professor of Philosophy at Georgetown University. His works include *Democratic Liberalism and Social Union* (1987) and *Hegel's Dialectic: The Explanation of Possibility* (1988). His most recent book is *Hegel's "Phenomenology": The Sociality of Reason* (1994).

RICHARD RORTY is University Professor of Humanities at the University of Virginia. He is the author of *Philosophy and the Mirror of Nature* (1979) and *Contingency, Irony, and Solidarity* (1989). He has published three volumes of essays: *Consequences of Pragmatism* (1982), *Objectivity, Relativism, and Truth* (1991), and *Essays on Heidegger and Others* (1991).

SUSAN SHELL is Associate Professor of Political Science at Boston College. Her first book was *The Rights of Reason: A Study of Kant's Philosophy and Politics* (1980). She is completing a new book on Kant's concept of community.

JERRY WEINBERGER is Professor of Political Science at Michigan State University. He is the author of *Science, Faith, and Politics: Francis Bacon and the Utopian Roots of the Modern Age* (1985) and editor of *Francis Bacon: "New Atlantis" and "The Great Instauration"* (1989). He is at work on an edition of Bacon's *Henry VII*. Professor Weinberger is a Director of the Symposium on Science, Reason, and Modern Democracy and an editor of its first volume of essays, *Technology in the Western Political Tradition* (1993).

M. RICHARD ZINMAN is Professor of Political Theory in James Madison College at Michigan State University. He is Executive Director of the Symposium on Science, Reason, and Modern Democracy and an editor of its first volume of essays, *Technology in the Western Political Tradition* (1993).

INDEX